International Law and Political Crisis

AN ANALYTIC CASEBOOK

INTERNATIONAL LAW AND POLITICAL CRISIS

AN ANALYTIC CASEBOOK

Lawrence Scheinman and David Wilkinson

UNIVERSITY OF CALIFORNIA, LOS ANGELES

LITTLE, BROWN AND COMPANY

BOSTON

Preface

International Law and Political Crisis is a series of cases designed to show how law in fact is employed in situations of political crisis. Unlike those standard treatises and works which traditionally concede too much or *a priori* grant too little to the role of international law in political confrontations, this book concentrates on what *practice* reveals as salient or secondary.

This is not a casebook as that term is normally understood — a set of abstracts of judicial decisions; nor is the attitude of the writers toward their cases a quasi-judicial one. Rather, the cases are analytic accounts of the legal aspects of various acute political conflicts (Suez, Cuba and Malaysia) and of the crucial phases of chronic conflicts (Berlin, Kashmir, and U.N. financing).

To focus only on the determinations of international tribunals, severely limited in authority and scope, would present a distorted picture of the practical content and employment of international legal norms. The central phenomenon of international politics is conflict: consequently, a realistic study of the relationship of law and politics must itself focus on conflict, and upon the employment of alleged norms of international law by the key actors in international politics — nation-states.

These cases are studies of what was done by states in crises: what norms they alleged in words and instituted in practice; what constraints, if any, law exercised in the decision-making process and on the selection of alternative courses of state action. While each author was left free to express his own opinion on the merits of the legal postures of the various parties, the common aim of all was to clarify those postures and their efficacy rather than to indict or to exonerate them. The task was to determine what relation those words that texts and treatises presented as "norms of international law" in fact bear to the practice of states in conflict, to the behavior of decision-makers operating under the pressures of crisis. Our specific objectives, then, were: (1) to give a description in each case of the legal positions and decisions of the participants against a factual background sufficient to make the broad outlines of the origins and evolution of the crisis clear; (2) to explain such decisions by reconstructing the apparent logic and motives of actors; and (3) to examine the implications of the norms that actors advanced (and settlements they achieved) for their objectives and values and for their past and prospective legal positions.

The first two matters are the concern of any normal narrative: What was done? Why was it done? The third relates to the analysis of means, action and outcomes: Were the consequences of the deliberate behavior of the actors those which were intended and desired? Did the norms advanced distort and confuse an established legal position which the actor might profitably have maintained; perpetuate an established but footless pose; or sustain the former and correct the latter? Did the words and acts strengthen the state's legal hand for the future, or did they constitute a prospective obstacle and future embarrassment? Did physical acts set, sustain or break precedents, and if so, to whose advantage? Did legalistic rhetoric and precedent-oriented acts aid or hinder the achievement of immediate objectives and long-run goals?

If the purpose of the casebook then was to explain the constraints and tactics of legal choice and to appraise the consequences of legal aspects of decisions of state, the working hypothesis was that actors, rather than seeing international law as a body of unambiguous norms which they strive to interpret correctly and then to enforce in international law, view pragmatically the mass of prescriptions which can be catalogued as alleged norms of law. Statesmen employ law as a technique or instrument of political conflict and/or conflict resolution; as a tool of policy with which to manage a crisis, containing or developing it, steering toward victory or toward compromise. Thus, in argument and decision, actors may use norms to justify immediate claims and concessions; to condemn or to approve the claims and concessions of others; to prepare a justification for claims they intend to make in the future; or to structure, and thereby attempt to legitimize the structure of, a claim or concession that is otherwise an improvised response to a new and immediate challenge. Stanley Hoffmann's introductory essay can be read as a commentary on how far the cases, written against the framework of description-explanation-appraisal, merely bear out or in fact lend elaboration to the working hypothesis that the alleged norms of law are, in the practice of states, more or less useful tools of policy.

If the projected method is accepted as valid and provocative then it can serve both the analysis and teaching of international law in the future. From the point of view of research, breadth and depth studies of international political relationships may lead to the advancing of testable propositions about the behavior of states and the relationship of law to that behavior.

From the point of view of teaching, the suggested method can be implemented by the selection of sets of cases in which the analysis applied in this book can be further employed, critiqued and refined. The application of this method for the study of international law would also yield sharper perceptions of the advisability, utility, and policy value of alternative legal postures, and of the consistency, continuity and coherence of state policies under a variety of crisis conditions.

Lawrence Scheinman
David Wilkinson

Contents

Introduction

The student of international law who examines its functions in the present international system and in the foreign policy of states will, unless he takes refuge in the comforting seclusion from reality that the pure theory of law once provided, be reduced to one of three attitudes. He will become a cynic, if he chooses to stress, like Giraudoux in *Tiger at the Gates*, the way in which legal claims are shaped to support any position a state deems useful or necessary on nonlegal grounds, or if he gets fascinated by the combination of cacophony and silence that characterizes international law as a system of world public order. He will become a hypocrite, if he chooses to rationalize either the conflicting interpretations and uses of law by states as a somehow converging effort destined to lead to some such system endowed with sufficient stability and solidity, or else if he endorses one particular construction (that of his own statesmen) as a privileged and enlightened contribution to the achievement of such a system. He will be overcome by consternation, if he reflects upon the gap between, on the one hand, the ideal of a world in which traditional self-help will be at least moderated by procedures and rules made even more indispensable by the proliferation both of states and of lethal weapons, and, on the other hand, the realities of inexpiable conflicts, sacred egoisms, and mutual recriminations.

Recent efforts to bridge the growing distance between international law and political science have underlined rather than eased the predicament[On the one hand, the analysis of international law as part of the national decision-making process (in which law, i.e., the making of authoritative and controlling decisions, aims at realizing certain values through the selection of a preferred policy alternative) has the merit of diverting the student's attention from the misleading notion of law as a set of rigid commands somehow independent from and superior to the political processes of statecraft.]But it has had the disastrous effect, not only of obscuring the differences between law as an instrument of policy and other, less solemn political and administrative techniques, but also of encouraging the second kind of hypocrisy deplored above — that which puts a legal-universalist coating on decisions that are essentially self-serving. On the other hand, the study of the role international law actually plays in the foreign policy process and in foreign policy decisions provides political scientists at last with empirical reasons for examining a body of material which, due to the combined impact of behavioral approaches and of so-called realism, they had tended to leave disdainfully to the lawyers; but such study may actually feed the very cynicism which the realists have displayed.

Most of the authors in this book are political scientists; their conclusions are stark and, on the whole, pessimistic. Their case studies provide the reader with a perceptive analysis of the functions international law performs for the policy-maker, and with a trenchant view of the reasons why international law plays a minor part not only in the policy process but also in the establishment and maintenance of world order.

1. Some of the functions of international law constitute *assets both for the policy-maker and from the viewpoint of world order,* i.e., of providing the international milieu with a framework of predictability and with procedures for the transaction of inter-state business.

(a) International law is an instrument of *communication.* To present one's claims in legal terms means, one, to signal to one's partner or opponent which "basic conduct norms" (to use Professor Scheinman's expression) one considers relevant or essential, and two, to indicate which procedures one intends to follow and would like the other side to follow. At a time when both the size of a highly heterogeneous international milieu and the imperatives of prudence in the resort to force make communication essential and often turn international relations into a psychological contest, international law provides a kind of common language that does not amount to a common code of legitimacy yet can serve as a joint frame of reference. (One must however remember, one, that communication is no guarantee against misperception and, two, that what is being communicated may well determine the other side's response to the message: if "we" communicate to "them" an understanding of the situation that threatens their basic values or goals — like our interpretation of the war in South Vietnam as a case of aggression — there will be no joint frame of reference at all, and in fact the competition may become fiercer.)

(b) International law affords means of *channeling conflict* — of diverting inevitable tensions and clashes from the resort to force. Whenever there have been strong independent reasons for avoiding armed conflict — in an international system in which the superpowers in particular have excellent reasons for "managing" their confrontations, either by keeping them nonviolent, or by using proxies — international law has provided statesmen both with alibis for shunning force, and with alternatives to violence. The case studies of the Berlin airlift crisis and of the Cuban missile crisis establish this point forcefully. In Berlin, both the Soviets and the West shaped their moves in such a way as to leave to the other side full responsibility for a first use of force, and to avoid the kind of frontal collision with the other side's legal claim that could have obliged the opponent to resort to force in order not to lose power or face. Thus, today as in earlier periods, law can indeed, as shown by Professor Falk, serve as an alternative to confrontation whenever states are eager or forced to look for an alternative.

2. International law also plays various useful roles in the policy process, which however do not *ipso facto* contribute to world order. Here, we are concerned with *law as a tool of policy* in the competition of state visions, objectives and tactics.

(a) The establishment of a network of rights and obligations, or the resort to legal arguments can be useful for the *protection or enhancement of a position:* if one wants to give oneself a full range of means with which to buttress a threatened status quo (cf. the present position of the West in Berlin; this is also what treaties of alliance frequently are for); if one wants to enhance one's power in a way that is demonstrably authorized by principles of international law (cf. Nasser's claim when he nationalized the Suez Canal, and Sukarno's invocation of the principle of self-determination against Malaysia); if one wants to restore a political position badly battered by an adversary's move, so that the resort to legal arguments becomes part of a strategy of restoring the *status quo ante* (Western position during the Berlin blockade; Kennedy's strategy during the

Cuban missile crisis; Western powers' attempts during the first phase of the Suez crisis; Soviet tactics in the U.N. General Assembly debates on the financing of peace-keeping operations).

(b) In all those instances, policy-makers use law as a way of putting pressure on an opponent by *mobilizing international support* behind the legal rules invoked: law serves as a focal point, as the tool for "internationalizing" a national interest and as the cement of a political coalition. States that may have political misgivings about pledging direct support to a certain power whose interests only partly coincide with theirs, or because they do not want to antagonize another power thereby, may find it both easier and useful to rally to the defense of a legal principle in whose maintenance or promotion they may have a stake.

(c) As Professor Gerberding points out, a policy-maker who ignores international law leaves the field of political-competition-through-legal-manipulation open to his opponents or rivals. International law provides one of the numerous *chessboards* on which state contests occur.

3. Obviously, this indicates not only that to the statesman international law provides an instrument rather than a guide for action, but also that this tool is often *not used*, when resort to it would hamper the state's interest as defined by the policy-maker.

(a) One of the reasons why international law often serves as a technique of political mobilization is the appeal of reciprocity: "you must support my invocation of the rule against him, because if you let the rule be violated at my expense, someday it may be breached at yours; and we both have an interest in its preservation." But *reciprocity cuts both ways:* my using a certain legal argument to buttress my case against him may encourage him, now or later, to resort to the same argument against me; I may therefore be unwise to play on a chessboard in which, given the solemn and abstract nature of legal rights and obligations, I may not be able to make the kind of distinction between my (good) case and your (bad) one, that can best be made by resort to ad hoc, political and circumstantial evidence which is irrelevant or ruled out in legal argumentation. Thus, Professor Gerberding points out that during the

Cuban crisis, when the United States tried to distinguish between Soviet missiles in Cuba and American ones in Turkey, in order to build its case and get support, America's use of the OAS Charter as the legal basis for its "quarantine" established a dangerous precedent which the Soviets could use some day, against the U.S. or its allies, on behalf of the Warsaw Pact. And in the tragicomedy of the battle over Article 19 of the U.N. Charter, one reason why the U.S. finally climbed down from its high legal horse and gave up the attempt to deprive the Soviets of their right to vote, unless they paid their share, was the growing awareness of the peril which the principle of the exercise of the U.N. taxing power by the General Assembly could constitute some day for the United States if it lost control of the Assembly.

(b) One of the things that international law "communicates" is the solemnity of a commitment: a treaty, or a provision of the Charter, serves as a kind of tripwire or burglar alarm. When it fails to deter, the victim and third parties have a fateful choice between upholding the legal principle by all means, at the cost of a possible escalation in violence, and choosing to settle the dispute more peacefully, at the cost of *fuzzing the legal issue*. For excellent political reasons, the latter course is frequently adopted, either in the form of dropping any reference to the legal principle at stake (cf. the U.S. retreat from Article 19) or in that of a *repli* on a less explosive or more procedural legal argument (cf. the U.N. organs' preference for invoking Chapter VI instead of VII, analyzed by Professor Miller with reference to Kashmir).

(c) The very *ambiguity* of international law, which in many essential areas displays either gaping holes or conflicting principles, allows policy-makers in an emergency to act as if international law were irrelevant — as if it were neither a restraint nor a guide. Professors Friedmann and Collins' analysis of the Suez crisis (second phase), and their comparison of Britain's and France's behavior with that of the U.S. and the Soviet Union in similar circumstances, are particularly eloquent in this respect. So are Professor Gerberding's conclusions about the small role played by legal considerations in the minds of President Kennedy and of his top advisers in October, 1962.

However, precisely because there is a legal chessboard for state competition, the fact that international law does not, in a crisis, really restrict one's freedom of action, does not mean that one will forgo legal rationalizations of the moves selected. Here we come to the last set of considerations about the role of law:

4. The resort to legal arguments by policy-makers may be *detrimental to world order and thereby counterproductive for the state* that used such arguments.

(a) In the legal vacuum or confusion which prevails in areas as vital to states as internal war or the use of force, each state tries to justify its conduct with legal rationalizations. The result is a kind of *escalation of claims and counterclaims,* whose consequence, in turn, is both a further devaluation of international law and a "credibility gap" at the expense of those states who have debased the currency. America's rather indiscriminate resort to highly debatable legal arguments to support its Vietnam policy is a case in point. The unsubtle reduction of international law to a mere storehouse of convenient *ex post* justifications (as in the case of British intervention at Suez, or American interventions in Santo Domingo and Vietnam) undermines the very pretense of contributing to world order with which these states have tried to justify their unilateral acts.

(b) Much of contemporary international law authorizes states to *increase their power.* In this connection, Nasser's nationalization of the Suez Canal Company was probably quite legal, and those who accept the rather tortured argument put forth by the State Department's legal advisers to justify the Cuban "quarantine" have concluded that this partial blockade was authorized by the OAS Charter and not in contradiction with the U.N. Charter. Yet it is obvious that a full exploitation by all states of all the permissions granted by international law would be a perfect recipe for chaos.

(c) *Attempts to enforce or to strengthen international law,* far from consolidating a system of desirable restraints on state (mis)behavior, may actually *backfire* if the political conditions are not ripe. This is the central lesson of the long story of the financing of U.N. peace-keeping operations. American self-intoxication with the importance of the rule of law, fed by misleading analogies between the U.N. Charter and the U.S. Constitution, resulted ultimately in a weakening of the influence of the World Court (which largely followed America's line of reasoning), and in an overplaying of America's hand during the "non-session" of the General Assembly in the fall of 1964 and winter of 1965.

These are sobering considerations. But what they tell us is not, as so many political scientists seem to believe, that international law is, at best, a farce, and, at worst, even a potential danger; what they tell us is that *the nature of the international system condemns international law to all the weaknesses and perversions that it is so easy to deride.* International law is merely a magnifying mirror that reflects faithfully and cruelly the essence and the logic of international politics. In a fragmented world, there is no "global perspective" from which anyone can authoritatively assess, endorse, or reject the separate national efforts at making international law serve national interests above all. Like the somber universe of Albert Camus' *Caligula*, this is a judgeless world where no one is innocent.

One may, however, find the picture presented in this book too gloomy for two different reasons. First, one could point out that the cases studied here are all within one corner of the international arena — the darkest: they all deal with tests involving the use or the threat of force, or the consequences of a resort to force. In other words, they deal with breakdowns of order; they do not deal with the innumerable placid instances in which the national policy process is permeated with international law, in which international law, reflecting a reciprocity of concerns or a community of tasks, plays an uncontroversial and accepted role as a restraint on and harness of state interests, as an almost seamless web of stability and predictability. Two, one could argue that a study of policy decisions in crisis situations would have led exactly to the same conclusions as this one, had it dealt with 19th century examples instead of with the period since the end of World War Two; and yet the 19th century was a golden age for international law.

Neither argument is convincing, for reasons that I have developed elsewhere at greater length.[1] One, it is the problem of war and peace that is both the distinctive feature of international politics, and the test

---

[1] See my contribution to: S. Hoffmann and Karl Deutsch (eds.), *The Relevance of International Law* (Cambridge: Schenkman Publ. Co., 1968, forthcoming); also, *The State of War* (New York: Praeger, 1965), Chaps. 4–5.

of any legal system. A legal system that breaks down in the area of greatest importance for its subjects is like a house without foundations. The solidity, scope and intensity of regular legal transactions is dependent on the preservation of moderation at the higher level of the states' essential interests. Two, what makes the weakness of international law at that level particularly dangerous today is the difference between the present international system and past ones: this one seems to breed more tests of will, i.e., to provide more cases of breakdown, in circumstances that leave little room for complacency.

What produces periodic crises is, first, the very complexity of an international system that covers the whole planet and includes a bewildering variety of units, regimes, ideologies, economic systems and class structures, with countless opportunities for conflict over territory, principles of legitimacy, or resources. Secondly, the new conditions of the use of force incite states to prudence in the resort to large-scale violence, but create a grave danger of escalation when violence breaks out, and also contribute to a recurrence of violence precisely because of the greater difficulty of settling disputes in a world teeming with causes of conflicts. These conflicts stay unresolved due to the very restraints on war, which used traditionally to be the most expeditious way of settling conflicts: hence lasting centers of trouble, such as the Middle East, Kashmir, Berlin, Indochina. It is the nature of the present international system which makes competitive attempts at building rival systems of law and at multiplying legal tripwires both inevitable and perilous. It is the nature of the system which makes premature worldwide attempts at regulating behavior through legal norms positively dangerous, yet keeps "informal" agreements and habits of restraint tactical and shifting, and insures that the grand principles or values that are invoked by most, and are of moral-political significance rather than of a legal nature, remain stakes in a contest for legitimacy and power.

The permanent plight of international law is that, now as before, it shows on its body of rules all the scars inflicted by the international state of war. The tragedy of contemporary international law in that of a double divorce: first, between the old liberal dream of a world rule of law, and the realities of an international system of multiple mini-dramas that always threaten to become major catastrophes; second, between the old dream and the new requirements of moderation, which in the circumstances of the present system suggest a *down-*

playing of formal law in the realm of peace-and-war issues, and an *upgrading* of more flexible techniques, until the system has become less fierce. The interest of international law for the political scientist is that there is no better way of grasping the continuing differences between order within a national society and the fragile order of international affairs than to study how and when states use legal language, symbols and documents, and with what results. One can only hope that case studies such as these, by showing at what points in the political process international law becomes relevant, will allow both students and statesmen to overcome consternation or sarcasm and to think of ways in which statecraft could combine the defense of national interests and the interest in world order, make the state's material power serve both, and harness both to that strategy and ethics of prudence that Raymond Aron has called for.

Stanley Hoffmann

International Law and Political Crisis

AN ANALYTIC CASEBOOK

LAWRENCE SCHEINMAN

The Berlin Blockade

I

That international law is a significant factor in international politics is a fundamental assumption of this essay. International legal norms, so-called, are used principally as tactics of political conflict, and many of the legal rules which are wheeled into action in the course of international political confrontations are sufficiently flexible to be applied with almost equal conviction to any side of a dispute. The very flexibility of these norms may account in large measure for the fact that appeals to international law are heard above the din of conflict — whether that conflict occurs within, or across, the zonal bounds of bipolarity, or among ideologically similar, or dissimilar, states. The flexibility of legal norms also may affect the manner and timing of the use of those norms: whoever first musters cogent legal arguments on behalf of his position frequently reaps the benefits which accrue to the initiator.

Whatever may be the tactical uses of international legal norms in political conflict, it may be argued that international law also has a dimension of constraint, without at the same time making untenable claims for the role of law in international relations. The crux of this argument is that in developing and promoting legal justification for their action, states (in a sense) draw the boundary lines of the game in play, thus it becomes more difficult for states to cast aside these ground rules. The more the states pursue legal argumentation in the public forum, the more difficult they find it to divest themselves of the legal paradigm of their own making. This observation may apply more to the Western democracies whose values are more clearly represented in what are claimed to be international legal norms, but

1

the same considerations might also have an impact on Soviet behavior.

Distinguishing between types of norms is another perspective from
which to evaluate the role of law. It could be argued that the provision in the Charter of the United Nations that "All Members shall refrain in their international relations from the threat or use of force . . ."
[Article 2(4)] is a fundamental-behavior, or basic-conduct, norm. It is
general in application and *proscriptive* in nature. The corollary Charter provision of Article 2(3) that "All Members shall settle their disputes by peaceful means . . ." also is a basic-conduct norm, but is
prescriptive in nature. The two rules respectively prohibit and impose a certain type of conduct in international relations. The basic-
conduct norms are fragile, and hedged by other provisions, such as
the inherent right of self-defense. They are abstract to the point of
ambiguity, and often are honored in the breach, for example, in the
cases of Korea, Suez, Indonesia, Kashmir, Hungary, Goa, Cuba, Berlin.

There also exist norms, qualitatively similar, which prescribe the
manner in which states shall fulfill the injunction of peaceful settlement, such as are found in Article 33 of the Charter. These are fundamentally methodological, or operational, norms; as states must not
resort to force but must settle their disputes peacefully, a menu is
provided from which to select means for peaceful settlement, an operational code for the basic-conduct norms.

States obviously have not discounted the use of force in international politics, and occasionally invoke the argument of the mailed
fist. Nevertheless, in the postwar world, states have sought to pursue
political and ideological goals without travelling all the way to Arma-
geddon. Once having breached the basic-conduct norm against the
use of force, states usually seek a way to avoid the full consequences
of their act. The methodological norms of conflict management frequently serve this purpose. These norms are flexible, do not irrevocably circumscribe state conduct, and do not tax states with weighty
obligations. In brief, they are factors which can, and do, induce states
to pursue more diverse and safer tactics than the use of force. The
argument for law as a constraining factor can be pushed too far; the
impact of technology on modern warfare has a greater claim as a restraint on state action, but this should not allow us *a priori* to totally
discount law's constraint on policy.

My personal conviction is that the United States, properly, has as-
pired to conduct international politics within the framework of the

broad, flexible rules of international behavior, but that it has not permitted these rules to stand in the way of the defense of vital interests as defined by the government of the United States. To the limit of the possible, American policy has by and large remained within the broad context of international law, but, as it must, has reserved to itself the right to weigh its interests against unfailing adherence to that law. Generally speaking, I believe the United States has correctly decided when national interests must be superior to, and served by, the law. The game of international politics is not lightly played; it is one in which all too frequently the ante is survival. We have not yet emerged from the jungle in certain respects, and there does not exist today any institution or organ above the state to which the state safely can entrust its survival. Until that time arrives, we may seek to approximate in international conduct the principles and mores we cherish as a nation, and try to induce others to follow; but we cannot allow the rules to absorb us. What follows is written in the spirit of the above comments.

II

The Berlin crisis ostensibly began on June 18/19, 1948 when the Soviet Military Government in Germany imposed severe restrictions on access to the city. In reality the problem was incipient in the wartime and immediate postwar agreements reached by the Allied powers. These agreements, like the Atlantic Charter which underpinned the nascent United Nations Organization, were predicated on the assumption of continued harmony between the Allied powers which had banded together to destroy the Axis threat. The Berlin crisis of 1948 was merely the most dramatic in a series of events which pointed to the fallaciousness of this earlier assumption. The crisis was also the point of departure for development of the defensive alliances which relate members of the North Atlantic world to one another.

At least since the time of this confrontation of the superpowers, Berlin has been in a critical state and periodically in crisis. It is unquestionably the geopolitical Vesuvius of the European continent, the place where the tensions and mutual frustrations which are ingredients of postwar East-West relations are found. Of all the situations presented in this book, that in Berlin is the only one where there has been a continuous physical relationship between the superpowers (the United States and the Soviet Union); Berlin is the only place where aggression and an increase in tension automatically entail the locking of horns by the nuclear giants of the mid-twentieth century. It is consequently an interesting locus in which to evaluate the manner in which these two states have employed legal norms and invoked legal argument to sustain their own positions and to weaken those of their adversary. Correspondingly, it presents a situation wherein we can judge the extent to which the international legal order serves as a constraint upon action.

Provisions for the management of Germany following her unconditional surrender had been worked out by the European Advisory Commission in 1944 and 1945.[1] The two principal agreements were the Protocol on Zones of Occupation and Administration of the Greater Berlin Area of September 12, 1944,[2] and the Agreement on Control Machinery in Germany of November 14, 1944.[3] The pertinent provisions of the Protocol allowed that "Germany . . . will, for the purposes of occupation, be divided into three zones, one of which will be allotted to each of the three Powers, and a special Berlin area, which will be under joint occupation by the three Powers." The principal stipulations of the Agreement were the establishment of Allied control machinery in Germany: an Allied Control Council which was to consist of the Commanders-in-Chief who would "constitute a supreme organ of control" (article 3) and an Inter-Allied Governing Authority (*Komendatura*) consisting of three (later a Frenchman was added) Commandants "to direct jointly the administration of the 'Greater Berlin' area" (article 7). These instruments were ratified at the Yalta Conference in February, 1945.

In light of later developments, three features of these instruments warrant attention. First, they were intended as interim provisions between the assumption of supreme authority by the Allied victors and the peace settlement which was expected to follow. This is evident from the provision in the Protocol that "for the purposes of occupation" Germany would be divided into zones and from the statement

[1] The European Advisory Commission was a high-level inter-Allied planning board created at the Moscow Conference in 1943 to expedite communication between the Big Three (the U.S., Britain and the U.S.S.R.) on nonmilitary problems related to enemy territory and for other problems referred to it by the three governments.
[2] Senate Committee on Foreign Relations, *Documents on Germany, 1944–1961*, 87th Congress, 1st Session (Washington: Government Printing Office, 1961), p. 1.
[3] *Ibid.*, p. 5.

in the Agreement that the control machinery would be operative while Germany is "carrying out the basic requirements of unconditional surrender." Second, in both instruments a distinction was made between the three occupation zones and the "Greater Berlin" area from which it may be deduced that Berlin was not a part of any occupation sector, but a separate and distinct entity. Third, in neither of the above instruments, nor in later Allied statements on the Zones of Occupation or on the Control Machinery in Germany were any explicit provisions made with regard to access to the "Greater Berlin" area from either of the two (later three) contiguous zones. In fact, Berlin was nestled well within the Soviet occupation zone.

The absence of an explicit written agreement concerning access to Berlin for all of the occupying powers proved embarrassing to the Western powers as the events of the blockade unfolded in 1948. It facilitated the Soviet gambit to isolate the city. But, of course, it does not follow that, even in the presence of written access agreements, the Soviet Union would have been deterred from taking the action it did. Indeed, if it had been so deterred, we would have reached beyond the present state of international relations to an order in which international law had begun to make marked inroads on the policy behavior of states. In the light of the political context in which the Berlin crisis took place, Soviet inaction would have been more than surprising.[4]

A brief review of the political milieu will serve to clarify the challenge, response, and evolution of events. The context in a nutshell was Soviet expansionism. Whether for ideological or power-politics reasons is irrelevant — the principal fact is that the Soviet Union was systematically pursuing a policy designed to modify the status quo to make it conform to what the Kremlin conceived to be its best interest. By the time of the coup in Czechoslovakia in February, 1948, the Soviet Union controlled all of Eastern and most of Central Europe, and apparently was bent on extending that control or influence over all of Germany, largely by obstructing the implementation of Allied agreements.

Harmonious relations among the victors began to erode shortly after the end of the war. The Soviets followed parallel policies of disrupting and impeding plans for economic recovery, while taking ad-

---

[4] We are assuming here that although Stalinist foreign policy was more cautious than it was often recognized as being, Germany represented a situation of extensive risk-taking up to, and *perhaps* including, armed conflict.

vantage of the autonomy of zonal control to Sovietize the Eastern sector under its charge. The Potsdam Agreement of 1945[5] to treat Germany as an economic unity never was implemented. Earlier disagreement in principle over the issue of reparations quickly translated into practical disputes. Administrative zonal boundaries hardened into economic zonal boundaries. The pursuit of economic disequilibrium proved one of the more artful tactics in the Soviet repertory. Quadripartite machinery in Germany in the form of an Allied Control Council[6] never functioned effectively beyond a purely technical level. This merely reflected discord at a higher level — the Council of Foreign Ministers.[7] Meeting twice for extensive periods in 1947 this Council only succeeded in clarifying the abyss between East and West.

Two principal problems raised in these Council meetings are of significance to this study. One was the continuing dispute over economic principles where no meeting of minds was possible. Out of this dispute came the decision to incorporate the Western zones of Germany into the European Recovery Program (ERP).[8] The other was the problem of the nature and timing of the political organization of Germany: The Soviets insisted on the creation of a centralized structure first, and then the tackling of economic issues, while the West was determined to institute a decentralized federal structure which would come into being on the heels of an economic settlement. These dichotomous and irreconcilable positions were made clear at the hapless Foreign Ministers' meeting in London in December, 1947.

The failure of the London meeting set the stage for the crisis which developed over Berlin. The ensuing decision of the Western powers (principally the United States and Great Britain) to incorporate their zones into the ERP, and to put German materiel and productive capacity to work to ensure the success of the ERP, created a major problem for the Soviet Union. For if the ERP were to succeed and the western zones of Germany were to undergo economic rectification and readjustment, Soviet potential in those zones would be cor-

---

[5] At this inter-Allied conference of August, 1945, earlier agreements on basic principles for the treatment of a defeated Germany were specified and given substance. The specifications extended to disarmament, demilitarization, reparations, and other issues.

[6] This was a body consisting of the Commanders-in-Chief of the occupying powers; the supreme organ of control in Germany at the termination of the war.

[7] This permanent body was designated to deal with questions relating to the war and to the establishment of the peace.

[8] Popularly, ERP was known as the "Marshall Plan."

respondingly diminished, indeed eliminated. This became even more clear when the Western powers, after much wrangling among themselves, decided not only on common economic policy, but also on the termination of military government, the political fusion of their zones, and the establishment of a federal republic. The implementation of these decisions would put an end to Soviet designs for eventual economic, political, or strategic control of Germany. The success of these steps was clearly a threat to important Soviet interests.

Without closing the door to cooperation with the Soviet Union, the three Western powers, in concert with the Benelux countries, moved to end the economic drain of Germany on Anglo-American treasuries and to establish a program of economic and political recovery. The results of these efforts were recorded in the London Agreements which were made public on June 8, 1948, but earlier communiqués had indicated the tenor and movement of events. In response to Western preparations for these talks, the Soviet government, in February, protested that "the calling of such a conference . . . would constitute a violation of the Potsdam Agreement and of other Four-Power decisions, according to which responsibility for the administration of Germany and for defining policy with regard to Germany lies jointly on the occupying Powers."[9] Having blocked any Four-Power action, the Soviet Union wanted to preclude positive action at any other level. When the Western powers persisted in conducting separate talks, the Soviet Union more forcefully demonstrated against Western action by walking out of the Allied Control Council on March 20, thus effectively putting an end to quadripartite action at this level as well.

Economic unification of the Western zones required a new and sound financial basis which would give the Germans confidence that production and work were tied to basic recovery and were not merely Sisyphean battles against spiralling inflation. It had been understood for some time that currency reform was an indispensible first step toward economic recovery, and it was originally intended that a uniform currency reform would be introduced in all four occupation zones. Systematic Soviet blockage of all attempts at concerted action meant that the Western zones would have to undergo a separate

[9] "Identical Notes from the Government of the U.S.S.R. to the Governments of the United States of America, the United Kingdom and France on the London Conference," February 13, 1948, in O. M. Von der Gablentz (ed.), *Documents on the Status of Berlin, 1944–1959* (Munich: R. Oldenbourg Verlag, 1959), p. 53.

currency reform. Recognizing the adverse effects such a reform would have for Soviet policy in Germany, but unable to intercede directly in the three Western zones, the Russians sought other means to overcome Western action. The answer was found where the West was most vulnerable in Germany — in the city of Berlin. The only thing needed was an excuse to apply pressure.

The opportunity came on June 18, 1948 when the Western powers announced the introduction of a currency reform, effective June 20, for the three Western zones (but not for the city of Berlin itself). Charging, in a public proclamation to the German people on June 19, that "the agreements providing for the control machinery in Germany and the Potsdam agreement which stipulated that Germany be treated as a single unit and that her currency remain uniform, have been violated,"[10] Soviet Military Governor Sokolovsky declared the new currency invalid in the Soviet zone "and in the area of great Berlin which comes within the Soviet zone . . . and is economically part of [it]"; that "in order to protect the interests of the population . . . and to prevent disruption of economic life . . . the Soviet Military Administration in Germany will take . . . necessary measures arising from the situation that has been created."[11] These measures were the blockade of Berlin.

On June 19 all rail and road passenger traffic between the Western zones and Berlin were suspended. Freight traffic by rail and waterway was restricted to 20 percent of normal capacity, but was not fully suspended until June 23, the first day of total blockade.[12] These were not novel measures. Harassment of civilian and military movement across zonal borders had been sporadically in play for several months. As early as January, 1948 the Soviets had begun to impose restrictions on Berliners travelling to the West. On March 30 they took the first steps against the free movement of military interzonal traffic. On that day, authorities of the Soviet Military Government informed the Western commanders of new communications provisions, effective April 1.[13] The main thrust of the new regulations was

---

[10] "Proclamation to the German People on the Western Currency Reform by Marshal Sokolovsky, June 19, 1948," in *ibid.*, pp. 53–54.

[11] *Ibid.*

[12] *New York Times,* June 23, 1948.

[13] "Report of the Exchange of Letters between General Dratvin and General Gailey regarding Soviet Interference with Allied Access to Berlin, March 30/31, 1948," in Von der Gablentz, *op. cit.*, pp. 55–56.

to submit Allied personnel and freight to Soviet inspection. Western military authorities sought to accommodate the Soviets by offering to submit freight manifests and passenger lists upon passing through border crossing points, but they refused to allow Soviet officials to board trains for purposes of inspection. When Allied trains tried to cross the border without inspection they were turned back. The Western response was a portent of things to come: a "little airlift" was improvised to avoid compliance with what were considered illegal and unilateral policy changes.[14]

Tensions momentarily receded but began to rise rapidly again in June in response to the London agreements. On June 9, new restrictions were imposed on Germans travelling into the Soviet zone. Two days later, all rail traffic was stopped only to be resumed a day later.[15] On June 12 the Elbe River bridge on the only autobahn open to Western use for travel between Berlin and the Western zones was closed "for repairs" although a detour route was provided until all road traffic was brought to a halt on June 19.

The events of June 19 themselves, however, were only a prelude of things to come. Throughout the ensuing days and months the Soviet Union gradually increased the pressure on Berlin and supplemented the rupture of communications with intensified activity in the city itself. Tactics ranged from manipulation of the city's electricity supply to the continuous barrage of propaganda warning Berliners of the impending departure of Western forces from the city and the implicit consequences of total Soviet control; from kidnapping of city officials and fomenting riots to the systematic undermining of the constitutionally elected authorities of the City Assembly and of the executive arm, the Magistrat. Furthermore, on June 22, following the breakdown of a last Western effort at accommodation on currency the Soviets announced a currency reform effective not only in the Soviet zone but also in Greater Berlin.[16] The immediate reaction of the Western powers, prepared for this contingency, was to extend the Western zone currency reform to the Western sectors of the city

[14] Lucius D. Clay, *Decision in Germany* (New York: Doubleday & Co., 1950), pp. 359–61.

[15] It is significant that this was on a Friday, the day of the week on which currency reform would most likely be announced after bank closing. It would appear to reveal Soviet anxiety to activate a blockade, but not without "cause."

[16] For a comprehensive analysis of the entire Berlin episode see the excellent study by W. P. Davison, *The Berlin Blockade* (Princeton: Princeton University Press, 1958), especially Chaps. 3 and 5.

and to declare the Soviet orders contrary to Four-Power agreements on Germany and Berlin and, consequently, null and void. Finally, in response to all of these Soviet actions, which spelled belligerency, the Western powers introduced what, in hindsight was their ultimate weapon, the Berlin airlift. With the introduction of land blockade and the announcement of dual currency reforms, the issue was joined and the battle for Berlin was on.

III

There is an abundant literature on the status of Berlin in which elaborate and impressive arguments have been put forth to sustain or contest the legality of continued Western occupation of the city, and, by implication, of the right of access to the enclave of West Berlin.[17] The present essay is not concerned with the legal correctness of the arguments or claims put forth on behalf of the contestants, but rather with another set of questions. First, how, if at all, did law or international legal norms act as a constraint on policy in the Berlin crisis? Second, how were legal arguments and international legal norms used by the parties to manage the crisis? The term "manage" is used here to express the purpose of intensifying and accelerating crisis as well as sustaining, controlling or decelerating crisis. To pose the question in these terms is not to imply that norms necessarily will contain crisis, although that well may be their ultimate effect. This logically follows from the more general proposition that law serves the purpose of expanding as well as consolidating and preserving power or authority.

The question of legal correctness of conflicting claims would be pertinent if the issue were before an adjudicatory tribunal. We would do well now to dispose of the general question of bringing disputes such as the Berlin crisis before a body like the International Court of Justice. At least one observer has suggested that the Berlin crisis, in its several forms (blockade of 1948, threatened unilateral peace treaty between the Soviet Union and East Germany in 1958, and the erection of the Berlin Wall in 1961), is reducible in great measure to iden-

---

[17] See, e.g., M. E. Bathurst, "Legal Aspects of the Berlin Problem," *British Yearbook of International Law*, XXXVIII (1962), 255–306; Lyman M. Tondel, Jr. (ed.), "The Issues in the Berlin-German Crisis," *The Hammarskjold Forums* (Dobbs Ferry: Oceana Publications, 1963); Roland J. Stanger (ed.), *West-Berlin: The Legal Context* (Columbus: Ohio State University Press, 1966); and W. Wewjura & I. Lukashek, "International Legal Aspects of the West Berlin Problem," *International Affairs* (Moscow) (April, 1963), pp. 37–42.

tifiable and justiciable issues, the resolution of which would clear the way for a final settlement over Berlin.[18] The line between justiciable and non-justiciable issues in international politics is so faint as to be often undiscoverable. Any dispute can be cast in terms of legal issues, but the real question is the utility and practicality of doing so in the first place.

There are at least three objections to regarding disputes such as the Berlin case as reducible to, and solvable under the aegis of an international tribunal. In the first place, resolution of the legal issues in no way guarantees solution of the dispute. Indeed, disposing of legal claims which are cloaking basic political issues only leaves the raw political dispute and the often irreconcilable political interests completely exposed; and it wipes away the opportunity for the contestants to contain the conflict behind the obfuscating wall of artificial legalisms. The stakes of the conflict are correspondingly raised and the disputants are carried to the brink, with all of the dolorous consequences of armed conflict. Secondly, even if an international tribunal were able to come to grips with and produce a legal solution, it is unlikely that the losing party would adhere to the decision of the court. This was amply demonstrated in the Corfu Channel case which involved far less in terms of prestige and importance than does Berlin. Finally, and as a corollary of the latter point, the only likely result of submitting a *machtpolitik* issue to an international tribunal in the contemporary international system would be the further destabilization of an already weak, unstable and minimal set of legal norms. In brief, to follow the suggested course might be a disservice both to the disputants and to the law.

IV

At the inception of the blockade the United States and her allies were faced with two interlocking issues. The first question was whether or not to stay in Berlin in the face of Soviet pressure. Second, if it were determined not to withdraw, how was this decision to be implemented. The latter essentially was a question of the use of force to assert alleged rights of access to the city. Legal considerations entered into the resolution of both of these issues although the constraints which such considerations imposed on policy outcomes were

[18] Arthur Larson, *When Nations Disagree* (Kingsport: Louisiana State University Press, 1961), pp. 103–106.

limited almost exclusively to providing an analytic framework for action.

Despite the fact that the crisis over Berlin in the form of a blockade had been expected for at least two months, when the crisis finally did break and consolidate in the five-day period between June 19 and June 24, Washington still was apparently undecided as to Berlin's importance to and place in the overall policy toward Europe. The Marshall Plan was in the process of being implemented, plans were being worked out to establish a West German State, but Berlin was not snugly fitted into American policy. In June, 1943 Berlin had no particular strategic value, and it was not yet a window to the West; nor was it yet, in Premier Nikita Khrushchev's gourmet turn of phrase of a decade later "a bone in our [the Soviet] throat." At the inception of the blockade, the city did not possess the symbolic value it eventually acquired and still maintains through present times. In brief, Berlin was not clearly accepted by all key policymakers as vital to American interests.[19]

There were, of course, rather concrete views in high quarters on what our Berlin policy should be. One of the most forceful statements of what that policy should be, and ultimately did become, was made by the U.S. Military Governor for Germany, General Lucius D. Clay. In a teleconference with the Department of the Army on April 10 in the midst of an earlier phase of the crisis, Clay remarked that,

We have lost Czechoslovakia. Norway [sic] is threatened. We retreat from Berlin. When Berlin falls, western Germany will be next. If we mean . . . to hold Europe against Communism we must not budge. . . . If we withdraw, our position in Europe is threatened. If America does not understand this now, does not know that the issue is cast, then it never will and communism will run rampant. I believe the future of democracy requires us to stay.[20]

The above appeal reveals a considerable part of what must have constituted the political factor in the determination not to withdraw from Berlin — that to do otherwise risked compromising America's

---

[19] This is a significant but delicate point. While many participants did appreciate Berlin's value, the principal thrust of this argument is that a consensus had not yet evolved on the Berlin issue. As in the case of most foreign policy crisis situations, however, the range of participants necessary to achieve consensus is rather limited as debate does not spill over into the larger public realm except *post facto*.

[20] Clay, *op. cit.*, p. 361.

position in Europe. The challenge had been thrown down and it was politically expedient to meet it in Berlin. Military factors undoubtedly entered into the decision to stay as well, but these considerations were more closely linked with the second issue — how to implement the decision to stay in Berlin — which will be treated below.

There is, however, another aspect of the decision to stay in Berlin which merits some attention. It is reported in *The Forrestal Diaries* that on June 25, at the first *structured* meeting in high policy quarters on the Berlin issues, discussion turned "on the controlling legal rights and undertakings."[21] This is significant from the point of view of the role of law as a possible constraint on state action, although the observation does not per se permit us to draw any far-reaching conclusions. The mere fact that discussion turned on legal considerations does not, for example, warrant the conclusion that it was the discovery of legal rights that irrevocably determined that we would stay in Berlin. It might be, and apparently was, a strong reason to do so, but the very nature of policymaking would perforce bring politico-strategic considerations into the picture, considerations which are invariably dominant factors. If, on the other hand, the answer to the question of legal rights had been negative, we could then deduce even to a lesser extent that we simply would have withdrawn to the zonal boundary leaving Berlin in the sole control of the Soviet Union.

To reiterate, at the time of these discussions the United States, although rapidly moving in that direction, was not yet firmly committed to the proposition that the defense of Berlin was a vital interest which could not be compromised.[22] Consequently, it was even more necessary from the point of view of domestic and world opinion to have firm legal ground on which to stand in making policy commitments which could lead to untold consequences. When, on June 28 at a White House meeting on Berlin, President Harry S. Truman finalized the American commitment to remain in Berlin regardless of the potential consequences, i.e., war, he remarked that "we were in Berlin by terms of an agreement and . . . the Russians had no right to get us out by either direct or indirect pressure."[23] More than a trace of

---

[21] Walter Millis (ed.), *The Forrestal Diaries* (New York: Viking Press, 1951), pp. 451–52.

[22] Davison, *op. cit.*, comments on page 149 that both Clay and Truman "had to take upon themselves the decision to attempt to hold out in Berlin, without the benefit of agreed staff recommendations."

[23] Millis, *op. cit.*, p. 455.

American moralism can be read between these lines. The significance of this statement lies in the fact that it was made to the President's advisors behind closed doors, and not to a concerned public opinion which had to be prodded into line in support of a dangerous policy. The statement smacks strongly of the injunction against the use or threat of force to attain political objectives found in Article 2 of the Charter of the United Nations, and of a moral posture against nations which would violate this injunction. At the same time it supports the proposition that, in thinking through our politico-strategic position, legal factors constituted one of the parameters, and that these factors were not purely post-decision instruments of policy justification.

Even if we grant law an important role in the pre-decision process, I do not believe the point can be pushed very far and remain valid. The assertion of a legal right created some breathing space for a more careful assessment of the situation. It also bolstered a questionable decision, and gave to that decision a legal quality it would otherwise have lacked. In other words, having decided to remain in Berlin for any of a number of reasons, law could be, and indeed was used to justify the decision — and to justify it to the decision-makers as well as to others. If it were eventually decided that Berlin was an untenable position because it could only be held by a war we were unwilling to engage in, law could serve admirably to cover the retreat — law-abiding nations whose political independence or territorial integrity is not challenged and who have not been victims of armed aggression (itself an elastic concept) have no alternative but to withdraw, and seek other means of conflict resolution.[24] It goes without saying that law could have served to support an initial decision to withdraw immediately. Either way, law serves more as a justification than as a determinant.

The second key issue was how to implement the commitment to remain in Berlin. This issue was inseparable from the initial question whether or not to remain in the city, for a positive answer to the latter question automatically invoked consideration of the former. Our ultimate response was the Berlin airlift but it is important to bear in mind that in the early days of the crisis and well into the summer, it

---

[24] The other side of this coin is that a legal argument pushed too far may make it unfeasible to withdraw from an untenable position without a serious loss of prestige — the threading of a legal needle requires an incisive eye.

was assumed by many of the participants (and very much so by the Russians) that the airlift simply was an expedient which could not be counted on to maintain the city at more than a subsistence level, and a device which would be of doubtful utility during the winter when fog and cold weather normally impeded air traffic into Berlin. It was not considered a suitable substitute for rail and road supply.[25]

Several alternative courses of action were explored during the first week of the crisis.[26] One was to seek to eliminate the problem through diplomatic channels in conjunction with the temporary expedient of the airlift and to meet further problems, such as the use of force, if and when they came. A second suggestion was to pursue diplomatic channels of activity with the possibility of using some kind of force if these negotiations did not succeed. A third was to send an armored convoy through on rail or on the road while the crisis was still in its early stages and before positions on both sides hardened to the point that a show of force would be tantamount to the outbreak of war. General Clay was an early and vigorous advocate of the use of an armored convoy and was firmly convinced that such an action would not have been met by Soviet force, but the idea temporarily was set aside.

There were several considerations which militated against the use of an armored convoy: technical, political, and military. From a technical point of view it would be relatively simple for the Soviets to neutralize the effort to use an armored convoy. A train convoy could be stopped simply by the removal of track in front of the train and, once it was within the Soviet zone, removal of track to the rear of the train, thus leaving the military convoy in an immobile, embarrassed position. Similarly, a road convoy could be effectively stopped by the blowing of several bridges. Unless the United States was prepared to make a major move, the use of an armored convoy at first did not appear to many to be a suitable alternative. From a political point of view, prudence and caution, as well as concern for public and world opinion, dictated a more graduated response to Soviet action. Militarily in terms of conventional force, the Western powers were at a decided disadvantage vis-à-vis the Russians. In contrast to 18,000 Soviet troops in Berlin and 300,000 more in the Soviet zone, the United States and her allies had 6,500 troops in Berlin and the pos-

---

[25] Davison, *op. cit.*, pp. 149–50.
[26] Millis, *op. cit.*, pp. 452–53.

sibility of activating a little over two divisions to back these troops up.[27] In the event of a major conflict, the United States, seriously outclassed on the ground, would have to fall back on its nuclear monopoly with all the consequences that would entail.[28] Nevertheless, the use of force to break the blockade was never discounted, but only placed to one side. General Clay once again advocated the idea to Secretary of Defense James Forrestal on July 21[29] and was questioned about the potential use of armored convoys by President Truman on July 22.[30]

There is hardly any evidence that legal considerations, and a commitment not to use force unless in self-defense, even partially motivated the American decision against the use of armored convoys. Neither territorial integrity nor political independence were threatened in the blockade, but rather rights based on agreements, so claims of self-defense would be difficult to sustain in law. The development of a cogent legal argument to justify the use of force to assert those rights would have taxed the ingenuity of the legal departments of the Western powers, but we can be fairly confident that a convincing argument would have been made. Admittedly, our right of access on the ground was fuzzy, implicit rather than explicit, but we cannot assume that these legal subtleties would have dominated our decision on the manner of response.

The only public indication that the legal parameter had not completely been shelved in the process of considering the use of force to break the blockade derives from a comment by General Clay. Noting Washington's decision against the use of an armored convoy Clay remarked: "I understand [Washington's] desire to avoid this risk of armed conflict *until* the issue had been placed before the United Nations"[31] [emphasis added]. From this together with the statement of Ambassador Phillip Jessup before the United Nations Security Council on October 19, 1948 — that "we could have used armed force against this Soviet threat," but that "what we actually did and are still doing is live up to our obligations under the Charter of the

[27] Davison, *op. cit.*, p. 150.
[28] That we were, nevertheless, prepared to face this possibility is reasonably clear.
[29] Millis, *op. cit.*, p. 459.
[30] Harry S. Truman, *Memoirs: Years of Trial and Hope* (Garden City: Doubleday & Co., 1956), p. 125.
[31] Clay, *op. cit.*, p. 374.

United Nations and to try to settle the question by peaceful discussions while continuing to discharge our obligations in Berlin"[32] — one might deduce the impact of legal norms on the decision of how to respond to the Soviet blockade. It is, however, a very slim reed on which to lean. It seems reasonably clear that these statements more appropriately fall in the category of tactics than into that of behavioral restraint. There were a number of reasons beside legal prescriptions for bringing the crisis to the United Nations before using force. These will be treated below.

V

The crisis passed through four phases between June 19, 1948 and May 4, 1949, at which time the Four Powers reached agreement on terminating the Berlin blockade. Schematically, these phases were: (1) technical negotiations at the level of the military commanders in Berlin which lasted from June 19 to July 3; (2) diplomatic negotiations in the form of diplomatic notes and direct talks between Western representatives and Vyacheslav Molotov and Joseph Stalin in Moscow, which lasted from July 6 through the end of the first week of September; (3) the United Nations' phase in which the Western powers brought the issue before the Security Council under Chapter VII of the U.N. Charter (October, 1948); and (4) bilateral contacts between American and Soviet representatives at the United Nations which later were expanded to include the French and British representatives, and the eventual reaching of agreement, a period lasting from February 15, 1949 to May 4, 1949.

The first two phases of the crisis can be treated more or less as a unit. The United States appeared to have little hope that anything fruitful could materialize from discussion between the military commanders. The less secure, more exposed French and British were concerned to keep the dispute at the lowest possible level merely out of fear that a shift of responsibility to the diplomatic level implied a more serious situation than they were disposed to admit. The French, because of their geographic location and their delicate internal political situation were the most cautious of the three powers, while the British tended to be most blunt and uncompromising in their public

---

[32] *Department of State Bulletin,* October 31, 1948, p. 543.

statements[33] but trod a more cautious path in the actual exchange with the Russians. Washington appeared to be still jockeying for the most acceptable position from which to maneuver during the first week of the crisis.

In retrospect, the principal division among the American authorities existed between the line and staff officials: those who held responsibility in Germany, whether from the military or diplomatic corps, favored a firmer response including the recommendation to use force to break the blockade; those who were responsible for policy in Washington appeared more apprehensive. In both quarters, however, there were internal divisions as well.[34] Finally, there was some movement in favor of immediately invoking the authority of the United Nations. Initiatives emanated from the United Nations Secretariat as well as from certain government sources, but on June 30 Lincoln White of the State Department made clear that for the United States the time for such action had not yet come: "We are deeply appreciative of the role which the United Nations might play should the situation in Berlin further deteriorate. Meanwhile this government is exploring every means of arriving at a settlement of the differences which have arisen."[35]

Although the crisis dialogue never became heavily laden with legal jargon and argumentation, both sides maneuvered from basic legal positions, the essentials of which emerged early in the crisis. As the crisis coursed its way through 1948, the Soviets adduced a number of justifications for the imposition of transport restrictions between Berlin and the Western zones: at first the restrictions were alleged to be the result of "technical" problems;[36] in the Soviet note of July 14 they were described as "urgent measures for the protection of the interests of the German population and also of the economy of the Soviet zone of occupation and the area of Greater Berlin"[37] resulting from the currency reform; in the August meetings between Stalin and representatives of the three Western powers in Moscow, the Russian Premier linked the defense of the introduction of restrictions to

[33] See, e.g., the statement of Foreign Minister Ernest Bevin, *New York Times,* July 1, 1948.

[34] Davison, *op. cit.,* pp. 149–50.

[35] *New York Times,* June 30, 1948.

[36] "ADN Report on the Closing of the Berlin-Helmstedt Railway, June 23, 1948," in Von der Gablentz, *op. cit.,* p. 63.

[37] "Identical Notes from the Government of the U.S.S.R. to the Three Western Governments on the Berlin Situation, July 14, 1948," in *ibid.,* p. 67.

the London decisions to establish a West German government,[38] while simultaneously stressing the currency reform in the Western zones and in the Western sector of Berlin.

None of the above justifications enjoy the color of legality, but underlying them there was a thread of legal argument which has remained a part of the Soviet case ever since. The crux of the Soviet argument was that "Berlin lies in the center of the Soviet zone and is a part of that zone."[39] Also, the Soviets continued, Western rights to participate in the administration of the city derived from Four-Power agreements concerning the administration of Berlin, and these agreements in turn were merely a part of a wider set of agreements designed to deal with the entire German problem. All of these agreements — Yalta, Potsdam, the control mechanism decisions — have been violated; indeed Western actions add up to "systematic violation."[40] As a result, the Western powers had "destroyed the system of quadripartite administration of Germany and . . . thereby undermined as well the very legal basis which assured their right to participation in the administration of Berlin."[41] That the Western powers no longer had a juridical right to occupy Berlin was an insistent part of the Soviet argument as negotiations unfolded in Moscow in August, 1948. Molotov vainly sought to incorporate implicitly in the directives of August 30 to the Military Commanders in Berlin a directive which later aborted. The claim was resurrected once again when Berlin's fever chart began to climb anew in November, 1958.

Predictably, the Western response (herein represented by the U.S. notes and aides-mémoire) vigorously challenged the Soviet thesis both with respect to the source of Western rights in Berlin and the implications which flowed from the Soviet argument. The first official response was voiced by Secretary of State Marshall on June 30 at a press conference where he stated that "we are in Berlin as a result of agreements between the Governments on the areas of occupation in Germany and we intend to stay."[42] In its first diplomatic note of July 6, the United States categorically denied that Berlin was in the Soviet zone or a part thereof and contended that it "is an international zone

[38] *New York Times,* September 27, 1948 (reproduction of Department of State: *The Berlin Crisis: A Report on the Moscow Discussions, 1948*).

[39] *Ibid.,* Soviet note of July 14.

[40] *Ibid.*

[41] *Ibid.*

[42] *New York Times,* June 30, 1948.

of occupation." The basis of Allied rights in Berlin was broadened to include not only Four-Power agreements but also rights deriving "from the total defeat and unconditional surrender of Germany." Thus, however strong a case the Soviets might muster to the effect that there had been violations of Four-Power agreements by the Western powers,[43] the latter still would be able to claim legal rights based on a general international legal principle independent of any particular agreements reached with the Soviet Union. Throughout the long summer months of negotiation the Western powers were to insist repeatedly on their "unquestionable and absolute"[44] right to be in Berlin; that the Soviets must recognize "our basic rights in Berlin";[45] and that any agreement between the Soviets and the West must "respect the juridical position of the Western Governments in Berlin."[46]

Although the right of the Western powers to be in Berlin was tolerably clear both in terms of general principles of international law and on the basis of specific agreements reached among the Four Powers, the right of access to the city from the Western zones over territory of the Soviet zone was less clear. The only explicit access agreements were those reached in November, 1945 with respect to the air corridors, and it was significantly in this medium of access that the Soviets avoided interfering beyond occasional harassment and verbal threats. Access rights over land, rail, or by waterway were never reduced to written agreement and the West had to rely almost exclusively on implication and usage. Thus, in the note of July 6, the United States emphasized that the Four-Power agreements reached in 1944 and 1945 "implied the right of free access to Berlin," and that "this right has long been confirmed by usage" and had been "directly specified" in correspondence between Truman and Stalin in June, 1945.[47] But after stressing the Truman-Stalin correspondence in which, unfortunately, Russian acceptance of access rights for the West had to be implied rather than specifically cited, the United States was

---

[43] These violations could give rise to a disavowal by the Soviet Union under general principles of international law.

[44] "Statement by Ambassador Walter Bedell Smith to Premier Stalin, August 2, 1948," *Documents on American Foreign Relations*, X (1948), 90.

[45] *Ibid.*, p. 94.

[46] At a meeting between Ambassador Smith and Premier Stalin on August 23, 1948 as reported in the *New York Times*, September 27, 1948.

[47] Occasional reference was also made to similar statements by Marshal Zhukov, former Commander-in-Chief of Soviet armies in Europe.

moved to fall back on what basically was an argument of political morality: "The facts are plain. Their meaning is clear. Any other interpretation would offend all the rules of comity and reason."[48] In fact, ' a substantial part of the Western case turned on appeals to reason and practicality on the one hand, and morality and humanitarianism on the other: "This Government now shares . . . the responsibility initially undertaken at Soviet request . . . for the physical well-being of 2,400,000 persons. . . . The responsibility which this Government bears for the . . . safety of the German population in its sector of Berlin is outstandingly humanitarian in character."[49] The legal dimension was developed as far as possible under the circumstances, but the lack of written access agreements once again placed the West at a disadvantage.

Throughout the period under consideration negotiations were conducted in secret. They were made public only in late September, 1948 when, in the midst of an impasse and the breakdown of direct negotiations, the Soviets released their version of all that had transpired in the previous months. This action in turn induced the publication of White Papers on the Western side to refute and rebut the Soviet claims, and to neutralize the propaganda advantage which naturally ensued from the Soviet action. While, as we have seen above, legal claims were asserted by both sides of the dispute, these appeals were limited and complex; they were what we might term "micro-legal" arguments — arguments designed to assert, support and sustain specific legal claims rather than to garner public support for one side or the other. It would be useful to recapitulate these fundamental propositions in a general manner.

The United States was insistent that the Soviet Union recognize the rights of the Western powers to be in Berlin and to have access thereto, while the Soviet Union operated from the premise that whatever rights the West did have with respect to Berlin had been lost as as a result of their activities in their respective zones with regard to reconstruction, monetary reform, reparations, and the like. The Soviets did not directly attack the existence of Western rights, but rather alleged a forfeiture of any such rights which did exist as a result of breach of agreements among the occupying powers. The So-

---

[48] "Identical Notes from the Governments of the United States of America, and the United Kingdom, to the Government of the U.S.S.R. on the Berlin Blockade, July 6, 1948," in Von der Gablentz, *op. cit.*, p. 65.
[49] *Ibid.*

viet Union, in other words, wanted to predicate all rights on written agreements. They therefore were led to postulate general principles of law which supported the claim that the breach of an essential part of an agreement between states allowed cancellation of the agreement by the aggrieved state. They implicitly rejected those principles of international law which would sustain rights acquired by virtue of conquest and the assumption of supreme authority over the vanquished (customary rules) at least insofar as Berlin was concerned. The dialogue did not develop in such pointed terms, but this was its essence.

Legal claims usually are developed with a twofold purpose in mind: as a justification of current state action and as a precaution against the future unfavorable evolution of the situation. Western arguments were not made simply in terms of "you have violated my rights and are culpable." Rather, their arguments attempted to bring about an agreement that would explicitly and implicitly shore up the legal claims of the West to be in, and have access to, Berlin — agreements the Soviets might later find more difficult to transgress. In this they did not succeed to any marked degree. The Soviets, on the other hand, maneuvered for an agreement which would imply that the Western powers were in Berlin on Soviet sufferance and that Berlin was, in fact, economically and politically a part of the Soviet zone. They attempted to word any agreement in such a manner as to imply that existing and future rights flowed from that new agreement. They too did not succeed.

It was this fundamental disparity of starting premises and negotiating objectives which foredoomed the success of any diplomatic negotiation between the parties in the summer of 1948. Law had developed as an important factor in the negotiations, but neither side had used the full potential of the law as a tactic of political conflict — this use remained for the next phase, the "open arena" phase of the Berlin crisis.

VI

An "in-principle" directive was agreed upon between the Soviet Union and the Western powers in Moscow on August 30, calling for the simultaneous lifting of transport restrictions and the introduction of the Soviet-zone mark as the sole currency in Berlin. The inability of the military commanders in Berlin to fulfill this directive made clear the disinterest of the Soviets in achieving any agreement. Not only had negotiations foundered on the issue of quadripartite control over the new currency, but the Soviet Union also made new demands for control over air traffic. A Western note to the Kremlin on September 22 concluded what long had been known: that the difficulties between the two sides derived "not from technical matters but from a fundamental difference of views . . . as to the rights and obligations of the occupying powers in Berlin, their right to have access . . . and to participate in the administration of the affairs of the city of Berlin."[50] The breakdown of direct negotiations which ensued brought about a change of forum, tactics, and rhetorical style.

The Western powers delivered a blistering note to the Soviet Union on September 26 heralding the next stage of the Berlin crisis. Soviet activity, they asserted, obliged them to refer the action of the Soviet government to the United Nations Security Council. This decision had not come easily, and France and Great Britain joined in the move as more or less reluctant allies; the United States, on the other hand, had been prepared to make this move as early as September 7, the day the Berlin discussion on the basis of the August 30 directive had broken down.[51] Washington was less concerned than London or Paris about the consequences of terminating direct negotiations with the Kremlin, and apparently less inclined to believe that the Soviets would abandon the United Nations than were many of the smaller powers. To say the least, the move was not popular.

Meticulously reciting how the Soviet Union had sought "to undermine and indeed to destroy, the rights of the three governments as occupying powers in Berlin as a price for lifting the blockade, illegally imposed in the first instance and still unlawfully maintained," the September 26 note charged that the Russians had resorted to acts of force rather than to the processes of peaceful settlement, had used coercive pressure in clear violation of the principles of the Charter of the United Nations (specifically citing Article 2 in a letter to the Secretary-General three days later) and thus had created a situation which "constitutes a threat to international peace and security"[52] (citing Chapter VII in the aforementioned letter).

While the Western powers, "conscious of their obligations to settle disputes by peaceful means," had had initial recourse to the provi-

[50] *New York Times,* September 27, 1948.
[51] Millis, *op. cit.,* p. 484.
[52] *Department of State Bulletin,* October 10, 1948, p. 455 — a note addressed to Secretary-General of the United Nations Trygve Lie.

sions of Article 33 of the Charter concerning the pacific settlement of disputes, this avenue of approach had been exhausted; it literally was strewn with distortions, violations, broken promises, and Soviet ill will, leaving the West no alternative but to turn to the United Nations. Patience and the continued pursuit of peaceful channels were not to be taken as weakness or ambivalence, and in appealing to the United Nations, the Western powers nevertheless reserved "full rights to take such measures as may be necessary to maintain . . . their positions in Berlin."[53] Thus, the Berlin crisis was escalated one step further to the level of multilateral consideration, the concept of a dispute gave way to the claim that there was a threat to international peace and security, and the language of specific rights, while still maintained, became absorbed in the broader rhetoric of international principles and obligation.

Throughout the crisis, the overriding objective of the Western powers was to get the blockade lifted, but by the time they decided to invoke the Security Council a second objective appeared on the horizon: to induce the world organization to censure the Soviet action in Berlin. This appears to have been the major thrust of at least American policy during the first weeks of consideration of the case by the Security Council. The whole United Nations' experience illustrates how international legal norms and legal argument are used as tactical devices in political crisis; it reveals the limits of even this dimension of international law in international conflict, and the highly circumscribed role the United Nations can play in a conflict involving the major powers. In the last analysis, neither international law nor the United Nations were principal factors in the recession of the Berlin crisis.

It was, of course, clear from the outset that, because of the Soviet veto power, the Security Council could not "solve" the Berlin crisis, and it was not primarily for the purpose of solving it that the Western powers brought the case before the United Nations. The memory of the Iranian situation of 1946 was still fresh. In that case, the failure of Soviet troops to withdraw from northern Iran despite an agreement to do so, led to Security Council consideration of the matter. The Soviet Union refused to participate in a discussion of the case but they eventually did what the Security Council had recommended — withdrew their troops. This and other Soviet behavior in-

[53] *New York Times,* September 27, 1948.

dicated that the Russians were not impervious to the weight of world opinion, factors which may well have induced the belief that even if the Soviet Union vetoed a resolution calling on them to lift the blockade, they eventually might respond positively to such a resolution.

Even if the moral judgment of the organized community of nations did not result in the Soviet Union bowing to the weight of this pressure, there was still much to gain from going to the United Nations. In the first place, it would clarify who was responsible for the tension over Berlin and give the West an invaluable opportunity to show the rest of the world the worth of a Soviet promise and the brutality of Soviet tactics in the pursuit of political goals. Most of the direct negotiations had been conducted in secret until September 25 when the Russians, in violation of an agreement to the contrary, publicized their version of the crisis. Consequently, there was a record to set straight. Secondly, an appeal to the United Nations enabled the United States and her allies to pose as staunch defenders of the principles and procedures of the Charter and thus to solidify public support for their position and policy. Finally, it might serve *a priori* to vindicate "defensive" measures eventually undertaken by the Western powers to assert their fundamental rights. For, if the overwhelming weight of world opinion could be marshalled behind the Western position, then the onus of committing a forcible act in defense of claimed rights would be largely neutralized.[54]

The decision to invoke the Security Council under Chapter VII of the Charter (Threats to the Peace) rather than under Chapter VI (Pacific Settlement of Disputes) was in one sense a matter of necessity rather than choice. Under either chapter of the Charter, seven votes were required to consider a case, but under Chapter VI parties to the dispute are not permitted to vote. Four of the eleven members of the Security Council were parties to the Berlin dispute, and one of the remaining seven, the Ukraine, was a member of the Soviet bloc. It was more than reasonable to assume that the Ukraine would vote against consideration of the case thus depriving the Security Council of its capacity to handle the matter under Chapter VI. Under Chapter VII, on the other hand, parties to a dispute may vote. While this

[54] There is some evidence that this support may already have materialized in the United States. In a national sample, four-fifths of the respondents to a poll on the Berlin situation were ready to go to war with the Soviet Union over Berlin. See Gabriel Almond, *The American People and Foreign Policy* (New York: Frederick A. Praeger, 1960), p. 105.

automatically meant that any condemning resolution would be vetoed by the Soviet Union, it still gave the Western powers the opportunity to publicly air their grievances.

There were other practical advantages to using Chapter VII, however, and these factors clearly played a role in the tactical decision to
invoke the Security Council under this Chapter. In doing so, the West
was able to lift the case out of the impasse of technicalities and legalities which had been used to thwart progress in the direct negotiations, to set aside momentarily the questions of currency and control, and to challenge the blockade alone.

This was a tactical shift of fundamental importance. The earlier insistence on the origin and nature of Western rights was now accompanied by stress on the existence of a threat to the peace, on the illegal use of coercive measures to attain political objectives to which
the Soviet Union was not entitled, and on the use of the threat of
force in derogation of the obligations of the Charter of the United
Nations. This was an appeal to general principles and rules of international conduct, to what we might call "macro-legal" norms; an appeal to public and world opinion in clear and unequivocal language.
No longer was it simply a "dispute" over rights between two parties;
now it was a contest between the aggressive Soviet Union and the
United Nations. *Whatever* might be the legal rights of the respective
parties, the *real* issue was whether, in the pursuit of political objectives, coercion might be used by one member of the United Nations
against other members in such a manner as to threaten the peace.
This was the new theme, and in an attempt to orchestrate the response of the community of nations the Deputy U.S. Representative
to the Security Council, Dr. Phillip Jessup, even went so far as to suggest that the whole *raison d'être* of the United Nations was at stake:
"The real question is whether in the present situation . . . the only
existing general international machinery for the preservation of peace
can be used to remove a threat to peace, or whether the Government
of the U.S.S.R. intends that the world be thrown back upon an unor-
ganized international community with all that that implies."[55]

However fuzzy the access rights of the Western powers to Berlin,
and whatever the precise legal obligations and rights of the disputant
with regard to currency control (the ostensible bone of contention),

[55] *Security Council Official Records* (hereafter cited as *SCOR*); 3rd year,
361st meeting, pp. 20–21.

the Western states had now staked out secure legal ground. They had responded to the blockade, a belligerent act, by flying over it; they had not resorted to forcible action; and they had followed the prescriptions of the Charter in the matter of settling disputes. And they fully intended to capitalize on their exemplary behavior. Thus the opening plea of Dr. Jessup before the Security Council on October 6:

The United States Government has sought by peaceful means to remove the threat to peace created by the Soviet Union which, while it remains, is the insuperable obstacle to free negotiations. Our very resort to the Security Council is a further use of the same peaceful means and is directed to the same end. The United States will be no party to encouraging or submitting to practices which would make a mockery of the Charter.[56]

We had come to the United Nations with "clean hands" so to speak, and we expected our chief protagonist to be judged accordingly.

Despite our disclaimer that "we do not bring this case to the Security Council with any cut-and-dried formula for its solution," and that it was only "our hope that the Security Council can assist in removing the threat to the peace,"[57] it was fairly evident at the time that the United States expected at least a resolution calling for the lifting of the blockade.[58] As it was the blockade which created the threat to the peace, such a resolution would have been an implicit condemnation of Soviet action and an indirect admission that the Soviets had violated the Charter of the United Nations. And, as suggested earlier, even a defeated resolution to this effect would greatly strengthen any later claim of legality for the use of force in the defense of claimed rights. Far less could have been expected under Chapter VI.

The true value of a tactical measure often may be measured by the response of the target state. Under this criterion it would appear the game was worth the candle, if not in resolving the issue or in securing a lifting of the blockade, then at least in reversing the roles of hunter and hunted. There can be no doubt but that the Soviet Union did not want the Berlin case before the United Nations, and they argued vigorously against its inclusion on the agenda of the Security Council. Losing this argument, they announced that the Soviet Union would not participate in the consideration of the question (which eventually proved to be poor tactics), but unlike their action in the

---

[56] *Department of State Bulletin,* October 17, 1948, p. 484.
[57] *Department of State Bulletin,* October 6, 1948, p. 487.
[58] *Ibid.*

1946 Iranian situation, the Soviets did not walk out. Rather, they remained to veto the fruits of the Security Council's labors to break the impasse.

The attempt of the Soviet Union to prevent Security Council discussion of the Berlin case is a classic example of Soviet "distortionism." The Soviet defense is worth exploring briefly, for it is instructive both on how the Soviets sought to develop a legal basis for precluding United Nations' involvement, and on the uses to which international legal norms may be put.

The Soviet Union contended that the Berlin issue did not come within the competence of the Security Council. It was part of a larger question, Germany, which was specifically excluded from United Nations' consideration by Article 107 of the Charter,[59] as well as by a host of international agreements ranging from Yalta and Potsdam through the specific agreements on control of Germany reached in 1944 and 1945. These agreements established the appropriate procedures for dealing with problems connected with Germany or any part thereof, and created the necessary instrument to handle them, the Council of Foreign Ministers. Secondly, there was no blockade and those transport restrictions which did exist "were simply counter-measures which the . . . Soviet Union have been forced to take on account of a separate currency reform introduced . . . in the western zone of Germany."[60] As there was no blockade there was no threat to the peace, and the claim that there was such a threat "is but a means of exerting pressure, an attempt to use the United Nations to further its [the United States'] own aggressive ends."[61] Finally, even conceding *arguendo* that a threat to the peace did exist, "Article 107 of the Charter excludes intervention in this matter by the United Nations Organization."

In what must unquestionably be considered a brilliant performance in hypocrisy, Andrei Vishinsky made the following legal arguments:

If we are to keep to the terms of . . . international agreements, and to respect the signatures appended to them, then it cannot be recognized as either legal or correct to refer to the Security Council any question concerning Germany, including that of Berlin.[62]

A decision to refer any such question to the Security Council would con-

---

[59] *SCOR*, No. 113, 361st meeting, pp. 9–10.
[60] *Ibid.*, p. 10.
[61] *Ibid.*
[62] *Ibid.*, p. 12.

stitute a direct violation of the United Nations Charter and of the international agreements . . . mentioned.[63]

The Governments of the United Kingdom, the United States . . . and
France must therefore choose the legal way, the way or procedure established in international agreements signed by them. . . . That is the legal
method. Those who follow it will not violate either the Charter . . . or the
international agreements which these Governments have signed.[64]

and then, the clincher:

. . . the only legal way of dealing with the matter is to have the Council of
Foreign Ministers examine the Berlin question. That way is in conformity
with the Charter . . . since Article 2 requires that Governments shall fulfill
in good faith the obligations assumed by them.

Pacta sunt servanda ("treaties are made to be observed") — such is the
basic principle of international law, of international cooperation. So, if you
please, carry out that fundamental requirement.[65]

Thus, in rapid-fire succession the Soviet Union charged the West
with violation of Four-Power and U.N. obligations, with attempting
to pervert the Charter of the United Nations, and with disregarding
fundamental principles of international law. The tactic was well
suited to the purpose. The principal aim of the Soviet Union was to
turn the Security Council's attention from the blockade to the broader
issue of the proper forum for handling disputes concerning Germany. The respective rights of the parties was immaterial; all that
mattered was that disputes regarding those rights be dealt with in
the prescribed manner. The West did not deny the basic principle,
but contended that what was before the Security Council was not the
German problem but a threat to the peace — the blockade — and that
the appropriate forum for this problem was the Security Council.
If the West had acceded to the Soviet demand to return to the Council of Foreign Ministers not only would they have had to negotiate
under the pressure of the blockade, but removal of the latter would
have been used as a *quid pro quo* for concessions the West was quite
unprepared to give. The Soviets were unable to sustain their claim.

To my knowledge, the only explicit reference to international law
was that made by Vishinsky above, although many of the arguments
made by the West in the course of Security Council discussion of the
Berlin issue implicitly were based on international obligation. The

[63] *Ibid.*
[64] *Ibid.*, p. 13.
[65] *Ibid.*, p. 14.

United States certainly made a strong case for having abided by the prescriptions of the Charter, and if anything, perhaps overdid the point. The following statement by Dr. Jessup is typical of many similar claims put forth by the Western powers:

The Governments . . . chose that [appeal to the Security Council in lieu of the use of force] alternative. It was the only alternative consistent with the obligations of a Member of the United Nations. It was a recognition of the conviction of the three Governments that the United Nations is and will remain the cornerstone on which the structure of peace must be built.[66]

It would be difficult to contest the sincerity of this claim which is strikingly representative of the legalistic-moralistic bias of the American political style. The postwar history of the United States displays an active support for the principles of the Charter, which essentially reflect the basic values of its system. However, as we saw earlier, there were a number of other, pragmatic, considerations which led the United States to refrain from immediately responding with force: the less dangerous overflight of the blockade with the airlift had created certain possibilities worth exploring; the conventional military weakness of the West and the political implications, in light of that weakness, of an atomic monopoly; the probability that a mere show of force might be insufficient and even counterproductive. As long as the airlift was sufficient to sustain Berlin there was every reason for probing all the diplomatic channels — bilateral and multilateral — to end a dangerous situation. That these policy decisions could be sustained and justified in support of general principles of international law and morality as inscribed in the Charter does not permit the conclusion that the tail was wagging the dog.[67]

Resort to the United Nations was prudent, morally correct, and perhaps a politically astute move for an administration five weeks away from a Presidential election. Furthermore, it made an important contribution by plugging all the legal gaps against the day when, if the case arose, force might be used — at least such force would be based on a moral consensus registered against the Soviet Union in the United Nations, and with legal remedies exhausted. We have insisted on a number of occasions that one factor of Western strategy was to legally cover an eventual use of force. While the point is conjectural,

[66] *Ibid.*, p. 22.
[67] It goes without saying that the same conclusions apply to the Soviet Union.

it is based on a pattern of thinking discernible in American foreign policy. It may be Machiavellian to view the use of the United Nations in so instrumental a fashion, but the use of the United Nations as a vehicle for legitimizing American policy has often been seen, and at the level of political crisis, both the Korean and Cuban missile cases would seem to sustain this point.

VII

Aside from the discomfort caused the Soviet Union, and the one-sided opportunity afforded the West to expound its case before world opinion, resort to the United Nations and to the evocation of fundamental norms for international behavior as inscribed in the Charter was of no service either in resolving the dispute or in mitigating the positions of the disputants. It was useful, however, in a negative sense. The situation proved in fact what long had been accepted in theory — that the world organization was not competent to handle serious disputes among the major powers. It also demonstrated the elasticity of international norms such as are recorded in Article 2 of the Charter — talismen of political morality and not much more. And, it may even suggest the advantages which can accrue to the state which first invokes general legal norms in support of its position.

The United States went to the United Nations in the hope that it could muster support for a resolution calling on Russia to lift its blockade. Within a week, however, it had become tolerably clear that the members of the Security Council who were not parties to the dispute, the so-called "neutral" nations (Argentina, Belgium, Canada, China, Colombia and Syria),[68] were unwilling to support a resolution condemning the Soviet Union for having created a threat to the peace. As it eventually turned out, this was not all they were unwilling to support. Efforts at mediation were undertaken by the six "neutral" nations under the guidance of the President of the Security Council, Dr. Juan Bramuglia of Argentina. The grave concern of these nations, and many others as well, in becoming entangled in a Great Power struggle was demonstrated in the Syrian delegate's comment that he preferred that the disputants would settle the problem among themselves.[69] The clear desire of many of the smaller nations

[68] The only other nonpermanent member, the Ukraine, followed the Soviet Union in nonparticipation in Security Council discussions.

[69] *New York Times,* October 16, 1948.

not to be forced into taking sides for or against the Great Powers probably goes far toward explaining why the United States did not go directly to the General Assembly where it would have avoided the Soviet veto.[70]

The mediatory efforts of the six nations passed through several stages between October 4 when the issue was formally opened before the Security Council and October 25 when the Soviet Union vetoed a compromise resolution put forth by the "neutrals." At first Dr. Bramuglia sought to get agreement on a formula in which the Western powers would drop their complaint and reopen discussion in the Council of Foreign Ministers with the understanding that in turn the Soviet Union would lift the blockade, but such a "gentlemen's agreement" was totally unacceptable to the West.[71] The United States remained insistent that any resolution at least contain a clause that there could be no negotiations on the Berlin question under the threat of force.[72] Secretary of State Marshall was adamant that any resolution transferring the question to the Council of Foreign Ministers include a demand that the Russians lift the blockade.[73] Preparedness to go to the Council of Foreign Ministers did not represent a change of position by the United States, for in his opening remarks Dr. Jessup had stated that "the moment the blockade is lifted, the United States is ready to have an immediate meeting of the Council of Foreign Ministers to discuss with the Soviet Union any questions relating to Germany."[74] As had been true all through the crisis, both sides always left open escape routes to retreat from the brink.

The "neutral" nations sought to buy time in their efforts to find some mutually satisfactory face-saving formula by asking both sides to clarify the nature of the transport and communications restrictions and the reasons why the August 30 directive to the Military Commanders had not been implemented. The Soviet Union refused to participate, in keeping with their earlier contention that the Security Council lacked jurisdiction, but the Western powers did respond,

---

[70] There was speculation that the United States would bring the Berlin case before the General Assembly following the Soviet veto of a Security Council resolution on October 25, 1948, but many delegations did not want a showdown between the superpowers and the idea was dropped. *New York Times,* October 27, 1948.

[71] *New York Times,* October 10, 1948.

[72] *Ibid.,* October 9, 1948.

[73] *Ibid.,* October 10, 1948.

[74] *Department of State Bulletin,* October 17, 1948, p. 487.

thus getting a second opportunity to rake the Soviet government over the coals. Finally, on October 21 the "neutrals" presented a compromise resolution calling for the removal of restrictions by both sides, continued negotiations on the basis of the August 30 directive, and a meeting of the Council of Foreign Ministers shortly after the negotiations among the Military Governors terminated.[75] The latter were given a definite time limit, November 10. The compromise resolution was a far cry from the initial Western demands: it did not censure the Soviet Union; it omitted any direct reference to the blockade; and in calling on both sides to reciprocally lift restrictions, it suggested at least implicitly a modicum of shared responsibility for the current impasse. Despite the concessions the Western powers accepted the compromise. The Soviet Union vetoed it.[76]

Mediatory efforts by the Security Council "neutrals" at a technical level were to continue through the winter months along with joint efforts by the Secretary-General and the President of the General Assembly.[77] But by October 25 the United Nations already had served its purpose. The West had come to the United Nations as an aggrieved party ostensibly seeking relief; it had exhausted all possibility of direct negotiation and had laid the facts before the court of world opinion. It had remonstrated against the brutality of Soviet action, the long line of broken promises, and the callous disregard of the fundamental norms of international behavior. As an editorial in the *New York Times* on the eve of the Soviet veto was to remark:

The veto cannot nullify the moral validity of the judgment. . . . There can be no further doubt as to who is responsible for the Berlin crisis. This, in turn, not only puts on Russia the onus for any further aggravation of the crisis but also frees the hands of the Western Powers to take all measures necessary and permissible under the Charter to cope with the situation.[78]

Public opinion had been brought to bear on a political crisis, but in

[75] *New York Times*, October 22, 1948; *ibid.*, October 25, 1948, in an editorial.

[76] *Ibid.*, October 26, 1948. In voting against the compromise, the Soviets argued that the August 30 directives called for a simultaneous introduction of Soviet currency and lifting of the blockade, whereas the compromise in essence made the former a precondition of the latter.

[77] Herbert Evatt, President of the General Assembly and Trygve Lie sent a joint letter on November 13 to the parties to the dispute calling for a peaceful settlement of the issues. See *Department of State Bulletin*, November 28, 1948, p. 655, and *New York Times*, November 14, 1948 (IV) for text and commentary, respectively.

[78] *New York Times*, October 26, 1948.

the absence of the willingness of a major power to accept the judgment of this opinion, the world organization had done all that it could.

The Soviet Union had been disadvantaged by its refusal to accept Security Council jurisdiction in more ways than one. In the first place, it forfeited the opportunity to use the forum of the United Nations to rebut the Western charges, and while silence is not acquiescence, presumptions ran against the Soviet Union. Secondly, the Soviets were precluded the chance of introducing a counterproposal which could shift the defensive burden to the West. In fact, Vishinsky had discussed an alternative with Dr. Bramuglia which called for a graduated lifting of restrictions as negotiations between the Military Commanders in Berlin progressed.[79] This would not have been accepted by the West but it would have provided grist for the Soviet propaganda mill. That the Russians were bothered by the image their veto had created and by the publicization of their truculence, became evident three days after the veto. On October 28, Stalin held an interview with *Pravda* in which he charged that the West had backed out of two "agreements" — the agreement of August 30, and an alleged agreement with Dr. Bramuglia for a staged withdrawal of restrictions geared to negotiations in Berlin.[80] It was evident, Stalin concluded, that the West did not want agreement "but [they] talk about agreement and cooperation so as to put the blame on the USSR."[81] For several days afterward the Russians hammered away at the supposed agreement for graduated return to the *status quo ante,* neglecting the elementary fact that as a go-between, rather than a representative of either side, Dr. Bramuglia had no capacity to bind the West or the Soviet Union to any agreement. The fact that the Russians invested considerable time and effort to "correcting" the record and that they spoke in terms of how the impasse might have been broken, rather than denying the existence of a blockade or a threat to the peace, might be taken as evidence that the Western gambit in going to the United Nations had borne fruit. But, when taken in conjunction with an increase of Soviet pressure in Berlin and no concrete move to de facto relieve the tension, little more than propaganda value can be assigned to the Soviet move.

For the United States, the United Nations eventually became more

[79] *Ibid.*
[80] *Ibid.,* October 29, 1948.
[81] *Ibid.*

of a liability than an asset. The Berlin case was left on the Security Council agenda, and its "neutral" members created a technical committee to try to work out an acceptable agreement on currency reform. Secretary-General Trygve Lie and Herbert Evatt, President of the General Assembly, also sought to induce a *démarche*. Only one element in these complex developments need concern us: the increasing tendency of these actors to treat the West as being as culpable as the Soviet Union, thus implicitly to distribute the responsibility between the two sides. Responding to the Lie-Evatt appeal for a resumption of conversations between East and West, Secretary of State George C. Marshall was at pains to stress that the basic issue in Berlin is "whether or not the Soviet Union can be permitted to use force, whether by way of blockade or of economic pressures involving currency, credit or trade . . . to deprive the Western Powers of participation in the administration of Berlin."[82] The United States however, once again ran into the snag that was implicit in the earlier unwillingness of the "neutrals" to censure the Soviet Union for committing a threat to the peace — that the small powers were less interested in vindicating rights than they were in maintaining the peace.

VIII

The Berlin blockade finally was broken as a result of considerations quite different than those of international law or the pressure of the United Nations. Indeed, by late January, 1949 the efforts of the world organization were recognized to have been a failure. The Berlin blockade had stimulated increased pressure by the United States for an independent West German government, had brought about the Brussels Pact, and had made clear to Washington the need to discard old shibboleths and to undertake new commitments — specifically, the North Atlantic Pact. The airlift had become an obvious success by the time winter set in, and the tensions engendered by the continuance of the blockade enabled the United States to exert pressure on both France and Germany to complete their respective metamorphoses. As early as October 26, the day following the Soviet veto, Secretary-General Lie asked Dr. Jessup: "Is it a fact that the United States wants a settlement?"[83] Remarking on the increasing effectiveness of the airlift and the value which was accruing to the United

[82] *Ibid.*, November 18, 1948.
[83] Trygve Lie, *In the Cause of Peace* (New York: Macmillan, 1954), p. 203.

States in terms of prestige, Lie also noted the "lack of anxiety for an immediate solution [which] characterized American circles in Germany."[84] Shortly afterward he was moved to conclude that both in London and Washington there were elements not interested in "a compromise solution from which no party would emerge wholly victorious."[85] These doubts were shared by the influential Paris daily, *Le Monde*.[86]

From the Soviet point of view, while the blockade was steadily becoming disadvantageous, it nevertheless was a useful shield behind which to consolidate the cleavage between East and West in Berlin. Throughout November, Soviet authorities in Berlin moved toward the establishment of a separate government for the Eastern sector of the city.[87] Correspondingly, the United States steadily hardened its position and by mid-January found itself a minority of one, rejecting efforts of the "neutrals" technical committee on currency and submitting counterproposals which clearly invited rejection.[88]

The embarrassing efficiency of the airlift and the economic effectiveness of the counterblockade which had been imposed on the flow of goods and raw materials to the Eastern zone by the Western powers finally led the Soviets to conclude that their blockade had become a distinct liability.[89] This was signalled to the West on January 31 when Premier Stalin, responding to a series of questions posed by American journalist Kingsbury Smith remarked that he saw no obstacle to lifting the blockade of Berlin if the West met two conditions: reciprocally removed their counterblockade and postponed establishment of a West German state pending a meeting of the Council of Foreign Ministers on the entire German question.[90] What was notably missing as a condition for the first time was settlement of the

---

[84] *Ibid.*, p. 210.

[85] *Ibid.*, p. 216.

[86] As quoted in *New York Times,* November 28, 1948 (IV).

[87] See, generally, Davison, *op. cit.*, pp. 208–209.

[88] *New York Times,* January 22, 1949.

[89] See, e.g., *New York Times,* March 2, 1949 where it is reported that Polish representatives made overtures to British authorities in Berlin to induce a reopening of the negotiations on currency reform. The alleged cause of Polish activity was the impact of the counterblockade on Polish economic recovery.

[90] *New York Times,* January 31, 1949. The United States refused to make this a condition, but in fact postponed establishment of the West German state until after the meeting of the Council of Foreign Ministers which, like its predecessors, achieved nothing.

currency issue. On February 15 Dr. Jessup casually asked the Soviet Representative on the Security Council, Jacob Malik, whether the omission had been "accidental." When, exactly one month later, Malik informed Jessup that the omission had not been "accidental," the way to a solution was opened.

Agreement finally was reached on May 4, 1949 and the blockade was lifted on May 12. Drew Middleton described this day which signaled the end of the first high tension confrontation between the two superpowers in these eloquent terms: "as the morning sun rose over the jagged skyline of this broken but defiant city a Soviet zone locomotive chugged wearily into Charlottenburg station . . . hauling the first train to reach Berlin from the West in 328 days."[91] Nothing had really been resolved except for the removal of the physical impediments to communication which had constituted the blockade and the counterblockade. The escutcheon of international law had been tarnished, but not too badly. The Communist bloc had violated the proscriptions of the Charter, and ignored its prescriptions. The removal of the blockade no more vindicated those principles than did the withdrawal of Anglo-French troops from the Suez in 1956.

Berlin still remains a festering sore in the center of Europe and the rights of the Western powers to be in Berlin and to have free and unimpeded access thereto are periodically challenged. The balance of nuclear terror — not a deeper commitment to the principles of international law against the use of force as an arm of policy — has caused a change in the manner of Soviet attack. The bluntness of blockade has given way to the subtleness of arguments couched in the language of the law. But the fundamental point remains the same: the Soviet Union can no more tolerate the perpetuation of a Western island in a Communist sea than can the West tolerate the absorption of that island and its two and a half million inhabitants into the Communist camp. What is clear for both sides, however, is that while they may parry and thrust with legal argument and innuendo, and while a legal framework may functionally serve the interests of non-conflagration, the only settlement attainable in Berlin is a political settlement. When the moment for that arrives, we may expect law to serve once again, this time to ratify and authenticate a new status quo.

[91] *New York Times,* May 12, 1949.

IX

The assiduous attention paid by the Western powers to proscriptions against the use of force, and the meticulous pursuit of prescriptions for the peaceful settlement of disputes first by direct negotiation and then through the medium of the United Nations, could be interpreted as evidence that international law has considerable constraining influence on state behavior. Similarly, the callousness of Soviet action in imposing the blockade and in consciously thwarting some of the attempts at peaceful settlement seems to lend strong support to the contention that the Communist bloc has little or no regard for the principles of international law. The latter proposition is more tenable than the former. Western action in pursuing the broad outlines traced in this essay cannot be tied to the proposition that the Western powers were acting in the service of international law, or in order to vindicate that law. All that can be sustained is the proposition that many states, and principally the established non-Communist states, where possible, will try to conduct their policy in a manner compatible with generally accepted international legal and moral principles. As most of the alleged norms reflect Western tradition and values and incline toward maintenance of the status quo, this is not an unforeseen conclusion.

As we have seen, the Western powers always reserved their "rights" (of self-defense) and pointedly noted that although they could have done otherwise, they refrained from the use of force. But we also have seen that military and political reasons strongly militated against the use of force until the point that a failure to use force would have meant the forfeiture of a vital interest. Fortunately, this point never was reached in the Berlin crisis. There is, therefore, no ground upon which to base a claim that reverence of law precluded or impeded a resort to force by the United States and its allies.

It is important to recognize the delicacy of the Western position. The Soviet blockade was not a case of clear-cut aggression against which the use of force is sanctioned; the first actual use of force (breaking the blockade) would have fallen principally to the United States. In light of the temperament both of American and other (uncommitted) publics and policymakers, it was important that the eventual use of force have sound moral and legal underpinnings. The United States, therefore, sought to put forth a strong legal case regarding (a) the nature of its right to be in and have access to Berlin, (b) Soviet violations of those rights, and (c) the threat to the peace created by the blockade.)

In agonizing its way through this dilemma, the United States tried to develop as strong a position as possible. It also tried to avoid facing the use of force to assert its rights, first by invoking the weight of world opinion through the medium of the United Nations, and secondly in accepting a very modest resolution in the Security Council. As the airlift revealed its tremendous potential as a substitute for force, the United States lost interest in compromising, or even in keeping the Berlin case actively on the agenda of the Security Council. To a great extent, in other words, the United States lost interest in promulgating its legal case. And, as the blockade turned from a burden into a benefit (as a catalyst for the completion of the West German state, and as a means for welding together defensive alliances against the Soviet Union), the United States became distinctly bothered by the continued attempts of the "neutrals" on the Security Council to find a solution to the problem.[92] This is rather compelling evidence for the central proposition of this essay — that legal argument is fundamentally a tactical device for the pursuit of policy. When such tactics no longer are instrumental for policy, and certainly when they threaten to upend policy, even the allegedly righteous supporters of international law are prepared to minimize, if not to discard, the law.

The Berlin crisis illustrates the uses and limits of law in political crisis. There is some evidence that legal considerations were an important ingredient in the initial Western decision to remain in Berlin. Once that decision was made, however, law became principally a tactical device for maneuvering through the crisis. The Western powers used legal argument to advertise their own good behavior and as a weapon to attack Soviet policy. The Soviet leaders found law a somewhat less serviceable device but they, too, did not fail to invoke law in justification of their own action and to undermine Western strategy in the conflict.

The problem of Berlin still is with us; it has become a permanent crisis. While threats of force are not alien to the situation, the dialogue over Berlin today is carried on much more in legal terms than it

---

[92] These attempts put the United States in the embarrassing position of having to sabotage them by imposing untenable conditions.

was in 1948. The use of force is not less conscionable, but more risky; and the Soviet Union, which was the only state ever to use force in the Berlin case, has adjusted its tactics accordingly. Neither side is satisfied with the status quo, but any change implies a shift in the power structure on the European continent. This is unacceptable, so the unnatural situation in Berlin is perpetuated. Law has found a useful role in this perpetuation — legal contentions serve as a means to probe the other side's commitment (a substitute for force), and by obscuring the underlying political confrontation in the jargon of the law, they blanket the volatility which characterizes the Berlin situation. This is a modest role, but it is all that reasonably can or should be expected of international law in view of the heterogeneous nature of the contemporary international political system.

LYNN H. MILLER

The Kashmir Dispute

I

Independence and Political Turmoil. On August 15, 1947, two independent states emerged on the Indian subcontinent out of the British Empire. For the new leaders of India, realization of the long-awaited dream of independence from British rule was marred seriously by the fact that self-rule had brought with it the division of the subcontinent into two nations. Their goal had been the creation of a single democratic and secular state, uniting Hindus and Moslems, as well as Christians, Buddhists, Jainists, Parsis and Sikhs, in one political allegiance. To Pakistani leaders, on the other hand, the birth of their nation represented the culmination of years of Moslem political ambitions on the subcontinent. The founders of Pakistan had sought to avoid their likely future domination by the more numerous Hindus through the creation of a Moslem state which, while not as large as its Indian neighbor, could aspire to leadership of the world of Islam and develop in freedom from Hindu rule. The political ideology of Mohammed Ali Jinnah and the Moslem League he led had triumphed in the creation of the Moslem state of Pakistan; that of Mahatma Gandhi, Jawaharlal Nehru, and their colleagues in the Indian National Congress had been challenged seriously by the same act.

The issue of partition was not the only problem which confronted British and local leaders in the years that they had prepared for the withdrawal of British authority on the subcontinent. Throughout the colonial period, the Crown had maintained a special treaty relation-

41

ship, that of "paramountcy," with the 584 princely states that were scattered across the subcontinent. For the most part, these states were thoroughly autocratic in their internal rule, although the paramount power of the British Crown regulated their foreign affairs and defense matters. When the British government agreed to grant independence to British India, the question immediately arose as to the relationship of the princely states to the new nation (or nations) once paramountcy was withdrawn.

In the spring of 1946, a Cabinet Mission memorandum was produced stating that after the transfer of power to an independent India ". . . His Majesty's Government will cease to exercise the powers of paramountcy. This means that the rights of the States which flow from their relationship to the Crown will no longer exist and that all the rights surrendered by the States to the paramount power will return to the States."[1] The princely states would then have the juridical right to remain independent entities or to accede either to India or Pakistan. Although both Moslem and Hindu leaders accepted this memorandum as the logical resolution of the British relationship with the princely states, they could not have been favorably disposed toward the possibility that many, or even any, of the princes would choose independence for themselves. Recognizing the obstacles such an option would place in the creation of viable Indian and Pakistani states, the Viceroy, Lord Mountbatten, repeatedly urged the princes to choose accession to one state or the other before the day of independence arrived. His assumption was that, in general, the Hindu states should accede to India and the Muslim states to Pakistan. Almost all the princes recognized their own impotence in the face of national independence on the subcontinent and chose union with one country or the other before the date of expiration of British paramountcy. Three princes, however, refused to make such a choice, and on August 15 their states of Hyderabad, Junagadh, and Kashmir became technically independent.[2]

In all three cases, this refusal to accede to one country or the other before independence resulted in serious political clashes between India and Pakistan. Yet it was only in the case of Kashmir that the chain

---

[1] *Cabinet Mission Memorandum*, Command Paper 6855 (May 12, 1946).

[2] "Jammu and Kashmir" is the full name of the state. Throughout this study, however, it will be referred to simply as "Kashmir," the commonly used abbreviation.

of events resulting from the refusal of the Maharaja to accede produced an intractable conflict, destined to embroil the subcontinent in hot and cold war for the next twenty years.[3]

Unlike either Hyderabad or Junagadh, both of which constituted enclaves within Indian territory, Kashmir bordered both India and Pakistan as well as China, the Soviet Union, and Afghanistan. Kashmir's proximity to both of the new states gave each an approximately equal claim to sovereignty over it on the basis of its location. And because of its position in an international frontier area, each of the new states regarded possession of Kashmir to be of enormous strategic importance. Additionally, both new countries were attracted by its large mineral and timber resources.

While Kashmir's size, location, and resources made it a highly desirable prize, then, the state's social and political composition formed the roots of the conflict which Kashmir's status was to produce in Indo-Pakistani relations. Kashmir's population was overwhelmingly Moslem, while its minority was composed largely of Hindus with much smaller percentages of Sikhs and Buddhists.[4] In spite of the predominance of Moslems, however, for a hundred years the state had been ruled by the Hindu Dogra dynasty.[5] By the 1930's, the growing political consciousness of the Moslem population was accelerated by the independence movement on the ascendancy throughout the subcontinent that was to produce organized political action in Kashmir for the first time, directed against the autocracy of the

[3] Junagadh, with a Moslem ruler and largely Hindu population, acceded to Pakistan in September, 1947, but, with the opposition among the populace to this move, the Indian army entered the state and guaranteed the people the right to determine their own future. When they voted for union with India, Junagadh's accession was transferred to that country.

In the case of Hyderabad, its Moslem Nizam apparently hoped to maintain his independence indefinitely. His subjects were predominantly Hindu, however, and his state an enclave in the midst of Indian territory. In September, 1948, the Indian army forced its way into Hyderabad and secured its accession to India.

[4] Estimates are that the population of Kashmir is between 70 and 80 percent Moslem, 20 percent Hindu, with 1–2 percent each of Sikhs and Buddhists.

[5] The founder of the Dogra dynasty had cooperated with the British in defeating the rulers of the Sikh Empire, which had included Kashmir. By the Treaty of Amritsar (1846), the first Maharaja acquired Kashmir in perpetuity from Britain in return for a payment of some 7.5 million rupees. A century later, Pakistani leaders and, finally, Sheikh Abdullah challenged the legitimacy of Dogra rule in Kashmir by condemning the "Sale Deed" of 1846 by which Gulab Singh obtained possession.

Maharaja. Leaving the details of that political movement aside, several factors in its development are particularly relevant to the conflict which was to follow after partition of the subcontinent. First, the most important political leader in Kashmir at the time, Sheikh Mohammed Abdullah, led an organization which became dedicated to the intercommunal principle — i.e., the necessity of political unity between Moslems and Hindus — and which maintained ties with the secularist Congress party outside Kashmir. Here was a Moslem-led and Moslem-dominated political movement which embraced most of the principles of the strongly Hindu Congress party. Secondly, Sheikh Abdullah's organization was sharply disputed by the Kashmir affiliate of the Moslem League led by Ghulam Abbas, which demanded a separate Moslem state and no political cooperation with the Hindus. Although both these groups had originated in opposition to the Maharaja's autocratic rule, their mutual rivalry was so great as to prevent concerted action against him. By the time of partition, the leaders of both groups had been imprisoned by the Maharaja, with the result that the nationalist movement in Kashmir — while far from suppressed — was temporarily halted.[6]

In the month before independence came to the subcontinent, Lord Mountbatten visited the Maharaja of Kashmir in his capital of Srinagar to urge him to accede either to India or Pakistan before August 15. As Mountbatten later explained,

. . . had he acceded to Pakistan before August 14, 1947, the future Government of India had allowed me to give His Highness an assurance that no objection whatever would be raised by them. . . . The only trouble that could have been raised was by non-accession to either side, and this was unfortunately the very course followed by the Maharaja.[7]

The ruler of Kashmir was able to continue his vacillation, thanks in large part to the outbreak of communal violence in the Punjab, which demanded the full attention of both Hindu and Moslem leaders in the following weeks. At the last moment before independence, the Maharaja attempted to negotiate Standstill Agreements with both the

[6] For a full discussion of the Kashmiri national and reformist movements before independence, see Michael Brecher, *The Struggle for Kashmir* (New York: Oxford University Press, 1953), Chap. 1.

[7] Address to the East India Association of June 29, 1948, in the *Asiatic Review,* London, XLIV (October, 1948), 353.

new states. These agreements would have granted the new governments the authority to operate Kashmir's telegraph and postal systems (before this, the responsibility of the unified government of India), and may have been desired by the Maharaja as confirmation of
his state's impartiality as to political ties with either Pakistan or India.
Although such a Standstill Agreement was signed with Pakistan on
the day of independence, none was concluded with India — whether
because of the Indian government's distraction by the communal riots
in the Punjab or because of her leaders' desire to avoid another source
of conflict with Pakistan.

Although this situation regarding the Standstill Agreements may
have led Pakistani leaders to suppose that Kashmir eventually would
accede to Pakistan, it also resulted, at least indirectly, in the straining
of relations between the Maharaja and the Karachi government in the
weeks following independence. For more than a month, the basic
foodstuffs which Pakistan was pledged by the terms of the Standstill
Agreement to supply to Kashmir failed to reach their destination.
Then railroad service between the two states was suspended. As
charges and countercharges flew between Karachi and Srinagar, huge
numbers of refugees from the Punjab poured into southern Jammu
province. Amidst rising tensions and confusion, there occurred the
"Poonch revolt" against the authority of the Maharaja. This event —
essentially a peasant uprising — soon was depicted by the Pakistanis
as another example of Hindu-Moslem conflict ruthlessly suppressed
by the Hindu government of the Maharaja. The latter, in turn, interpreted the revolt as a plot to force him to accede to Pakistan, for he
charged that the region had been infiltrated by Moslem bands from
across the Pakistani border. During September and October, regular
reports were heard of the movements of tribesmen and other Pakistanis into Kashmir. Finally, on October 21, 1947, several thousand
tribesmen living in the remote regions of Pakistan south of Afghanistan's border marched through Pakistani West Punjab and invaded
Kashmir.

Within five days virtually all Kashmir was in danger of being over-
run by the tribal invasion. The Maharaja could no longer remain am-
bivalent or impartial toward India and Pakistan if he hoped to secure
the safety of his own government. On October 26, the Maharaja formally agreed to Kashmir's accession to India so that the Indian government would provide him with protection against the tribal in-

vaders. In a letter to Mountbatten (now Governor-General of India)
he wrote,

. . . with the conditions obtaining at present in my State and the great
emergency of the situation as it exists, I have no option but to ask for help
from the Indian Dominion. Naturally they cannot send the help asked for
by me without my State acceding to the Dominion of India. I have accordingly decided to do so, and I attach the instrument of accession for acceptance by your Government. The other alternative is to leave my State and
the people to freebooters. . . .[8]

In the same letter, the Maharaja also informed Mountbatten of his
decision to request Sheikh Abdullah to form an "interim" government
for Kashmir.

The next day, in his letter accepting the Maharaja's accession offer
on behalf of the Indian government, Mountbatten wrote,

In consistence with their policy that in the case of any State where the issue of accession has been the subject of dispute, the question of accession
should be decided in accordance with the wishes of the people of the
State, it is my Government's wish that, as soon as law and order have been
restored in Kashmir and its soil cleared of the invader, the question of the
State's accession should be settled by a reference to the people.[9]

Even as the accession offer was being accepted, units of the Indian
army were dispatched to Srinagar to repel the invasion. When the
troops arrived, the tribesmen were within five miles of the capital.
Quickly repulsed by the Indian army, they soon withdrew to the
state's western regions where they were able to maintain their control
and continue their fight — now against the government of India.

Upon learning of the entry of Indian troops into the fighting in
Kashmir, the first response of the Governor-General of Pakistan, Mohammed Ali Jinnah, was to order the acting commander-in-chief of
the Pakistani army to dispatch troops to Kashmir. Instead, that officer
asked first to consult the supreme commander in charge of administering partition of the Indian army, who persuaded Jinnah to rescind
his order. Thus, an immediate confrontation between the recently
divided armies was avoided. It was at this point that Jinnah invited
the Indian leaders to come to Lahore to discuss the situation. The

---

[8] For a full text of the Maharaja's letter and Mountbatten's reply, see Lord
Birdwood, *Two Nations and Kashmir* (London: Robert Hale, 1956), Appendix
5, pp. 213–14.

[9] Government of India, *White Paper on Jammu and Kashmir* (no date), pp.
46–48.

negotiations which followed ended in complete failure and the fighting in Kashmir continued. Within a few months, the irregular troops of the Moslem tribesmen were to be supplemented by regular Pakistani forces, and the war in Kashmir became an overt military contest between India and Pakistan. When, more than a year after the outbreak of violence, the armed conflict was halted by a cease-fire order, the political division between India and Pakistan over Kashmir remained as deep and pervasive as it had ever been.

In the years since the cease-fire of January 1, 1949, the Kashmir dispute has come to be recognized by the world as one of those long-term conflicts between states which remains essentially insoluble by means of peaceful settlement. Throughout most of that period, military settlement — although not sporadic military conflict — has been effectively precluded in large part by the actors themselves, under pressure from the international community not to attempt it. Rather, the Kashmir dispute has been contained so that it has not, as yet, engulfed the rest of the world or resulted in the absolute military defeat of either protagonist. To say that the dispute has been and remains insoluble, at least for the foreseeable future, implies that the mutually exclusive interests both states claim to possess in Kashmir are not negotiable. Before proceeding to an examination of the legal claims each state has made to Kashmir, it may help us to understand why these claims are held and asserted with such intensity if the deep symbolic significance of the dispute is noted.

It is not much of an oversimplification to state that the ideological *raison d'être* for either India or Pakistan would be seriously undermined if they were to drop their claims to authority over Kashmir. The case of Pakistan is perhaps the more obvious, since the nation is firmly predicated on the doctrine of two nations for the subcontinent — one Moslem and the other Hindu. According to this ideology, India should be granted jurisdiction over the predominantly Hindu regions of the subcontinent, and Pakistani territory should include all those areas where Moslems are in the majority. If the Indians were to accept this theory, they would, of course, have scant claim to most of Kashmir. But their leaders have never adhered to the communalist concept, and have dedicated themselves consistently to the proposition that the subcontinent constitutes one nation, composed of diverse ethnic and religious groups, but bound together in a common history and in common political and social aspirations. Pakistan would lose its *raison d'être* if her people were to abandon the two-nations

theory; India would face fragmentation and witness the death of secularism on the subcontinent if her leaders were to adopt the reverse
Pakistani outlook.

So far as Kashmir is concerned, it may well be that, had the Maharaja acceded to Pakistan before the transfer of sovereignty from the
British, the Indians would have accepted that move — albeit reluc-
tantly, and possibly not without short-term conflict — just as they accepted the accession of other areas on the subcontinent to Pakistan.
Yet, once Kashmir's accession to India was completed and Indian
troops were called in to defend the territory against invaders, the intercommunal, one-nation theory did not permit her to grant the legitimacy of Pakistani claims to the area. Conversely, Pakistan's ideology
prevented her rulers from accepting the legitimacy of an action which
brought an area that was predominantly Moslem and adjacent to
Pakistan under Hindu-Indian rule. The longer the dispute has lasted,
the more clear-cut the logic of these uncompromising claims seems to
have become to the actors themselves. This fact should emerge more
clearly as we examine the legal claims put forward both by India and
Pakistan over the course of nearly two decades.

II

The First Phase in the Security Council. It is clear that in the immediate aftermath of invasion and accession, neither Indian nor Pakistani officials asserted an exclusivist claim to Kashmir. This may be
explained partly because Kashmir then constituted but one of a great
number of problems both governments had to deal with in the turmoil and confusion of partition. On the other hand, we may suppose
that even if both groups of leaders were fully cognizant of the pre-
eminent importance of Kashmir's status to their political well-being,
neither had the opportunity in the first days and weeks of the conflict
to recognize fully the implications of its own claims and suggestions
for settlement. Thus, proposals were advanced on both sides which
were later found unacceptable by their proponents — either because
of growing intransigence between the parties or, quite probably, because of the later discovery of logical weaknesses in some of those
proposals when used to buttress the basic, exclusivist claims.

For example, at the very first meeting of Indian and Pakistani leaders following the accession of Kashmir to India — that in Lahore on
November 1, 1947 — Jinnah's proposal for a settlement contained the
following passage: "We have no control over the forces of the Pro-

visional Government of Kashmir or the tribesmen engaged in the fighting, but we will warn them in the clearest terms that if they do not obey the order to cease fire immediately the forces of both Dominions will make war on them."[10] Here was an explicit suggestion that the Pakistani government would regard the Moslem invaders of Kashmir — presumably Pakistani nationals — as outlaws and enemies if they did not cease fighting. Such a suggestion, however, could be regarded as assuming the illegality of the invasion and the legality of Indian military action to repel it — an assumption that no Pakistani leader wished to promote as the conflict lengthened. Subsequently, the Pakistani position with regard to the invaders shifted significantly, i.e., the tribesmen were viewed as having undertaken a just and holy war to permit the union of the Moslem territory with the Moslem state of Pakistan.

At the same meeting in Lahore, Lord Mountbatten reportedly suggested a plebiscite in Kashmir carried out under United Nations' auspices. The suggestion was repeated by Prime Minister Nehru in New Delhi the next day, even though the Pakistani Governor-General already had rejected it. Then, two weeks later, the Prime Minister of Pakistan, Liaquat Ali Khan, suddenly accepted the U.N.-sponsored plebiscite idea, at which point Nehru rejected it, arguing that the United Nations could do nothing until the fighting was stopped. With the vision of hindsight, it is clear that, as the leaders in both countries began to examine the implications of U.N. entry into the arena, both were inclined to reverse their positions on the matter. U.N. participation in the issue came to appeal to the Pakistanis as a way of weakening the Indian assertion (only half-formulated, at this point) of sole jurisdiction in the territory. When, as we shall see, the Indians finally took the issue to the international forum, they went seeking a collective action against Pakistan rather than a neutral agency that would separate the contestants.

By the end of 1947, statements and accusations made by both Indians and Pakistanis revealed that already both sides were coming to regard the Kashmir issue as the latest and most threatening manifestation of the long-standing ideological cleavage between them. Liaquat Ali Khan expressed the Pakistani fear of the Indian one-nation theory in a telegram to Nehru when he said,

It is a matter for deep regret that even today responsible members of the Government of India, including yourself, openly declare their intention or

[10] *Ibid.*, p. 60.

hope of bringing Pakistan back into the Indian Union well knowing that this could be done only through conquest of arms. . . . In other words Pakistan's very existence is the chief "casus belli" so far as India is concerned. . . . India never wholeheartedly accepted the partition scheme but her leaders paid lip service to it merely in order to get the British out of the country. . . . The fraudulent procurement of the accession of Jammu and Kashmir State [is an act] of hostility against Pakistan whose destruction is India's immediate objective.[11]

Nehru's reply denied these allegations, and at the same time stressed the legality of Kashmir's accession in Indian eyes by insisting that Pakistan's encouragement of the invaders constituted "an act of aggression" against India.[12]

On January 1, 1948, India called upon the United Nations Security Council to intervene in the Kashmir situation on the grounds that the conflict was a threat to international peace and security.[13] The Indian letter described the invaders as receiving aid from the government of Pakistan to be used against Kashmir, "a State which has acceded to the Dominion of India and is part of India." Further, the Indian letter stated, "The Government of India request the Security Council to call upon Pakistan to put an end immediately to the giving of such assistance which is an act of aggression against India."[14] When the Council met to take up the Indian complaint, the spokesman for India reiterated the theme of Pakistani aggression in Kashmir, elaborating what constituted the proof in his government's view of Pakistan's connivance in the invasion from the beginning. Indeed, even before the invasion, Pakistan had begun an economic blockade of Kashmir, "to coerce Kashmir into acceding to the Dominion of Pakistan."[15]

The Indian case was characterized, on the one hand, by this attempt to stress the facts of the case, as interpreted by India, specifically as they revolved about the invasion and accession of Kashmir. In this respect, the legality of the act of accession was emphasized repeatedly and the Indian government made to appear above reproach with regard to the legality of her subsequent action, in contrast to Pakistan, which had engaged in subterfuge and in overt de-

---

[11] *Ibid.,* p. 83.

[12] *Ibid.,* p. 85.

[13] India brought the dispute to the Council under Articles 34 and 35 of the U.N. Charter, which authorize any U.N. member to bring such a dispute to the attention of the Council, and the Council to take action on it.

[14] *Security Council Official Records* (hereafter cited as SCOR): 3rd Year, Supplement for January, February and March 1948 (S/628, January 2, 1948).

[15] SCOR: 3rd Year, 227th Mtg. (January 15, 1948), p. 14.

fiance of legal standards once accession had taken place. All of this was meant to limit the focus of the Security Council's attention to the immediate, specific issues of the fighting. Yet, on the other hand, the representative of India also emphasized his government's desire to be fair and impartial with regard to the larger, long-run issue of Kashmir's permanent attachment. Thus, the Indian spokesman insisted that,

. . . in accepting the accession [India] refused to take advantage of the immediate peril in which the State found itself and informed the Ruler that the accession should finally be settled by plebiscite as soon as peace had been restored. They have subsequently made it quite clear that they are agreeable to the plebiscite being conducted if necessary under international auspices.[16]

However much the Indian pledge to conduct a plebiscite might be praised in the abstract, as an example of high principle and dedication to democracy, there is no question but that its emphasis in the Security Council served to weaken the argument against Pakistan as an aggressor. The pledge itself seemed to indicate that the Indian government regarded the accession as provisional upon the outcome of the plebiscite. Although the Indians later denied vehemently that there was anything provisional about the accession when Pakistani spokesmen chose to interpret the plebiscite pledge in this way, their own spokesman at this first Security Council consideration of the issue did admit the possibility of Kashmir's *withdrawal* from accession. He stated of Kashmir, "whether she should withdraw from her accession to India, and either accede to India or remain independent with a right to claim admission as a Member of the United Nations — all this we have recognized to be a matter for unfettered decision by the people of Kashmir after normal life is restored to them."[17] Never again did an Indian spokesman suggest that there had been anything conditional or temporary about the act of accession.

Nor was it simply that the Indian representative discussed the plebiscite so often that it detracted from the force of the appeal to condemn Pakistan as an aggressor. The entire Indian case rested upon the legality of the act of accession, and yet the spokesman for India may well have left many of the members with the impression that that act could only be regarded as legally binding *in the event that a future plebiscite supported it*. In fact, according to the terms of the

[16] *Ibid.*, p. 20.
[17] *Ibid.*

Partition Agreements laid down before the departure of the British —
to which future Pakistani leaders were a party — the accession of
Kashmir's ruler should have been regarded as binding and permanent. When Mountbatten suggested to the Maharaja that plebiscite
of the people was regarded by his government as desirable, he was, in
effect, committing the Indian government to a further unilateral step
than was required for the legality of the accession.[18] None of this was
made clear by the Indian spokesman at Lake Success, who spoke instead of India's "high-principled statesmanship" in her desire to conduct a plebiscite in Kashmir.

In contrast to the Indian presentation which focussed on accession
and Pakistan's aid to the invaders, the subsequent Pakistani presentation to the Security Council depicted the Kashmir situation as simply
one of many areas of friction that had developed in the partition of
the subcontinent. In keeping with this theme, the legal elements of
the situation were played down, to minimize the question of legal
rights in Kashmir and avoid the aggression issue. A large part of the
Pakistan delegate's testimony was devoted to descriptions of the
communal upheavals and alleged extermination of Muslim minorities
by Hindu authorities. Furthermore, the conflict in Kashmir had
started as the result of a Sikh conspiracy against Moslem neighbors,
of which the Indian government was allegedly aware. When the
Poonch revolt took place, the Pakistani spokesman charged, the Maharaja armed Hindu and Sikh refugees from the Punjab, encouraging
them to kill the Moslems. In such a situation, "it makes no difference
who commits the aggression and who the victim is; wherever there
is human suffering it is to be highly deplored."[19]

This emphasis on the "human aspect" of the Kashmir situation — as
merely one facet of the social upheaval convulsing the subcontinent
— clearly had a greater impact on the members of the Security Council than did the much more restricted Indian appraisal. Evidence of
this soon came in the Council's first important action on the issue. On

---

[18] Indeed, one of the ironies of the Kashmir situation is that it was the leaders of the Moslem League — not those of the Congress party — who had insisted
in the Partition Agreements that accession to India or Pakistan by the princely
states would be determined by the option of their rulers. They no doubt hoped,
thereby, to obtain Hindu Hyderabad from its Moslem ruler, and perhaps expected
to be able to place sufficient pressure on the Maharaja of Kashmir to secure that
border territory as well. See Charles Burton Marshall on this point in "India and
Pakistan at War," *The New Republic*, CLIII, No. 13 (September 25, 1965), 20.

[19] SCOR: 3rd Year, 228th Mtg. (January 16, 1948), p. 43.

January 20, 1948, a resolution was passed providing for the establishment of a three-member investigatory and mediatory commission (later enlarged to five). This commission, designated the United Nations Commission for India and Pakistan (UNCIP) was expected "to investigate the facts pursuant to Article 34 of the Charter," and "to exercise . . . any mediatory influence likely to smooth away difficulties."[20] Significantly, the Commission was expected to deal, not only with the Kashmir issue, but also with those broader issues which had been mentioned repeatedly by the delegate of Pakistan. The Indian delegate agreed to this mandate for the Commission — although he made it clear that his government expected it to deal with Kashmir first and foremost — and he accepted designation of the body as the Commission for India and Pakistan, rather than for Jammu and Kashmir.

With this decision taken, the Security Council then decided to alter the listing of the agenda item under discussion to read "the India-Pakistan question," rather than, as it had been described at first, as "the Jammu and Kashmir question." Again the Indian delegate acquiesced in this change, apparently not realizing the larger implications of what appeared to be a semantic quibble. Not only did this casting of the question concede the Pakistanis' point that the issue was not "as simple or as straightforward as the representative of India has tried to make out,"[21] it also provided the Pakistanis with a new basis for approaching the issue that was to plague the Indians for years to come. By implication, India and Pakistan could now be regarded as equal parties to the dispute, each with its own complaints and claims to make to the Security Council. This clearly has not been the Indian view of the matter at any time.

As a result of these apparently minor procedural decisions taken in the Council in 1948, the Pakistani delegate was able, fourteen years later, to say in the Security Council:

It is argued . . . that Pakistan is no party. Pakistan is no party? Look at the agenda which the Security Council approved only today; "The India-Pakistan question." Look at the resolutions of the Security Council: "The dispute between India and Pakistan," "the situation between India and Pakistan."[22]

[20] SCOR: 3rd Year, Supplement for January, February and March 1948 (S/654, January 20, 1948).
[21] SCOR: 3rd Year, 227th Mtg. (January 15, 1948), p. 31.
[22] SCOR: 17th Year, 1008th Mtg. (May 2, 1962), pp. 53–54.

And, fourteen years later, the Indian representative was far more vehement than his predecessor in 1948 had been in insisting that Pakistan had no *locus standi* before the Security Council in the issue. Yet, the passage of fourteen years in which the agenda item had been listed as "the India-Pakistan question," rather than "the Indian complaint against Pakistan" seemed to contradict him.

In the Security Council debate which followed immediately after the agreement to establish UNCIP, the Indian delegate again attempted to focus the attention of the Council upon the specific issue of Pakistan's aid to the invaders of Kashmir. Perhaps sensing that the argument as to the legality of Kashmir's accession had not proved to be as potent as expected, he now sought to strengthen that point by emphasizing the relevant duties of states in international law. Two such duties, in particular, were stressed: (a) that prescribing non-intervention by outside powers in support of insurgents in other states, and (b) that forbidding the state to permit warlike passage through its territory by armed bands. In elaboration of the first point, the Indian delegate stated,

Even if India went into Kashmir not as a Dominion to which Kashmir had acceded, but as an independent neighbouring country, we were within our rights. Pakistan, as a similar independent neighbouring country, has not the right to go to the help of insurgents in a neighbouring State. I think the Security Council must recognize this principle of international law.[23]

Reference here is to the traditional norm forbidding external aid to insurgent groups but permitting — indeed, condoning — such aid to the "legitimate" authority of a state threatened by insurrection. It is perhaps not surprising that the Indian delegate did not spell out this principle of international law in more detail, since it is clearly a principle designed to maintain a political status quo at almost any cost and, as such, was never universally accepted — certainly not by the "revolutionary" states of either the nineteenth or twentieth centuries.[24] As such, this principle inevitably would sound strangely hollow coming from Indian mouths — it could have been turned against them in the case of Junagadh, for example — and has not been urged seriously by them in support of their position in more recent years.

As to the second duty which Pakistan allegedly did not uphold,

[23] SCOR: 3rd Year, 236th Mtg. (January 28, 1948), p. 276.
[24] Since the time of Grotius, the more generally acceptable rule of international law has been that of the neutrality of states vis-à-vis a situation of civil strife within another sovereign state.

the Indian delegate undoubtedly felt himself on safer ground, for he reiterated and elaborated it. As one Indian spokesman put it,

Pakistan protests that it is anxious to discharge its international obligations, but that it is unable to keep these tribesmen from going into Jammu and Kashmir. That is, I am sure the members of the Security Council are well aware, no answer. A state cannot say that it is unable to restrain warlike passage through its territory to others, and permit an invasion of a neighbouring State.[25]

Here was a more telling accusation of the illegality of Pakistan's role in the Kashmir situation, and variations of this argument were to serve as one of the principal Indian charges against her neighbor. Yet the strategy of the Pakistanis again was to gloss over the question of international obligations by stressing the illegitimacy of the Maharaja's regime — i.e., the Dogra dynasty constituted alien rule, the result of a land purchase rather than constitutional accession — and the ambiguity of the legal situation with regard to Kashmir. Thus, the Pakistani spokesman argued,

. . . paramountcy having been withdrawn — and almost simultaneously with the withdrawal of paramountcy the Maharaja having started a campaign of atrocities and extermination of his subjects — the validity of his rule had ceased, and those subjects were not entitled, since there was no paramount Power there to make the Maharaja behave, to settle matters for themselves. The movement in Kashmir was a movement of that kind.

That being the state of affairs, it is a very delicate question . . . to determine what, if any, international obligations arise out of the situation. It was for that reason that I said it was profitless to enter upon academic discussions of international obligations.[26]

As this phase of the debate continued, primary attention came to be focussed on the conditions of a plebiscite in Kashmir. India's case had been predicated upon the need for a cease-fire first and a plebiscite afterward. The United Nations' primary responsibility was to help effect a cease-fire. Thus, although the Indians had referred to the possibility of supervision of the plebiscite by an international body, they maintained that in the interim before such a plebiscite could be carried out, Sheikh Abdullah's government would continue to function, administering elections to a National Assembly and arranging for the plebiscite. The Pakistanis, on the other hand, placed priority

---

[25] SCOR: 3rd Year, 232nd Mtg. (January 23, 1948), p. 181; 237th Mtg. (January 29, 1948), pp. 298–99.
[26] SCOR: 3rd Year, 242nd Mtg. (February 6, 1948), pp. 44–46.

on the plebiscite rather than the cease-fire. They wished to see UNCIP given the authority to arrange for an impartial interim administration in Kashmir followed by the withdrawal of forces and the holding of a plebiscite. In their view, agreement on an international arrangement for the plebiscite was essential before the fighting could be stopped. These divergent views conformed to the logic of the claims made by each state, i.e., for India, Kashmir's act of accession precluded the acceptability of outside interference in the administration of Kashmir, while for Pakistan, the territory was a subject of dispute between the two states and the issue of its legitimate accession could be determined only on the basis of an impartial administration of the state and an internationally controlled plebiscite.

On January 29, two draft resolutions were submitted to the Council by the Belgian delegation, purportedly as an attempt to reconcile the diametrically opposed views of India and Pakistan. In fact, however, taken together these resolutions granted the Pakistanis the substance of their position at the expense of the Indian claim. The first resolution called for a plebiscite to be "organized, held and supervised under its [the Security Council's] authority."[27] The second informed UNCIP that "among the duties incumbent upon it, are included those which would tend towards promoting the cessation of acts of hostility and violence."[28] Such cautious language scarcely could be regarded as placing the issue of demilitarization in a position of priority. Nine members of the Council supported these resolutions, and the comments of most of those supporters indicated their acceptance of Pakistan's point of view.[29] The Indian spokesman responded with sarcasm on the refusal of the Council to address itself single-mindedly to the issue of the termination of hostilities, and shortly thereafter returned to New Delhi for a lengthy period of consultation with his government. Indian leaders obviously were alarmed by the way in which their case had been received in the Security Council.

[27] SCOR: 3rd Year, Supplement for January, February and March, 1948 (S/661, January 29, 1948).

[28] SCOR: 3rd Year, Supplement for January, February and March, 1948 (S/662, January 29, 1948).

[29] For example, the U.S. delegate asked on February 2: "How is it possible to induce the tribesmen to retire from Jammu and Kashmir without warfare and without driving them out? That is the only way it can be done, unless the tribesmen are satisfied that there is to be a fair plebiscite assured through an interim government that is in fact, and that has the appearance of being, non-partisan...." SCOR: 3rd Year, 240th Mtg. (February 2, 1948), p. 369.

That state which had brought the original complaint to the United Nations, convinced of the righteousness of its own position, had now to take the defensive. It was in that position that India would remain during much of the succeeding U.N. debate.

Once India returned to the Council after an interval of several weeks, the deadlock in discussion continued for more than a month. A Chinese draft resolution on March 18 was somewhat more favorable to the Indian point of view than any earlier proposals had been — e.g., it "permitted India to maintain part of its armed forces in Kashmir after the fighting ceased in order to ensure security and law and order"[30] — but was, for that reason, unacceptable to Pakistan. Finally, on April 21, 1948, a resolution jointly sponsored by six Council members was passed by a vote of 9 to 0 (the Soviet Union and the Ukraine abstaining) which went far beyond any previous proposals in the attempt to reach a settlement on the Kashmir problem *in toto*. Even though neither India nor Pakistan found this resolution generally acceptable — for reasons which will be considered below — its adoption by the Council made it the effective instrument of U.N. action on Kashmir for a considerable period to come. With its passage, the first phase of the Security Council's consideration of the dispute soon drew to a close.

The resolution of April 21 began by enlarging UNCIP to five members and directing that body to proceed immediately to the subcontinent for purposes of conducting mediation between the parties so that the other terms of the resolution could be implemented. It then considered the three basic practical problems that had emerged from the weeks and months of debate: (a) the cessation of hostilities and withdrawal of forces, (b) the interim government, and (c) the plebiscite. On the first point, the resolution favored the Indian point of view, calling on Pakistan to secure the withdrawal of tribesmen and Pakistani nationals from Kashmir, after which India should reduce her troop strength in the territory to "the minimum . . . required . . . in the maintenance of law and order." Secondly, it asked for an interim government in Kashmir which would represent all major political groups (including pro-Pakistan forces, as well as Sheikh Abdullah's party). This section of the resolution was a clear attempt to reconcile the contradictory demands of India and Pakistan — the one

[30] SCOR: 3rd Year, Supplement for January, February and March 1948 (S/699, March 18, 1948).

insisting upon the retention of the Abdullah government in the interim before a plebiscite, the other on an "impartial" administration. Thirdly, the resolution clearly favored the position of Pakistan regarding the plebiscite. It envisaged the nomination by the U.N. Secretary-General of a plebiscite administrator with powers to direct and supervise the state's police and military forces for purposes of insuring fairness in the reference to the people.[31]

India's strong objection to much of the resolution stressed her bitterness over the Council's refusal to brand Pakistan as the aggressor. Rather, said the Indian spokesman, the Council "has gone even further and been apologetic to Pakistan for reminding it of its duty."[32] He also criticized the plebiscite provisions which granted the administrator authority over Kashmir (Indian) forces, and insisted that while India had no objection to governmental representation to the major political groups in Kashmir, any such selection would have to be made by Abdullah himself, who directed the legitimate government in the state. In this same response, the Indian delegate stressed more strongly than ever before the binding and unconditional nature of Kashmir's accession to India. It would lapse only in the event that the plebiscite favored Pakistan, not before, and as a result Pakistan had no right to participate in the plebiscite arrangements. At last it had become clear to the Indian delegation that their previous emphasis upon their own fair-mindedness in tying accession to the outcome of a plebiscite had had the unfortunate effect of permitting Council members to interpret the original accession as conditional. Although India refused to accept the resolution as binding her in any way, she did agree to receive the U.N. Commission in New Delhi or elsewhere, and to confer with it.

Pakistan's reaction to the resolution was that in the attempt to placate India and "compromise" with her, the Council had backed away from some of its previous assurances to Pakistan. Specifically, the spokesman for Pakistan charged, guarantees for the impartiality of the plebiscite were inadequate, the provision regarding the interim government too vague, and the use of Indian troops alone to police the plebiscite unacceptable.[33] Yet, considering the nature of the charges that had been brought by India against Pakistan on January

---

[31] SCOR: 3rd Year, Supplement for April, May and June 1948 (S/726, April 22, 1948).

[32] SCOR: 3rd Year, 285th Mtg. (April 19, 1948), p. 12.

[33] These arguments are to be found in Zafrullah Khan's speech as contained in SCOR: 3rd Year, 285th Mtg. (April 19, 1948), pp. 20–47.

1, 1948, the degree to which the Pakistani rather than the Indian position had been accepted by the Council was rather striking. This is not to say that the Council refused to accept India's charges and instead agreed with the countercharges brought by Pakistan. For the most part, the Council had indeed attempted to act impartially as between the two sides. Yet, in doing so, they had granted Pakistan the logic of her position before the Council and denied the Indian claim that she alone had a legitimate complaint.

III

UNCIP and the Failure of Mediation. During the next phase of the dispute, which was marked by the shift in the instrumentalities of settlement from the Security Council to UNCIP, the situation in Kashmir changed dramatically. When the Commission arrived in Karachi early in July, they were informed by the Pakistan Foreign Minister that three brigades of regular Pakistani forces had been sent into Kashmir some two months previously because of the threatening advance of Indian troops there.[34] The Foreign Minister added that "the presence of Pakistan troops in Kashmir did not raise the question of international obligations since Pakistan had never accepted any with regard to non-interference in Kashmir."[35] Somewhat later it was acknowledged in Karachi that "the Pakistan Army is at present responsible for the overall command of Azad ["free," i.e., Moslem] Kashmir forces."

This development complicated the work of the Commission considerably, for it seemed to call into question a number of the provisions of the resolutions which UNCIP was expected to help implement. And, not surprisingly, this entrance of regular Pakistani forces into Kashmir served to raise once more India's demands upon the U.N. to condemn Pakistan as an aggressor. When the Commission arrived in New Delhi, the Indian Secretary-General of the Ministry for External Affairs warned the members that his government attached

. . . the highest importance to the declaration of Pakistan's guilt. . . . Until this matter was settled there could be no question of discussing the details of a plebiscite. . . . If the future of Jammu and Kashmir was to be determined by the arbitrament of the sword, then, without in any way wishing

---

[34] See Josef Korbel, *Danger in Kashmir* (Princeton: Princeton University Press, 1954), p. 121.

[35] *Interim Report of the United Nations Commission for India and Pakistan,* SCOR: 3rd Year, Supplement for November, 1948 (S/1100, November 9, 1948), para. 40.

to utter a threat . . . I should like the Commission, as realists, to recognize that the offer of plebiscite could not remain open. If Pakistan wanted a decision by force and that decision went against Pakistan, it could not invoke the machinery of the United Nations to obtain what it had failed to secure by its chosen weapon of force.[36]

Here was a clear warning from the Indians that they would no longer consider themselves bound morally (and they never had considered themselves bound legally) to the idea of an internationally supervised plebiscite if Pakistani troops were to remain on what was legally Indian soil.

The members of the Commission worked feverishly to construct a new resolution which could be made acceptable to both the contestants as a basis of further negotiation. When it finally emerged, it indicated a considerable shift in the U.N. attitude toward the Indian position. There was no question but that the Pakistani claim of legal ambiguity with regard to Kashmir was not acceptable to UNCIP when stretched to permit the overt entrance of Pakistani troops into Kashmir territory. Still, the Commission's resolution of August 13, 1948, fell considerably short of constituting the outright condemnation of Pakistan that India demanded — undoubtedly because its framers recognized the necessity of achieving adherence to it from both sides if the work of mediation were to continue. The resolution began by observing that "As the presence of troops of Pakistan in the territory of the State . . . constitutes a material change in the situation since it was represented by . . . Pakistan before the Security Council . . . Pakistan agrees to withdraw its troops from that State."[37] Although Nehru later described this provision as a "feeble" slap at Pakistan, he nonetheless accepted the resolution as admitting the illegality of Pakistan's military presence in Kashmir. Its substantive provisions called on Pakistan to withdraw all her troops — both regular and irregular — after which India was "to begin to withdraw the bulk of their forces." Both sides were asked to reconfirm their acceptance of the plebiscite, once peaceful conditions had been restored. Significantly, however, the Commission members agreed to India's interpretation of this provision, which was that it did not recognize Pakistan's right to take any part in the plebiscite.

The government of Pakistan also "accepted" UNCIP's resolution of

[36] *Ibid.*, pp. 126–27.
[37] SCOR: 3rd Year, Supplement for July, August and September, 1948 (S/995, September 13, 1948), p. 3.

August 13, but with such qualifications as to vitiate their adherence. Perhaps the most interesting clarification in Pakistan's position with regard to the resolution was the sharp distinction made between the Pakistani and Azad Kashmir governments, which permitted them to claim the autonomy of the latter and the necessity of including them as a separate party to any settlement. Indeed, a government had been set up sometime previously in the portions of Kashmir controlled by the pro-Pakistani forces which was led by the old rival of Sheikh Abdullah in the days before partition, Ghulam Abbas. Here was an effective move on the part of the Pakistanis to counter the Indian charge of aggression by stressing the autonomy of the Azad forces even more strongly than had been done before the Security Council in the winter.

The consequences of this development were to be far-reaching and, for the short run, led directly to an impasse in the truce negotiations. One commentator has noted the effect of UNCIP's handling of this situation:

With regard to the Azad Kashmir Government, it [UNCIP] assured Nehru at the end of August, 1948, that this Government had no legal status, but at the very same time acknowledged its *de facto* status in its communications with Zafrullah Khan. . . . On the question of the plebiscite, it accepted Nehru's view that Pakistan had no right to participate in the plebiscite but by its very negotiations with Pakistan, it acknowledged, at least *de facto*, the Pakistani claim to be considered a party to such a plebiscite.[38]

The Commission was confronted with an impossible task in its attempt to draw areas of accommodation and agreement out of two positions that were essentially irreconcilable. Nonetheless, as the above quotation makes clear, their actions at this stage had the unfortunate effect of granting to each party its own legal claims, and these were claims that were mutually exclusive. The positions of India and Pakistan had hardened into the forms in which they would remain, with few modifications, for years to come.

The military situation in Kashmir, however, did not remain dormant in the meantime. By the autumn of 1948, the tide which had been running slightly in Pakistan's favor, since the introduction of regular forces that spring, began to be reversed, and by November the Indian army returned to the offensive in many areas. It was in this atmosphere that UNCIP moved to supplement and strengthen the

[38] Brecher, *op. cit.*, p. 95.

resolution of August 13 with a new group of proposals advanced on December 11, 1948.[39] Whether because of the Indian advance on the military front or because of other, domestic political factors, the Pakistani government accepted these new proposals — as did India — even though they reflected the shift in favor of the Indian position in much the same way as the August 13 resolution had.[40] As subsequent events were to prove, neither side actually had modified its claims in accepting these proposals; rather, the net effect "was the achievement of temporary agreement by India and Pakistan at the expense of long-run deadlock."[41] In the future, India would refuse to make the preparations for a plebiscite called for in these resolutions on the grounds that the Pakistani army had not been withdrawn from Kashmir as directed and that the Azad Kashmir force had not been substantially disarmed. Pakistan would continue to insist on the autonomy of the Azad forces and government, averring that India had reneged on her plebiscite agreement.

Yet the temporary agreement achieved in the adherence of both parties to the UNCIP proposals of December 11 did permit an immediate step to bring the military conflict to a halt. A cease-fire agreement finally was signed by India and Pakistan which took effect on January 1, 1949. Then began the arduous task of demarcating the cease-fire line and agreeing upon the procedures to maintain it during the period (which, it was hoped, would be comparatively brief) before opposing forces would be withdrawn and the plebiscite held. To aid in this task of demarcation and supervision, a group of United Nations military observers from various U.N. member states was dispatched to Kashmir. This group (the United Nations Military Observer Group for India and Pakistan — UNMOGIP), varying in size between forty to sixty members, continues in its supervisory duties nineteen years later.

Meanwhile, the negotiations carried on by UNCIP in Karachi and New Delhi throughout 1949 with a view to securing the withdrawal of forces on both sides ended in complete failure. When, at one point in the deadlock, President Truman and Prime Minister Attlee intervened to propose arbitration of all the remaining differences between

---

[39] The full text of UNCIP's proposals of December 11, 1948, is to be found in the Second Interim Report of the Commission to the Security Council, SCOR: 4th Year, Supplement for January, February and March, 1949 (S/1196, January 10, 1949, Annex 3).

[40] For further speculation as to the reasons for Pakistan's acceptance of these proposals, see Brecher, op. cit., pp. 97–98.

[41] Ibid., p. 96.

the two governments, Pandit Nehru rejected the offer, reminding the world once again of Pakistan's "unwarranted aggression against international law."[42] Arbitration was out of the question for a government which regarded its opponent's case as thoroughly illicit. The mandate for mediation with which UNCIP had been supplied finally had to be recognized as insufficient to resolve the differences between the contestants. In December, 1949, the Commission's final report was published, recommending its own replacement by a single mediator with broad powers to settle the problem.[43]

With this last report of UNCIP, the issue was returned once more to the lap of the Security Council. In its turn, the Council acted on the recommendation of the Commission and appointed an "informal mediator" to represent the Council in negotiations with the two governments. The Canadian representative on the Security Council, General McNaughton, was given the post temporarily, and before the end of the year he submitted several proposals to India and Pakistan for demilitarizing Kashmir. Although the proposals were effectively rejected by India and nothing of a substantive nature was to come of them, they are interesting for purposes of our inquiry because of one of the recommendations. Withdrawal of forces was not to be limited to the Pakistani, Azad Kashmir, and Indian troops alone, as previous resolutions had called for, but also was to include disbanding and disarming the armed forces and militia of the (Indian) State of Kashmir.[44] To the Indians, this constituted further confirmation of the U.N.'s predilection for treating the two parties to the dispute as equals, and must have been particularly odious to them after UNCIP's two resolutions of the previous year which had called for the withdrawal of Pakistani troops. Nor had those resolutions so much as mentioned the militia of the Kashmir state. Thus, while the Pakistanis accepted McNaughton's proposals wholeheartedly, the Indians criticized the mediator for having ignored "the basic legal and moral issues at stake."[45]

It seems that the balanced view of the contestants implicit in McNaughton's proposals — i.e., the Pakistani and Azad forces vis-à-vis the Indian and Kashmiri forces — and the equal responsibility of each

[42] From Nehru's speech in Allahabad, September 4, 1949.
[43] SCOR: 4th Year, Special Supplement, No. 7.
[44] SCOR: 5th Year, Supplement for January, February and March 1950 (S/1453, February 6, 1950). This document contains the full text of the McNaughton report and the reaction to it of India and Pakistan.
[45] *Times of India*, February 9, 1949.

to withdraw from the area was the inevitable result of the fact that a *de facto* government in the Pakistan-occupied sector of Kashmir had continued in existence for more than a year. Whatever the merits of the Indian claim in 1947 or even 1948 that the entire responsibility for the conflict lay on the shoulders of the Pakistanis and the Azad forces they sponsored, such a claim seemed irrelevant to the hard realities of the situation if settlement were still the goal late in 1949. Nonetheless, so long as the Indians clung to their position as the only legitimate stance, the changed political realities could not induce them to seek a settlement on the basis of equal claims between the parties. As for the Security Council, McNaughton's proposals were received warmly. Whereas Council members had been inclined to favor the Indian position in the period immediately after the introduction of regular Pakistani forces into Kashmir in 1948, now that another year and a half had dragged by and the issue remained unresolved, most agreed that the changed political conditions had to be dealt with in some such way as McNaughton had proposed.

Following McNaughton's brief foray into the issue — which had not been meant to be more than an exploratory endeavor — a single U.N. Mediator was appointed by the Council in April, 1950. Sir Owen Dixon, an Australian jurist, was selected for the post. His mission, too, was to end in failure, but not before it had furnished both contestants with new arguments for maintaining their intransigent claims. In the first place, Dixon made clear that he was favorably disposed toward granting the Indians most of the heart of their position and proceeding from there to try to effect a settlement. As he put it later in his report,

. . . without going into the causes or reasons why it happened . . . I was prepared to adopt the view that when the frontier of the State of Jammu and Kashmir was crossed . . . by hostile elements, it was contrary to international law, and that when, in May, 1948 . . . units of the regular Pakistan forces moved into the territory of the State, that too was inconsistent with international law.[46]

Although this statement went farther than that of any previous U.N. spokesman in criticizing the Pakistani position, the substantive proposals which flowed from it were not sufficiently pro-Indian to secure that country's acceptance. Dixon had suggested that, because of Pakistan's original breach of international law, her troops should be

[46] The Dixon Report, SCOR: 5th Year, Supplement for July, August and September, 1950 (S/1791, September 15, 1950).

withdrawn first from Kashmir. This was to be followed, however, by the withdrawal of Indian troops and the disbanding of both Azad and Kashmir government forces. It was the latter proposal which was not acceptable to India, any more than it had been in the McNaughton recommendations.

After complete deadlock had been reached on this and other issues, Dixon finally broached the idea of a permanent partition of Kashmir, recognizing as he did so that the idea of a plebiscite throughout the state was becoming increasingly unrealistic. Here, it was Pakistan that rejected the suggestion, presumably in principle, while India accepted it but with territorial demands of a sort which the Mediator knew could not be made acceptable to the Pakistanis. For both governments, the idea of partition was distasteful — not surprisingly, given the claims of each to sole jurisdiction over the entire territory. Numerous official and unofficial statements in both countries echoed the sentiments of a Pakistani newspaper which said of Dixon that "he sought to create in this sub-continent another Korea."[47]

Once Dixon admitted his failure and left the subcontinent in August, 1950, the Pakistanis were quick to place all the blame for the failure of his mediation efforts on the shoulders of India. In fact, India had rejected most of the substantive proposals of demilitarization and preparation for plebiscite that the Mediator had put forward.[48] Pakistani leaders undoubtedly were able to increase their stature in later discussions of the Kashmir issue by pointing out that it was India which had obstructed most of the work of the Mediator. The Indians, for their part, never tired of citing Dixon's evaluation of Pakistan as the aggressor in Kashmir. Meanwhile, for a number of months after Dixon's departure, the Kashmir issue lay dormant before the Security Council. Dixon had recommended that, all else having failed, it might now be best to allow the contestants to seek agreement through direct negotiations. The members of the Council seemed willing to concur with this suggestion.

IV

An Uneasy Maintenance of the Status Quo. Throughout most of the 1950's, the United Nations played a somewhat less important role in the Kashmir issue than it had earlier. The question of Kashmir re-

---

[47] *Civil and Military Gazette,* August 23, 1950.
[48] A number of these are left unmentioned here. For a full account of those proposals, see the Dixon Report, *loc. cit.*

mained on the U.N.'s agenda, however, and from time to time was debated before the Security Council. For approximately two years after April, 1951, the principal U.N. settlement effort was focussed on the mission of a new mediator appointed by the Security Council — this time bearing the title of U.N. Representative for India and Pakistan — Dr. Frank Graham of the United States. Dr. Graham's mandate was extended several times by the Council, and over the course of the next two years he met repeatedly with the Indian and Pakistani leaders. Although he succeeded in narrowing many of the differences regarding the problem of troop withdrawals, there remained at the end of his efforts a basic core of disagreement that could not be overcome as to the size of the Indian force to be maintained in Kashmir after demilitarization.[49] Interspersed among Graham's various attempts at mediation on the subcontinent were periods of largely fruitless bilateral negotiations between the prime ministers of India and Pakistan.[50]

If something of the crisis quality had gone out of the Kashmir dispute, it was not because the situation was very much less threatening to the peace of the area than before. Rather, every avenue of settlement seemed to have been exhausted and the parties to the dispute found themselves forced to live with a situation neither could accept as settled. More than once in this period, fighting threatened to break out again. That it did not do so on a large scale may have been due in part to the efforts of the U.N. Representative and to the presence of UNMOGIP at the cease-fire line, but the recognition by the contestants of the impossibility of a satisfactory settlement by force of arms perhaps was as important a deterrent. In one sense, however, the almost continual attempts at mediation and negotiation served also to postpone, perhaps indefinitely, an ultimate day of reck-

---

[49] For the complete texts of Graham's five reports to the Security Council, see SCOR: Supplement for October, November and December, 1951 (S/2375, October 15, 1951); ibid. (S/2448, December 18, 1951); Supplement for April, May and June, 1952 (S/2611, April 22, 1952); Supplement for July, August and September, 1952 (S/2783, September 19, 1952); and Supplement for January, February and March, 1953 (S/2910, January 23, 1953).

[50] For accounts of this exchange, see especially Government of Pakistan, White Paper: *India's Threat to Pakistan: Correspondence between the Prime Ministers of Pakistan and India, July 15–August 11, 1951*, Karachi, 1951; and Government of India, White Paper: *Indo-Pakistan Relations. Correspondence between the Prime Ministers of India and Pakistan from July 15, 1951 to April 9, 1951*, New Delhi, 1951.

oning in Kashmir and to permit far-reaching changes on the political scene — particularly within the Indian-occupied sector of Kashmir.

By 1953 Sheikh Abdullah, who had emerged as prime minister of Kashmir shortly after the accession of the state to India, found himself in deep political trouble within his own government. As leader of the Kashmir National Conference, Abdullah's political philosophy had long been closely akin to that of Jawaharlal Nehru and the Indian Congress party. Once in power, the Sheikh had moved quickly to proscribe the authority of the Maharaja who appointed him. Then, while apparently maintaining his opposition to communalism and his allegiance to India, he worked to secure special privileges for his state within the Indian union. Within a few years, this Moslem opponent of union with Pakistan was regarded with increasing suspicion by the advocates within Kashmir of closer ties with India. In the face of growing political opposition, especially from Hindu groups, to his strong-man rule, Abdullah began to hint at the necessity for an even more independent status for his state. Finally, in August, 1953, Sheikh Abdullah was dismissed as prime minister in a cabinet shake-up and replaced by his deputy, Bakshi Ghulam Mohammed — also a Moslem — who had opposed vehemently the Sheikh's recent drift from India. Abdullah was arrested and imprisoned, and his successor began the task of restoring harmonious ties with India and responding to the growing political unrest within his state.[51]

These events soon brought India-Pakistan relations to another low point, for the Pakistanis were quick to see Abdullah's downfall — correctly so, as events were to show — as removing the last real obstacle to the complete integration of most of the state of Jammu and Kashmir into India. In February, 1954, a Kashmiri Constituent Assembly clearly subservient to the Bakshi government duly ratified, presumably on behalf of all the people of Kashmir, the act of accession with India that had been entered into by the Maharaja nearly seven years before. For India, this act was to become one of the pillars of her future argument that the people of Kashmir had freely expressed themselves on the issue of accession; for Pakistan, it constituted action contrary to India's various pledges as contained in Security Council resolutions to support a free and impartial plebiscite

---

[51] For an especially good account of the events surrounding Abdullah's downfall, see especially Josef Korbel, *op. cit.*, Chap. 8.

throughout the entire state. For the time being, however, India had not yet backed away from the idea of an eventual plebiscite as envisaged by the United Nations. Rather, her leaders professed to see no violation of that pledge in the ratification of accession by the Kashmiri Constituent Assembly.

One further change in the balance of forces in the situation during this period remains to be noted. Beginning in 1954, the United States began to supply Pakistan with substantial amounts of military aid. Although U.S. government officials attempted to make clear to the world (and perhaps especially to India) that this aid was only intended to prevent Communist aggression against Pakistan, Indian spokesmen were understandably alarmed. To some, the likelihood appeared strong that the Pakistanis would be emboldened thereby to attempt a forceful settlement of the Kashmir issue; others objected most strenuously on the grounds that this action "introduced the Cold War to the Asian subcontinent." Unquestionably, for the short run, U.S. military aid to Pakistan served to exacerbate the long-strained relations between Karachi and New Delhi, and by the 1960's the Indians would see those arms turned against themselves.[52]

After a hiatus of several years in which the United Nations was not actively engaged in consideration of the Kashmir issue, the Security Council again met for this purpose in January, 1957, at the request of Pakistan. The Karachi government had complained that India was proceeding to integrate the portion of Kashmir which she occupied into the Indian union in defiance of Security Council resolutions on the subject which had called for an impartial, statewide plebiscite. The debate which followed — which was largely a recapitulation of familiar arguments from both sides — contained several nuances that differed from previous presentations, reflecting certain new conditions.[53]

Although India's case had always rested strongly on the alleged legality of her position in Kashmir, perhaps never before had she buttressed her appeal more strongly by reference to legal rights and standards. This is not surprising considering the fact that her position was now a defensive one before the Council. Moreover, the Pakistani charge against India was that she had violated specific in-

[52] For an analysis of the effect of U.S. military aid to Pakistan on Indo-Pakistan relations during this period, see Birdwood, *op. cit.*, Chap. 11.

[53] This series of meetings is contained in SCOR: 12th Year, 761st–774th Mtgs. (January 16–February 21, 1957).

ternational commitments undertaken through U.N. resolutions, and the majority of Council members clearly were disposed to regard the burden of proof as resting upon India. The Indian response, in addition to that familiar argument charging Pakistan with the original delict in Kashmir, was essentially threefold. First, as to violation of international agreements, India pled not guilty. One of her legal commitments had been to accept Kashmir's offer of accession in 1947, and she had never entered into any kind of international understanding that contradicted the legality of that act. As the Indian spokesman put it,

> . . . even if there were, and there is not, a high-level treaty as between our two countries [India and Pakistan], or an agreement of the nature of a treaty obligation, either registered with the United Nations or entered into with the Secretary-General, it would still be bound by these commitments [involving Kashmir's accession].[54]

Any resolutions that had been accepted by India could not, then, be interpreted as having jeopardized the legality of accession.

Secondly, with specific regard to the plebiscite, the representative of India attempted to reverse the accusation and place the blame on the Pakistanis. It was the Karachi government which had the first responsibility to withdraw its troops from Kashmir before general demilitarization and a plebiscite could take place. As the Indian spokesman put it at this time, "There is no international agreement for a plebiscite; there is international agreement on a plan for which there are certain pre-conditions. In these matters we must not jump from one thing to another; it does not mean the same thing."[55]

The third strand in India's argument in her own defense was her spokesman's extremely equivocal application of the doctrine of *rebus sic stantibus*.[56] In his first presentation, the Indian delegate did not name this doctrine as applicable to his government's case, but the Pakistani delegate was quick to declare that this was really what his opponent had in mind. He added that the doctrine was not generally accepted in international law and that, even if it were, the Indian delegate had not demonstrated that the conditions had changed in

[54] SCOR: 12th Year, 763rd Mtg. (January 23, 1957), p. 50.
[55] SCOR: 12th Year, 764th Mtg. (January 24, 1957), p. 42.
[56] "While things thus stand." This is a well-known but controversial doctrine in international law, i.e., the tacit assumption in all international agreements that they cease to be binding on the parties when the conditions upon which the agreement was based have been changed "substantially."

such a way as to relieve India of her obligation to support a general plebiscite. At this, the Indian spokesman elaborated the doctrine of *rebus sic stantibus* to the Security Council at great length, demonstrating both its common acceptance and the need for a principle to permit release from obligations when conditions had changed to the point that their fulfillment "should imperil the existence or vital development of one of the parties."[57] He then asserted that such a change had taken place with the introduction of regular Pakistani forces into Kashmir in the spring of 1948. Yet, curiously, he then declared that he did not intend to rely upon this doctrine to sustain his government's case.

This constituted an interesting twist in the Indian presentation revealing, no doubt, on the one hand a growing desire to be rid of the plebiscite pledge made almost a decade earlier, and on the other a continued reluctance to renounce that pledge altogether. In spite of the fact that the Indian spokesman took pains in 1957 *not* to disavow that pledge unequivocally, the implications of his three main arguments were tantamount to such a disavowal. In response to these arguments, the Security Council once again declared that any action undertaken to ascertain the will of the people in Indian Kashmir alone — i.e., through the Constituent Assembly and general elections within the territory — would not constitute fulfillment of U.N. plebiscite resolutions. A somewhat stronger resolution sponsored by the Western powers was vetoed by the Soviet Union, an action which reflected new Great-Power divisions on the issue since the extension of U.S. aid to Pakistan in 1954. At this and subsequent meetings of the Council, the U.S.S.R. emerged more clearly as the ally of India's position than had been the case — and this in spite of the fact that Western spokesmen generally were still careful to assert their neutrality on the issue.

The only other action of the Council at this time was passage of a resolution which requested its president, Gunnar Jarring of Sweden, to meet with Indian and Pakistani officials to revive the mediation process. The eventual outcome of these talks resulted in little more than a Security Council decision to call once again upon Dr. Frank Graham (still officially the U.N. Representative for India and Pakistan) to continue the mediatory efforts begun by Jarring. Predictably, too, Graham's recommendations, embodied in his report to the Se-

[57] SCOR: 12th Year, 767th Mtg. (February 8, 1957), p. 49.

curity Council of March 28, 1958, resulted in no substantial agreement between the parties.[58]

When the Security Council took up the issue of Kashmir once again — after another interval of more than four years — it was once more at the request of Pakistan. There were some interesting differences in the arguments used by the contestants this time, in 1962, as compared to those of the first U.N. consideration of the issue in 1948. Yet the same basic positions of each remained largely unchanged. The familiar charges of Pakistan's aggression and of the legality of Kashmir's accession to India remained at the heart of the Indian case. Insistence on the unsettled nature of Kashmir's affiliation and the necessity of a U.N.-sponsored plebiscite throughout the territory was as strong as ever on the part of the Pakistanis. In reading the verbatim accounts of these presentations, however, one senses a much greater sensitivity in 1962 than in 1948 both (a) to the logical implications of the claims made on both sides, and (b) to the need to substantiate those claims more fully through more elaborate legal arguments. Undoubtedly this emphasis in the 1962 debates reflected principally the fact that both states now had been constructing and improving their cases for many years.

On the Indian side, the delegate in the Security Council sought a somewhat more sophisticated "proof" for his government's claim of the absolute and unconditional legality of Kashmir's accession. He argued that of the two states carved out of British India on the subcontinent, it was only India which became the legal successor state to Britain there, and not Pakistan. In his words, Pakistan "is a new state, admitted to the United Nations as a new member. We were not admitted as a new State; we were here. We have taken on all the obligations, the assets and liabilities of the British Government . . . and . . . inherited the functions of paramountcy."[59] The Indian delegate could not, of course, use this argument to claim that the former princely states thus automatically came under the jurisdiction of India at the time of partition. The Partition Agreements specifically had given those states a choice in the matter of accession. Rather, this argument was advanced in the Council to assert the absolute sovereignty of India over any and all such states — including Kashmir — which had acceded to the Indian union. Sovereignty, he argued, is indivisi-

---

[58] For the text of Graham's 1958 report to the Council, see SCOR: 13th Year, Supplement for January, February and March, 1958 (S/3984, March 28, 1958).

[59] SCOR: 17th Year, 1009th Mtg. (May 3, 1962), p. 9.

ble and unconditional. India had done nothing after Kashmir's accession to compromise the exercise of that sovereignty in any way.

This thesis then provided the Indian delegate with somewhat heavier ammunition in his argument as to why the Kashmir issue was not negotiable from the Indian point of view. As he put it,

> We shall not at any time submit this matter to what is called mediation or arbitration, and we are not frightened by having it thrown in our face that this is a normal method of international settlement. There are many matters on which we will go to arbitration . . . but we will not agree to arbitration or mediation on the question of the sovereignty of our territory. . . . The sovereignty of a country and its independence, like the honor of a man, are not the subject of arbitration. . . . Not one other country would be free if its sovereignty were to be subject to arbitration. . . .[60]

This seemed an even more obdurate and uncompromising claim to sovereignty over the whole territory than had been made in the past. In the mid-1950's, it will be recalled, India had accepted in principle the U.N. Mediator's suggestion that the territory might be partitioned permanently. However, it was difficult to imagine that New Delhi still entertained such a view after the above statement. Even so, in themselves, these demonstrations of India's *de jure* sovereignty over all of Kashmir did not deny the legal possibility of a statewide plebiscite. Rather, they served to emphasize that any such decision could not be imposed on India from without.

Secondly, however, the Indian spokesman went on to declare — this time, quite straightforwardly — that the plebiscite to which his government had once agreed now was unacceptable to India due to changed conditions over the course of time. Without stating specifically that the doctrine of *rebus sic stantibus* had released India from a previous obligation to cooperate in the holding of a plebiscite — such a statement would have admitted what the Indians had long denied, i.e., that they had ever entered into an *international* agreement to conduct such a plebiscite — the Indian delegate did argue that conditions had changed to the point that the Security Council itself should recognize the present inapplicability of past resolutions on the subject. Among those changed conditions were listed, not only the "ancient history" of Pakistan's introduction of her regular army in Kashmir, but also more recent alleged changes such as (1) the increase in Pakistan's military strength on her side of the cease-fire line,

[60] SCOR: 17th Year, 1011th Mtg. (May 4, 1962), p. 49.

(2) suppression of the population in Azad Kashmir, (3) a widening disparity in each section of the territory in economic and industrial advance, and finally, (4) the *de facto* integration (although he carefully did not use the word) of Indian Kashmir into the union. [61]

Thirdly, the Indian delegate also raised a different justification for his government's having backed down from the idea of the plebiscite when he argued at considerable length that such references to the people had never been accepted as necessary to determine sovereignty in international law. In addition to citing numerous precedents (most notably, perhaps, those involving the United States) in which the incorporation of territory into a state without a plebiscite had been regarded as legal, he quoted an international lawyer to the effect that "the rules governing the intercourse of states do neither demand nor recognize the universal application of the plebiscite in the determination of sovereignty."[62] Obviously, this was not a case that India could have built for herself until after she had stopped paying lip service to the idea of a plebiscite.

Fourthly, the Indian spokesman went somewhat further than previously to articulate his government's contention that the Kashmir issue was not a "dispute" at all in terms of the U.N. Charter. This was really another means of asserting that Pakistan had no *locus standi* in the case – as the Indians had long contended – for it was Article 33 of the Charter, specifically, which was asserted to be inapplicable. This article states in part that

The parties to any dispute, the continuance of which is likely to endanger the maintenance of international peace and security, shall, first of all, seek a solution by negotiation, enquiry, mediation, conciliation, arbitration, judicial settlement, resort to regional agencies or arrangements, or other peaceful means of their own choice.

Confronted with the clear fact that the Kashmir situation had long been treated by the United Nations as falling within the scope of Article 33 and of Chapter VI generally, the Indian delegate could only assert that his government had been willing to seek peaceful settlement on "grounds of good conscience."[63] It should be clear at this point that this particular claim of India's was, in fact, difficult if not impossible to square with her own long-standing acquiescence in

[61] SCOR: 17th Year, 1009th Mtg. (May 3, 1962), pp. 53–54.
[62] *Ibid.*, p. 43.
[63] SCOR: 17th Year, 1016th Mtg. (June 22, 1962), p. 10.

peaceful settlement attempts as opposed to enforcement action against Pakistan. We shall be confronted with this issue — which has its roots in U.N. constitutional provisions and practice — again in the concluding section of this chapter. For the moment, however, it is sufficient to note that this claim was rather sharply challenged by the Pakistani delegate in 1962, who had only to look to past U.N. treatment of the issue as a dispute for proofs against India's contention.

Finally, the delegate of India sought international legal evidence to challenge the implications of Pakistan's warning that she could not be held responsible for the actions of the Azad forces if hostilities should break out once again. In this connection, the Indian spokesman quoted Oppenheim as having written "that a State's responsibility concerning international duties is a legal responsibility; a State must, according to international law, bear vicarious responsibility for the injuries and acts of private individuals."[64] Also cited was a ruling by the International Court of Justice to the effect that every state has the obligation not to permit its territory to be used for acts contrary to the rights of other states. He then added, "if Pakistan . . . either connives at or even permits — if Pakistan cannot control its citizens, it has little right to be a State and Government under the laws of civilized nations."[65]

The specific responses of the Pakistani spokesman to the Indian case at the 1962 meetings need not be considered here in any detail. As previously, the heart of Pakistan's presentation challenged India's claim that the accession of Kashmir had been *de jure* as well as *de facto*. Thus, he averred, the territory was indeed the subject of a dispute as understood in Article 33 of the Charter.[66] Additionally, India's refusal to permit preparations for a plebiscite was challenged as a disavowal of an international commitment. On this issue, debate soon centered about the question as to whether or not Part I of the UNCIP resolution of August 13, 1948, had been implemented. According to Pakistan it had been, since the cease-fire it called for had come into effect shortly thereafter. Thus, the Pakistanis argued, India was at fault for having obstructed implementation of the rest of the resolution, calling for demilitarization and a plebiscite. India, in turn, charged that only the cease-fire paragraph of Part I had been implemented, that the next paragraph of the same section — which pledged the contestants not to augment their military potential in Kashmir —

[64] SCOR: 17th Year, 1011th Mtg. (May 4, 1962), pp. 23–24.
[65] *Ibid.*
[66] SCOR: 17th Year, 1008th Mtg. (May 2, 1962), p. 5.

had been violated by Pakistan. It was for this reason that India had not consented to measures designed to implement the resolution's later provisions.[67]

The Pakistani case rested on the assertion that all of the issues that were currently disputed in this case could be resolved by the methods of peaceful settlement. As the spokesman for Pakistan put it,

. . . accession, aggression, the determination of the parties' obligations and of any default committed in carrying them out, the passage of time — all of the questions that have been raised are susceptible of determination. Most of them are questions of law, some of them are questions of fact. One method of resolving a dispute of that character . . . would be through arbitration. . . . What are the obligations of the parties? What has each to do? . . . These are questions which are susceptible of determination through arbitration or through judicial settlement.[68]

Here was an articulation, once again, of the apparent Pakistani interest in the kind of negotiated settlement between equals that the Indians continued to repudiate as strongly as ever.

At the conclusion of this series of meetings on Kashmir, a Security Council draft resolution calling on both parties to negotiate their differences at the earliest convenient time, and appealing for an atmosphere favorable to the conduct of such negotiations was vetoed by the Soviet Union. The Soviet delegate explained his veto to have been cast because of his government's conviction that the Western powers were only trying to fish in troubled waters in their attempt to reopen negotiations. He viewed many of the Council members as having adopted a pro-Pakistan stance on this issue at a time when the still-volatile Kashmir situation should be left to cool off by the passage of time. The existing situation, the Soviet delegate argued, was not intolerable to either party or to international peace. Renewed U.N. intervention into the affair could only exacerbate tensions and solve nothing, as numerous previous attempts at negotiation had shown.[69]

V

War on the Indian Subcontinent. As of this writing, the latest crisis in the Kashmir dispute (although it probably will not be the final one) erupted in 1965, beginning with wide-scale violations of the cease-fire during the month of August. Soon, the government of Pakistan pro-

[67] SCOR: 17th Year, 1009th Mtg. (May 3, 1962), pp. 36–37.
[68] SCOR: 17th Year, 1008th Mtg. (May 2, 1962), p. 55.
[69] SCOR: 17th Year, 1016th Mtg. (June 22, 1962), pp. 30–32.

fessed to see a popular insurrection taking place in Indian Kashmir, which was abetted by Pakistani "freedom fighters" and "volunteers." India immediately charged Pakistan with aggression by the use of her regular troops, and the attempted infiltration of Indian Kashmir by guerrillas. By early September, full-scale border warfare was in progress, extending south to the international border between India and West Pakistan as well as to the area on each side of the cease-fire line in Kashmir.

As the fighting continued and was extended, theatening eventually to turn into a full-scale war on the subcontinent, the Security Council met to consider the situation. At the first meeting, on September 4, the Indian delegate reviewed the history of the Kashmir issue, placing great stress upon the alleged culpability of Pakistan from the very beginning — first, in sponsoring the irregular Azad forces, then in sending regular troops into Kashmir, and finally, in repeating both actions again in recent weeks. The illegality of Pakistan's action had always been perfectly clear, the Indian delegate maintained, and the only reason that the Kashmir question remained a serious issue after so many years was because the Security Council had refused throughout "to face the simple fact of aggression by Pakistan." He concluded by demanding that Pakistan be condemned by the Council as an aggressor and instructed to withdraw from all parts of the Indian state of Kashmir.[70]

Two days later, at the next Council meeting on the subject, the representative of Pakistan focussed much of his attention on the recent Indian attacks across the international border against West Pakistan. This invasion had no parallel in United Nations' history, he claimed, and could only be compared to the aggressions of the Nazis in Europe. He vowed that Pakistan would continue to exercise its right to individual and collective self-defense until the Security Council took effective action, including enforcement measures, to end India's aggression both against Pakistan and against Kashmir.[71]

As these presentations in the Security Council make clear, the military engagements initiated by both countries in this flare-up of hostilities were meant to give expression to their very different interpre-

---

[70] A summary statement of the Indian presentation on this date is to be found in the *UN Monthly Chronicle,* United Nations Office of Public Information, II, No. 9 (October, 1965), 5–6.

[71] *Ibid.,* pp. 8–9.

tations of Kashmir's status. Since, for Pakistan, the territory was the subject of an international dispute and was being ruled, in large part, by an alien and illegal government, the August military action constituted the beginnings of a popular insurrection by the people of Kashmir against their rulers. Pakistani "aid" to these insurgents thus naturally was extended within the state of Kashmir itself, to help the Kashmiris "liberate" themselves. Any action initiated by the Pakistani army in territory acknowledged to be legally Indian would have been very hard to justify on the basis of this position. Yet for India, Kashmir was a full, constituent member of the Indian union; an attack across the cease-fire line in that state constituted an attack against India. Thus, Indian officials felt fully justified in responding to this "aggression" by retaliating directly against Pakistan elsewhere than in Kashmir.

The members of the Security Council, however, were most concerned to bring an immediate halt to the fighting, and tacitly recognized that they would inevitably meet with failure if they attempted to decide between these dichotomous claims first. It was in this light that the Council passed its first two resolutions — those of September 4 and September 6 — which attempted to secure pledges from the governments of India and Pakistan that they would respect the 1949 cease-fire line and withdraw all armed personnel to the positions they held on August 5, before the outbreak of hostilities.[72] In accepting these resolutions, the two governments crippled them by attaching sweeping conditions — conditions which revealed each government's reluctance to accept any resolution which refused to consider the issue of guilt and to initiate enforcement action in accordance with it. Therefore, New Delhi's acceptance was subject to a guarantee against further Pakistani infiltration and "aggression," and stated that no amount of pressure would prevent the Indian government from maintaining its sovereignty over Jammu and Kashmir. Pakistan's acceptance was predicated on the condition that the cease-fire arrangement would provide for a resolution of the "real" cause of the conflict. This meant that the cease-fire should be followed immediately by the complete withdrawal of Indian and Pakistan forces from Kashmir, the induction of a U.N.–sponsored, African-Asian peace-

[72] SCOR: 20th Year, S/6661 (September 4, 1965), and S/6683 (September 6, 1965).

keeping force into the territory to maintain order, and the holding of a plebiscite within three months.[73]

Undoubtedly the Indian conditions to acceptance of the cease-fire at this point were somewhat less sweeping in their implications than those of Pakistan; it also would appear that in U.N. circles at the time there was a good deal more sympathy for India than for Pakistan. In fact, the Indian response to the cease-fire proposals was widely interpreted as a conditional acceptance, and that of the Pakistanis as a virtual rejection.[74] In view of the fact that Pakistan's forces generally were regarded as having initiated warlike action in this instance, the reaction on the part of the international community is perhaps not surprising: had India, rather than Pakistan, initiated a wide-scale hostile action in Kashmir, there is every reason to suppose that the Security Council would have been more inclined to sympathize with Pakistan. Nonetheless, it is interesting to speculate whether or not the sentiments that did prevail, favoring India, may not have constituted evidence also of the way in which India's exercise of *de facto* sovereignty over much of Kashmir for a period of eighteen years had come to be accepted by most other national actors. The Indian retaliation across the Indo-Pakistan frontier in the Punjab, while viewed with dismay at the United Nations, certainly did not elicit the same kind of reaction against India that had been directed against Pakistan when fighting broke out in Kashmir.[75] In any event, if Pakistani officials sought to demonstrate to the world through armed action that their just demands regarding Kashmir had gone unanswered by the world community, they miscalculated rather badly in this instance. If anything, the events of the autumn of 1965 reaffirmed that the only tolerable means of living with the Kashmir issue was to enforce the "temporary" partition of the state that was the direct result of military factors nearly seventeen years earlier.

[73] Summary statements of U.N. debate and action in September, 1965, and of the responses of President Ayub Khan and Premier Lal Bahadur Shastri to that action are to be found in the *UN Monthly Chronicle,* II, No. 9 (October, 1965), 9–11.

[74] For example, see the *New York Times* of September 12, 1965, p. 1E.

[75] It should be noted that, at the beginning of the Security Council consideration of the issue in September, the Secretary-General reported the findings of the UNMOGIP commander regarding the first violations of the cease-fire line. As U Thant summarized that report, "The series of violations that began on 5 August were to a considerable extent in subsequent days in the form of armed men, generally not in uniform, crossing the cease-fire line from the Pakistan side for the purpose of armed action on the Indian side."

By almost entirely ignoring the conditions imposed by both India and Pakistan on the cease-fire resolutions passed early in September, the Security Council finally managed to secure an effective cease-fire through its resolution of September 20. Undoubtedly, much of the reason for the success of this resolution where previous ones had failed resulted from the fact that both belligerents had taken fright at the prospects for enlarging the conflict further. India's attitude revealed a willingness to continue living with the *de facto* partition of the state which may have seemed surprising in the light of her perennial claim to *de jure* authority over all Kashmir. Pakistani leaders were forced to turn cautious when they were unable to secure their goals quickly and all prospects of obtaining effective military allies began to vanish.[76] Thus, for Pakistan, it became a war that could not be won, and for India, a war which she had no desire to fight. Once these attitudes began to prevail in Rawalpindi and New Delhi, an effective cease-fire became possible.

While the resolution of September 20 did not attempt to respond directly to the conditions placed on previous resolutions by the two governments, it did contain provisions designed to placate each. In addition to ordering a cease-fire and the withdrawal of all armed personnel away from the cease-fire lines, the resolution stated that as soon as these measures were implemented the Council would decide "what steps could be taken to assist towards a settlement of the political problem underlying the present conflict."[77] Although this stipulation was noncommital in the extreme, it did permit Pakistan's grudging acceptance of the resolution without serious loss of face, since she had insisted previously that all cease-fire arrangements be tied directly to settlement action. On the other hand, it was, no doubt, the very vagueness of this provision that also permitted the Indian government to accept it.

India's demands for some sort of guarantee against future Pakistani infiltration were sidestepped in the resolution, but firm provisions for U.N. supervision of the withdrawal of troops were included, which helped to resolve the most pressing Indian insistence for a return to the *status quo ante bellum*. These provisions merit consideration here

[76] As one wag has put it with reference to the much-vaunted military superiority of the Pakistani troops: "It may be true that one Pakistani soldier is a match for three Indians. The difficulty is that there are four Indians for every Pakistani."

[77] For the text of the resolution, see SCOR: 20th Year, Supplement for July, August and September (S/6699, September 20, 1965).

because of the way in which they sought to resolve the disparate demands of the belligerents. Since the war had been extended south of Kashmir along the international boundary in the Punjab, the immediate issue was whether or not UNMOGIP — long in operation to maintain the cease-fire line in Kashmir — should be given a mandate to supervise the cease-fire along the India–West Pakistan border as well. Not surprisingly, the Indians argued that it should be, for their retaliation in West Pakistan had been in direct response to the Pakistani infiltration of Indian Kashmir. Pakistan's attack on an area where India claimed sovereignty was met with an Indian attack on territory that was admittedly Pakistan's. On the basis of India's claims, then, UNMOGIP's supervision of a cease-fire in the latter area would be just as logical as in Kashmir.

Such an interpretation was not acceptable, however, to the Pakistanis, who maintained that the action in Kashmir had constituted an attempted war of liberation by Pakistani civilians in an area under dispute, where India maintained *de facto,* but not *de jure,* control. India's attack on Pakistan in the Punjab had constituted an entirely separate issue — a case of Indian aggression — that demanded a new U.N. observation group with a distinct mandate. Since the Pakistanis required more appeasement in this situation than the Indians (India had the most to gain from a return to the status quo), it was the basic Pakistani position which eventually was subscribed to by the United Nations — without, of course, any condemnation of India. A new observer group — the United Nations India-Pakistan Observer Mission, or UNIPOM — was created to supervise the cease-fire and troop withdrawals along the international border, while UNMOGIP continued its similar mission in Kashmir. Once the cease-fire was accepted and the new observer group set up, UNIPOM's officials then agreed with India that the international boundary was to be regarded as the cease-fire line — not the line dividing the contestants at the time the fighting stopped, which would have given the Pakistanis more than a thousand square miles of Indian territory, as Pakistan argued. The result of this decision, too, was to facilitate restoration of the *status quo ante bellum,* with all of the frustrations that involved for Pakistan to press her claims in Kashmir.[78]

The cease-fire remained somewhat tenuous until, several months later, the Indian Prime Minister and the President of Pakistan met in

[78] Much of the information in the preceding paragraphs regarding the creation of UNIPOM was obtained from a high U.N. official involved in organizing the mission.

Tashkent at the invitation of the Soviet Premier to work out agreements for the withdrawal of forces. The meetings were a conspicuous success, and demilitarization of the frontier areas soon was stepped up. By the end of February, 1966, the U.N. Secretary-General was able to report to the Security Council that the troops of both nations had been withdrawn to the positions held before the infiltration of Kashmir began, in August, 1965.[79] Soon it was possible to dismantle UNIPOM, its work having been completed, and to reduce the number of observers in UNMOGIP recruited since September, 1965.

In spite of these rather sanguine developments, however, there was little reason to hope that the issue of Kashmir had been resolved in any final sense. With U.N. officials and national statesmen keeping a wary eye on the situation, no one was able to suggest measures to help solve this far-reaching political conflict. There had been an ominous note in Pakistan's acceptance of the resolution of September 20: her Foreign Minister had warned that his country would leave the world organization if, after an unspecified period of time, the basic problem of Kashmir remained unsolved.[80] More than two years later there had been almost no suggestion that such a solution was in the offing but, at the same time, neither had Pakistan reissued its threat.

While there was every reason to suppose, then, that the Kashmir issue would again demand the attention of the United Nations at some point in the future, there were, nonetheless, equally strong reasons for believing that the dispute could continue to be contained without involving a major conflagration. More than that, the experience of the 1965 outburst was convincing evidence that neither party could possibly hope to satisfy its full claims to the area by the use of force. Thus, every prospect pointed toward a prolonged continuation of the uneasy cease-fire situation with its concomitant *de facto* partition. Perhaps the day will come when both parties will be willing to regard this situation as an acceptable solution, rather than only as an enforced truce.

VI

Legal Claims to Kashmir and the Role of the United Nations. One of the characteristic features of the Kashmir issue throughout most of its

[79] *UN Monthly Chronicle,* III, No. 3 (March, 1966), 10–11.

[80] According to the *New York Times* of September 23, 1965, "Zulfikar Ali Bhutto, the Pakistani Foreign Minister, told the Council that his country would set a time limit for such a settlement. But he did not specify how long and he insisted that this was not an ultimatum."

long history has been the deep involvement in it of the organs of the United Nations. This fact naturally has affected the manner in which the issue has been treated; moreover, it reveals much about the effect of U.N. procedures and practices upon the foreign policy goals — claims made and advanced — of states. Without entering into a general analysis of U.N. practice in the field of peace and security, a few observations relating to the United Nations in Kashmir are called for.

First, what of India's long-standing and oft-repeated assertion that Pakistan had no *locus standi* in the Kashmir situation, that the issue was one which should have entailed condemnation of the aggressor rather than the treatment of the two countries as equal parties to a dispute — like "peas in a pod," in the sarcastic words of the Indian delegate? By the 1960's, it will be recalled, India elaborated at great length her contention that the Kashmir issue was not a "dispute" under the terms of Article 33 of the U.N. Charter. This position points up a dilemma inherent in U.N. constitutional practice, and one that has always been particularly painful for India in this situation. India had first brought the matter to the Security Council under the terms of Articles 34 and 35, which permit the Security Council to investigate situations which may "endanger the maintenance of international peace and security," and which permit any U.N. member to bring such a situation to the attention of the Council. Yet these articles, including Article 33, constitute much of the substance of Chapter VI of the Charter, entitled "Pacific Settlement of Disputes." The main thrust of its provisions assumes that the situations covered are, in fact, disputes rather than breaches of the peace involving culpability by one party or parties. It is Chapter VII of the Charter that treats the kinds of *enforcement* action that may be taken by the Council once it has determined that such action is necessary. Yet, Chapter VII has never been invoked by the Council with regard to Kashmir, in spite of India's continued insistence that such action was called for.[81]

So, although the Security Council legally could have adopted the Indian position at any time and undertaken enforcement action against Pakistan under the terms of Chapter VII, it chose to treat the issue within the framework where it was first introduced, of necessity, by India — i.e., that of Chapter VI. Since this kind of practice has

---

[81] Indeed, in all its history, the Security Council has invoked the enforcement measures of Chapter VII only once, during the Rhodesian situation of 1966 which was brought on by that colony's unilateral declaration of independence from the United Kingdom.

been very typical, rather than exceptional, for the Security Council throughout its history, we must conclude that any state which goes to the Council, as did India, seeking enforcement action is quite likely to be disappointed. In practice, the Security Council almost always has treated such issues as disputes within the meaning of Article 33. It is interesting to speculate whether India would have introduced the question to the Council at all if it had arisen in the 1960's, say, rather than in 1947. The U.N.'s history had been far too short in 1947 to make any such pattern discernible. India first took the issue to the Council secure in the righteousness of her position in Kashmir, and no doubt hopeful that a quick condemnation of Pakistan would follow. Instead, she found the United Nations treating Pakistan as an equal party to a dispute, able to assert claims of her own against India. As a result, the Indian position shifted to the defensive and remained there most of the time until the outbreak of hostilities in 1965.

Secondly, precisely because the Kashmir issue has been regarded as falling within the terms of Chapter VI, all U.N. action that has resulted has been in the nature of peaceful settlement action, i.e., negotiation, mediation, conciliation, etc. These kinds of procedures almost never are successful in the absence of at least a modicum of mutual faith between the parties. That this element has been lacking throughout almost the entire history of the Kashmir issue is seen in the fact that almost none of the paper agreements — for demilitarization, the conducting of a plebiscite, etc. — between the parties has been implemented. The essence of settlement by the above-named procedures is the desire to solve conflicts through compromise, for no third-party mediator or conciliator has the power to impose a settlement.

In a situation such as that involving Kashmir, where the prerequisites for peaceful settlement are not present, the continued use of these techniques may, nonetheless, be worth pursuing for the following reasons: (a) the alternatives, such as collective action by the international organization or resolution by military force, may be regarded as too destabilizing to be permissible; (b) while these techniques are being pursued, the parties undertake at least a tacit obligation not to resort to forceful measures, and thus, a somewhat unsatisfactory peace is kept. Such practice does little to insure that objective justice is done in the case, but the United Nations is far too political a body to mete out justice impartially around the world. It has accomplished quite a lot if it is able to prevent a conflict from spreading into a conflagration, even though, in doing so, it may perforce leave certain injuries to states unremedied.

Thirdly, it is useful to consider the effect on the Kashmir dispute of the fact that so much of it has been so highly publicized within the international forum. Apart from the fact that the Council always has been inclined to treat the parties as equals rather than as plaintiff and defendant, in what other ways has the debating situation typical of Security Council procedure affected the parties' claims?

When the Council first considered the issue in 1948, it appeared that India's tendency to present her case largely in legalistic terms was less well received by the other members than Pakistan's far more "political" presentation. While the Indian spokesman sought to narrow the scope of the issue and emphasized the legality of India's position, the Pakistani delegate succeeded in expanding the focus of attention, placing the issue squarely within the context of the myriad of political issues then confronting the subcontinent. Particularly impressive at these first meetings of the Council on the subject was Pakistan's lengthy charge of genocide and political repression in Indian-controlled Kashmir. This was the sort of dramatic issue which naturally would receive much attention and sympathy in a public forum and in the world press. One commentator has criticized India's presentation at that time, noting, "had the Indian case always been presented as a matter of a secular principle in conflict with the theocratic State, I have a feeling that the sympathies of a great community of intelligent observers all over the world would have supported India. . . ."[82]

Yet it would be erroneous to conclude that the Indian case fared less well than that of Pakistan in these first presentations because the former was narrow and predominantly legal, and the latter broad and non-legalistic. While it is certainly true that it would be foolish to argue a case before the Security Council in the same terms one would use before the International Court of Justice, it does not follow that legal claims cannot be made persuasive to the Council. Rather, one can criticize the initial Indian presentation for having introduced extraneous, non-legal issues which served to weaken her strictly legal claims. The most obvious example was her delegate's treatment of the plebiscite pledge. By failing to stress the clear legality of the act of Kashmir's accession as it stood, he undoubtedly gave the impression in his discussion of the plebiscite that the accession was conditional.

[82] Birdwood, *op. cit.*, p. 94.

In later presentations before the Security Council, the Indian spokesmen did not make the same mistake — although it was then difficult to undo the earlier impression left with the Council — and they argued quite forcibly both the legality of the accession and the irrelevance of a plebiscite from a legal point of view.

In fact, in more recent debates before the Council, Pakistan has relied more heavily than previously on legal argumentation as well. In part, this no doubt was due to the need to answer specific Indian claims with counterclaims that also relied upon the justification of law. In part, this later emphasis may have reflected Pakistan's realization that her own case against India could be made with greater precision if more legal analysis were included. Thus, for example, by 1962 the Pakistani delegate stressed heavily his government's contention that it was precisely because many legal rights and obligations were in doubt regarding Kashmir that solutions should be sought through the (judicial) technique of arbitration.[83]

Unquestionably, Pakistan's most telling argument against India through the years has been that of the need for, and India's refusal to permit, a plebiscite throughout Kashmir. It was, of course, United Nations' involvement in the dispute that gave rise to a serious plan for an internationally-supervised reference to the people. Since this is the sort of procedure that an international body is best equipped to handle, it is difficult to imagine that the plebiscite plan ever would have been developed to the extent that it was had there been no Security Council participation in the issue. Moreover, once India's unilateral pledge to conduct a plebiscite became tied to United Nations' resolutions upholding that pledge, the plebiscite plan took on a quasi-legal status it had not had before. International obligations now were undertaken — or so India's opponents could claim — which transformed a domestic political matter (i.e., India's unilateral pledge) into an international, quasi-legal one.

Without attempting to assess the blame here as to which state was

[83] Although the typical techniques of peaceful settlement mentioned throughout in connection with Kashmir — i.e., negotiation, mediation, conciliation — are characterized by the lack of third-party authority to impose settlement on the contestants, this is not the case with arbitration. When that technique is adopted, the arbitrator is empowered to decide a settlement — always within a rather narrow mandate agreed to by the parties — which the parties are pledged in advance to accept. Hence, arbitration should be regarded as essentially a judicial process, while mediation and conciliation entail negotiating processes, dependent for their success on the willingness of the parties to abide by the suggested terms of settlement.

most in default for not having implemented the measures called for in preparation for the plebiscite, it is clear that India's long-standing lip service to the plan made somewhat less satisfactory her eventual disavowal of any legal obligation to see it carried out. The entire issue of legal obligation in this matter remains ambiguous because of the U.N.'s mediatory, rather than judicial, role in the dispute. Thus, ironically, it was the U.N.'s consideration of the dispute in terms of Chapter VI rather than Chapter VII — treatment which was so detrimental to India's basic claim — that later prevented India's disavowal of the plebiscite from being branded as illegal action. On balance, then, the U.N. role in the Kashmir issue has served to weaken India's paramount claim of a legal right to jurisdiction although, in the process, it probably has aided her in consolidating her control over a large portion of the disputed territory.

On the other side, India's most forceful criticism of Pakistan before the United Nations no doubt has been that challenging Pakistan's contention that she has little or no control over military forays from Azad Kashmir. To a great extent, the Security Council and its agents seem to have regarded this criticism as justifiable (for evidence, note the U.N. resolutions calling on Pakistan to withdraw its forces first from Kashmir); yet, the United Nations may have drawn some rather different conclusions from that criticism than India intended in voicing it. Instead of leading to an outright condemnation of Pakistan for violating traditional rules of international law, this charge against her may have encouraged the Security Council to introduce a U.N. "presence" into Kashmir. Throughout its history, the United Nations has been very much inclined to send observers or a peace-keeping force into areas where the domestic authorities either are unable, or unwilling, to prevent infiltrations of armed personnel and to control civil strife. However much India may have welcomed UNMOGIP to secure the cease-fire in Kashmir, she has sometimes complained of United Nations' interference in her affairs through the work of the various mediatory agents. As long as a U.N. presence is maintained in Kashmir and a U.N. involvement in the issue persists on the agenda in New York, India's claim of complete "sovereignty" over the state is placed in some degree of doubt. While U.N. participation in the dispute often may be regarded by the Indians as the lesser of two evils, it remains, for them, something of an evil, nonetheless.

It has been contended here that much of the reason for the insolu-

bility of the Kashmir dispute lies in its symbolic nature, for it constitutes a challenge to two incompatible ideologies. India and Pakistan
have pressed their claims to the area so strongly in order to justify and
vindicate their dichotomous views of nationhood. Yet, throughout this
study there has been a sprinkling of evidence which would seem to
indicate that the actors themselves have not always kept this consistently rigid view of their interests in maintaining claims to all Kashmir.

Superficial analysis of this issue might lead to the suggestion that
the Pakistanis have been less uncompromising in their claims than
the Indians, for it is the former who consistently have stressed their
willingness to negotiate differences, even going so far on occasion as
to suggest their desire for an equitable settlement. To leave the issue
here would be misleading, however, for the reason that the Pakistanis
often have sounded less obdurate than the Indians is because of their
less favorable position as to *de facto* control of the territory. That
they were not willing seriously to consider a *de jure* division of the
state was made clear when they — not the Indians — rejected Sir
Owen Dixon's recommendation of permanent partition. In contrast,
India's acceptance of that same proposal, although qualified by rather
extreme territorial demands, revealed a willingness to compromise on
the principle of her sole right of jurisdiction if it would mean international acceptance of her sovereignty over most of the state. Yet India has continued to press her absolutist claim to sovereignty in all
succeeding debates on the issue. How are these contradictory actions
and statements on the part of both governments to be reconciled?

On the Indian side, the most plausible explanation is that continued
de facto control over what is by far the most desirable portion of
Kashmir has served to encourage her statesmen, on the one hand, to
prefer international acceptance of her authority there to the pressing
of a larger claim, but one that is unattainable. Since Indian Kashmir
does include a largely Moslem government of a predominantly Moslem population, *de jure* partition along the cease-fire line would entail no defeat for the Indian philosophy of secularism. On the other
hand, as long as Pakistan shows no willingness to agree to such a division, India maintains a more satisfactory bargaining and debating
position by continuing her legal claim to sole jurisdiction. Today she
only reasserts that claim when the legality of her position in Indian
Kashmir is challenged by Pakistan. India continued to pay lip service
to the plebiscite idea long after she had any real intention of supporting it actively. No doubt she did so not only because of her

apparent moral obligation under the terms of U.N. resolutions to do so but also because the principle of a statewide plebiscite harmonized with her own claim as to the indivisibility of the state, which in turn stemmed from her insistence that Pakistan's occupation of a piece of that territory was illegal. When in 1962 India finally rejected the plebiscite idea before the Security Council, that action could be read, perhaps, as a tacit abandonment of her "united Kashmir" thesis. The ideology of secularism was, by then, rather clearly vindicated in Indian Kashmir and throughout the Indian Union. Yet the legal claim to all of Kashmir could not be dropped without seeming to absolve Pakistan of her delict in occupying Azad Kashmir. Such absolution would not become politically feasible until Pakistan renounced all claims, in turn, to Indian Kashmir.

The Pakistanis, for their part, have had much less incentive to see the *de facto* situation accepted as *de jure*. Her two-nations ideology demands Pakistani rule over areas where Moslems are in the majority. However unrealistic it may appear that Pakistan will ever succeed in wresting most of Kashmir from India, her leaders must maintain their claims in support of Moslem-Pakistani rule over a Moslem state if they are to uphold the principle of Pakistan's nationhood. Although this principle, abstractly considered, might even encourage Pakistan to grant India sovereignty over those portions of the state where Moslems do not predominate, their bargaining position has been enhanced in practice by their refusal to concede even this much. If Pakistan were in *de facto* control of central Kashmir rather than India, such a concession might be wise politically; since she is not in control there — where a Moslem community remains under the authority of India — Pakistan has nothing to lose by asserting a claim to the entire state.

Thus, Pakistan's refusal to countenance a transformation of the current *de facto* situation into a *de jure* division should not really be regarded as contradicted by her profession of interest in an equitable settlement, perhaps through arbitration. Any such settlement, her leaders must reason, almost certainly would take account of the ethnic and religious composition of the state of Jammu and Kashmir and, as a result, award a larger piece of it to Pakistan than she now possesses. It is likely such a settlement would be reached on terms more in keeping with the Pakistani two-nations theory than with Indian secularism. The result would be, or could be made by the Pakistanis to appear, a vindication of Pakistan's basic political ideology. Whether or not these imagined views of the results of an arbitral settlement are completely realistic, they are at least more desirable than the perpetuation of the status quo.

The asserted interests of India and Pakistan in Kashmir remain as essentially irreconcilable as ever. In fact, it is possible to read the history of their dispute as a process in which those conflicting claims have been continually sharpened into ever more precise and unyielding arguments. But now that an attempted military settlement has resulted in a complete impasse, there now may be greater reason to suppose that the claims themselves may be modified in the future. Any *de jure* settlement of the issue acceptable to both the parties must remain, however, a distant goal.

WOLFGANG FRIEDMANN

LAWRENCE A. COLLINS

The Suez Canal Crisis
of 1956

I

Nationalization of the Suez Canal Company. The proximate, though most certainly not the underlying, cause of the Suez crisis of 1956 was the withdrawal of the offer of Western aid for Egypt's mighty Aswan Dam project. By late 1955 the United States and the United Kingdom had agreed in principle to contribute financial aid toward the construction of the Dam. At this stage the amounts to be involved were grants of $56 million from the United States and $14 million from the United Kingdom, and in addition a loan of $200 million from the World Bank.

The Western allies, however, were not satisfied with the developing situation in Egypt: President Gamal Abdel Nasser was already using his now familiar technique of playing the large powers off against each other. He began to publicize offers of aid from the Soviet Union; arms were being bought from Czechoslovakia in large quantities; in May, 1956, Nasser recognized Communist China. He was becoming increasingly restive at the conditions that were being attached to the offer of aid: that he would give the Dam priority over all else, that he must award contracts on a competitive basis, and, above all, that aid from the Communist bloc should be refused.

On July 19, 1956, the United States announced its withdrawal of financial support for the construction of the High Dam.[1] The circum-

[1] See 35 Department of State Bulletin 188 (1956).

stances of the announcements were doubly significant. First, Nasser had staked much of his prestige on the project, and as a developing leader among the uncommitted nations, he was especially wounded when the news of the withdrawal came while he was conferring with Jawaharlal Nehru and Marshal Tito. Second, this was the first of many times throughout the crisis in the ensuing months when the United States and the United Kingdom were out of step on major policy decisions. The British government, although it knew that a withdrawal of the offer of aid would be made, was not consulted about the timing of the announcement. Nevertheless, it followed suit and made a similar announcement on the following day. The influence of the United States in the World Bank is apparent, and for obvious reasons the loan from the Bank never materialized.

It was one week later, on July 26, 1956, that Nasser announced the nationalization of the Suez Canal Company. In an angry and highly emotional speech he emphasized the dangers of economic domination by outside powers, and resolved to build the Dam and restore the usurped rights of Egypt.[2] The Presidential decree of nationalization, issued the same day, noted the Egyptian character of the company, and provided compensation for the shareholders in accordance with the value of the shares as shown in the Paris Stock Exchange quotations of the preceding day. Payment was to be made after Egypt had taken delivery of all the assets of the company, including those situated abroad.[3] The Suez Canal was to be managed by an organization annexed to the Egyptian Ministry of Commerce.[4]

The main concern and interest of the United States in the Middle East was to keep the influence of the Communist bloc to a minimum. The Suez Canal was not the economic or strategic lifeline of the United States. Although American investors were making substantial profits from the oil of the Middle East, the United States did not depend on that area for her oil supplies. Peace and stability were more important issues than the control of the Canal.

For Britain and France, Suez was a more burning issue. British influence was on the wane in the Middle East. British troops had first occupied Egypt in 1882 when they were invited to quell a local rebellion, and they had remained for over seventy years. In 1914

---

[2] U.S. Department of State, *The Suez Canal Problem* [hereafter cited as *Suez Canal Problem*] (1956), pp. 25–30.

[3] Article I, English translation in *Suez Canal Problem*, pp. 30–32.

[4] Article II.

Britain declared the Turkish suzerainty over Egypt to be at an end, and established a protectorate. In 1922 Egypt was proclaimed an independent state, but the British government reserved to itself powers relating to the defense of Egypt from foreign aggression and, more significantly, to the security and communications of the British Empire. British military occupation of Egypt as a whole was terminated by the Treaty of Alliance of 1936,[5] but the defense of the Canal was entrusted to British troops who remained in the Suez Canal Zone. Their withdrawal was finally secured by the 1954 Anglo-Egyptian Agreement Regarding the Suez Canal Base.[6] Under this agreement British forces would be permitted to return in the event of an attack by an outside power. But Israel was expressly excluded from the powers whose attack would provide a justification for the reactivation of the base.

The Baghdad Pact was seen by Britain as a possible foothold in the Middle East; however, only Iraq was a member, and in 1956 Jordan was loath to join any bloc. Britain's historic and emotional ties with Suez were strong, but the Empire east of Suez was dwindling. As Britain's political influence in the Middle East declined, so — with the developing industrialization and economic expansion of Western Europe — did her economic dependence on the oil route through the Suez Canal increase.

France, too, had a substantial economic stake in the Canal. But her historical ties with that part of the Middle East were looser than those of Britain. It became apparent during the crisis that France, more a friend of Israel than of the Arabs, was interested above all in the downfall of Nasser. To France it was no coincidence that the war in Algeria began in 1954, the year in which Nasser came to power. France was interested in the control of the Canal, but perhaps more in overthrowing a regime which was aiding and encouraging the rebels in Algeria.

The Western powers were momentarily taken aback by the announcement of the nationalization of the Suez Canal Company. Sir Anthony Eden wrote to President Eisenhower on July 27:

We should not allow ourselves to become involved in legal quibbles about the rights of the Egyptian Government to nationalize what is technically an Egyptian company, or in financial arguments about their capacity to pay

---

[5] 173 League of Nations Treaty Series 401.
[6] Text in *Suez Canal Problem,* pp. 20–23.

the compensation which they have offered. I feel sure that we should take issue with Nasser on the broader international grounds.[7]

But in the House of Commons that same day he laid down the initial outlines of a legal argument which the United States, Great Britain and France were to press in greater detail for some months to come. As the crisis developed, the legal arguments became steadily more sophisticated, but they were always directed to the same aim. They should be read not so much in the context of the international law of expropriation, but rather with the understanding that the Western powers were concerned, above all else, with the control of the Canal. Nasser had taken not the Canal but the company which managed and operated it. The task of the governments and their legal advisers was to persuade world opinion that the Suez Canal must be run by an international authority, preferably by a restored Suez Canal Company. If that was not possible, then it must be operated by some alternative body representing the interests of the principal users. But it was necessary for them to avoid using arguments which could be turned against them. One of the reasons for the support which the United States gave to Britain and France was that it, too, had a strong interest in a canal, the Panama Canal. But although in Panama the interests of the United States were against nationalization, they were also against internationalization. Britain and France were pressing for the continued international operation of the Suez Canal, and so it was necessary for the United States, throughout the dispute, to ensure that its legal arguments for the internationalization of the operation of the Suez Canal could not be made applicable to the Panama Canal and so be used to wrest it from the control of the United States. Secretary of State John Foster Dulles was at pains to distinguish the legal and economic situations of Suez and Panama.[8]

On the day after the nationalization decree Eden told the House of Commons that the unilateral decision of the Egyptian government to expropriate the Suez Canal Company was in breach of the concession agreements, and that consultations would take place on the effect of the "arbitrary" action of Egypt on the operation of the Canal.[9] At this

[7] *The Memoirs of Sir Anthony Eden, Full Circle* (London: Cassell, 1960), pp. 476–77.

[8] *Suez Canal Problem*, p. 301.

[9] *House of Commons Debates* [hereafter cited as *H. C. Deb.*], Vol. 557, Col. 777, July 27, 1956.

stage, the United States contented itself with a protest at the tone of Nasser's speech.[10] Three-Power talks in London followed, and on August 2 the governments of the United States, the United Kingdom and France issued a joint statement incorporating what must now be regarded as their provisional view of the law. They did not question the right of a sovereign nation to nationalize assets subject to its political authority. But, they said, the action of the Egyptian government went beyond simple nationalization, for it involved the "arbitrary and unilateral seizure by one nation of an international agency which has the responsibility to maintain and operate the Suez Canal."[11]

The basic instruments governing the legal status of the Universal Suez Maritime Company were as follows: there were two unilateral concessions granted by the Viceroy of Egypt in 1854 and 1856, followed by a bilateral agreement of 1866 between the Viceroy and the company, which, *inter alia,* approved the articles of the company. The concession of 1854 authorized Ferdinand de Lesseps to establish a company to cut through the Isthmus of Suez and to operate its passage.[12] The duration of the concession was to be ninety-nine years from the opening of the Canal. On the expiration of the concession, the Egyptian government was to take the place of the company. The concession of 1856 further detailed the rights and obligations of the parties. Under Article XVI the *life of the company* was to be ninety-nine years, but it also provided for the possible renewal of the concession for successive periods of ninety-nine years. The Viceroy declared that the Canal would be open to every merchant vessel without distinction.[13] The 1866 agreement stipulated that

the maritime canal and all its appurtenances shall remain under the jurisdiction of the Egyptian police, who shall operate freely as at any other point of the territory, so as to assure good order, public safety, and observance of the laws and regulations of the country.[14]

[10] *Suez Canal Problem*, p. 33.

[11] *Id*. at p. 35.

[12] English translation in *Suez Canal Problem*, pp. 1–3; French text in Society of Comparative Legislation, *The Suez Canal — A Selection of Documents* [hereafter cited as *Suez Canal — Documents*] (1956), pp. 1–4.

[13] An English translation of the 1856 concession is in *Suez Canal Problem*, pp. 4–9. The French text appears in *Suez Canal — Documents*, pp. 4–10.

[14] Article IX. English translation in *Suez Canal Problem*, pp. 9–16. French text in *Suez Canal — Documents*, pp. 32–39.

As for the status of the company it provided that

> In as much as the Compagnie Universelle du Canal Maritime de Suez is Egyptian, it is governed by the laws and customs of the country; however, as regards its constitution as a corporation and the relations of its partners . . . it is . . . governed by the laws which, in France, govern joint stock companies.[15]

Disputes regarding the relations of the partners were to be settled by arbitration in France. Disputes arising in Egypt between the company and private individuals were to be settled by the local courts, and disputes between the company and the Egyptian government were subject to the jurisdiction and law of Egypt.[16]

The statutes of the company provided that the company was to have its seat at Alexandria and its administrative domicile in Paris.[17] The duration of the company was to be equal to the duration of the concession.[18] Article 73 read

> The Company being organized, with the approval of the Egyptian Government, as a joint stock company, by analogy to the joint stock companies authorized by the French Government, is governed by the principles of these latter companies.

If these were the only relevant instruments it would be legitimate to conclude that Egypt had the power to nationalize the company on payment of proper compensation. From these instruments the company would appear to be Egyptian. The French text of the phrase which the State Department translates as "in as much as [the company] is Egyptian" reads "La Compagnie Universelle du Canal Maritime de Suez étant Egyptienne."[19] But even if the reference to French law is a choice of law rather than an incorporation of foreign law, there was no reason why the company could not be expropriated on payment of proper compensation. Although there were suggestions that the compensation offered was not adequate or that Egypt would be unable to pay,[20] the efforts of the allies were directed at establish-

---

[15] Article XVI.

[16] *Ibid.*

[17] Article 3. French text in *Suez Canal — Documents,* pp. 11–29.

[18] Article 4.

[19] Egyptian Ministry of Foreign Affairs, *White Paper on the Nationalisation of the Suez Maritime Canal Company* (1956), p. 33 translates these words as "Since the Universal Company of the Maritime Suez Canal is an Egyptian Company."

[20] E.g., *H. C. Deb.,* Vol. 557, Col. 1605, August 2, 1956; *House of Lords Debates* [hereafter cited as *H. L. Deb.*], Vol. 199, Col. 711, September 12, 1966.

ing that the taking was unlawful *ab initio,* with a resultant obligation not so much to compensate as to restore the company or replace it with some international authority.

The first line of attack, therefore, was a traditional one. The Western allies alleged that the company had been taken for a narrow national purpose, that of financing the Aswan Dam, that the taking was arbitrary and unilateral.[21] The difficulty with these arguments was that Egypt was entitled to use the nationalization and its fruits for the public purpose of constructing the Dam, provided that it lived up to its international obligations with respect to the Canal. Although the withdrawal of the offers of aid for the construction of the Dam was the occasion for the expropriation, Egypt did not attempt to justify the taking on this ground, and Dulles later admitted that the nationalization would have occurred anyway.[22] If Egypt had the power to expropriate, then the power could be exercised unilaterally.

Because of the weakness of these rather tentative arguments based on the customary law, the allies found it necessary to relate their arguments to a conventional basis of obligation, and they found the answer chiefly in the Constantinople Convention of 1888, which regulated the free navigation of the Suez Canal. The Convention of 1888 was designed to ensure that the Canal would be open to all ships, whether merchants or men-of-war. Under Article I, "The Suez Maritime Canal shall always be free and open, in time of war as in time of peace, to every vessel of commerce or of war, without distinction of flag." The contracting parties took cognizance of the engagements of His Highness the Khedive towards the Universal Suez Canal Company[23] but agreed "that the engagements resulting from the present Treaty shall not be limited by the duration of the Acts of Concession of the Universal Suez Canal Company." The Egyptian government was to "take the necessary measures for enforcing the execution" of the treaty.[24] The obligations were not to "stand in the way of any measures" which the rulers of Egypt "might find it necessary to take to assure . . . the defense of Egypt and the maintenance of public order,"[25] but these measures were not to interfere with the free use of the Canal.[26]

---

[21] See, e.g., Tripartite Statement of August 2, in *Suez Canal Problem,* pp. 34–35.

[22] *Id.* at pp. 297–98.

[23] Article II.

[24] Article IX.

[25] Article X.

[26] Article XI.

The Three-Power statement of August 2 argued that the Suez Canal Company had an international character in terms of shareholders and management, and that since the Convention of 1888 provided for the internationalization of the Suez Canal, the nationalization of the company threatened the freedom and security of the Canal as guaranteed by the Convention.[27] But it did not follow from the fact that the company had a strong international element that the Convention guaranteed that type of management for all time. It was only later that the allies made a serious attempt to link the concessions to the Convention.

The United States, Britain and France proposed a conference of the nations principally concerned in the use of the Suez Canal. The conference was to be held in London from August 16. On August 12 President Nasser rejected an invitation to the conference. He accused the allies of attempting "to use every possible means to impart to the Suez Canal Company a status which it does not possess, simply in order to create reasons which will help in interfering with . . . Egypt's sovereignty."[28] The company, he declared, was Egyptian, and the British government had recognized this fact before the Mixed Courts of Egypt. That the company was called the *Universal* Suez Canal Maritime Company did not alter its Egyptian character. The Convention of 1888 was not linked to the concessions, as the Convention specifically provided that the obligation to permit free transit was not limited by the duration of the concessions, and on its expiration the Egyptian government was to take the place of the company. Although Article 8 of the 1954 Agreement with Britain recognized that the Canal was a "waterway economically, commercially and strategically of international importance," it also recognized that it was "an integral part of Egypt." Nasser charged that the proposed establishment of an international operating authority was "international colonization." A White Paper from the Egyptian Ministry of Foreign Affairs, issued also on August 12, concluded

the proposed conference has no right whatsoever to discuss any matter falling within the jurisdiction of Egypt or relating to its sovereignty over any part of its territory. The invitation to it cannot, therefore, be accepted by Egypt.[29]

[27] *Suez Canal Problem*, p. 34.
[28] *Id.* at p. 47.
[29] *White Paper*, p. 72.

The conference, then, was convened without the presence of a representative of the Egyptian government. By the end of the conference the twenty-two states represented were divided into two groups. First, there were the Eighteen Powers, led by the United States, Britain and France, who were seeking *international operation* of the Canal. A second group of four powers, including India and the Soviet Union, were for *international supervision*, without international operation.

By the time of the first London conference, hope had apparently been given up for the restoration of the Suez Canal Company. The Swedish delegate noted that the nationalization was regarded as a *fait accompli*.[30] Dulles said that the United States reserved its legal position and was prepared to explore the new situation to find a fair and just solution. In similar vein, the British and French delegates, perhaps because the concession would in any case have expired by 1968, though still contesting the legality of the nationalization, were more concerned with their proposals for a new international operating authority.

A new element had been injected into the allies' legal arguments. Although it was as early as August 2 that Eden had claimed a direct link between the concessions and the 1888 Convention, it was at the London Conference that the real attempt was made to find the link. Dulles and Selwyn Lloyd, the British Foreign Secretary, both argued that the preamble to the Convention supplied this missing link. The preamble stated that the contracting parties were desirous of establishing

a definitive system intended to guarantee, at all times and to all the Powers, the free use of the Suez Maritime Canal, and thus to complete the system under which the navigation of this canal has been placed by the Firman of His Imperial Majesty the Sultan, dated February 22, 1866.

The key phrase was "complete the system." On the basis of this reference to the concession agreement Dulles asserted that the concession had been incorporated into the Convention, and that the cancellation of the concession was therefore a breach of the treaty.[31] Selwyn Lloyd's approach was slightly different. He placed greater emphasis on the international character of the company, as did the French delegate, and though he referred to the preamble, it was for him more in the

[30] *Suez Canal Problem*, p. 79.
[31] *Id.* at p. 73.

nature of confirmation of the international character of the company rather than a separate treaty obligation not to expropriate.[32] A variant on the British view was made some weeks later by the Lord Chancellor when he said that the Convention of 1888 was based on the assumption that the concession would continue for its full period, and so the terms of the concession became implied terms of the Convention.[33]

Lloyd appealed to the delegates to look to the substance rather than the form, to disregard the fact that the company was incorporated in Egypt. But, he continued, "we must look to the future rather than to the past. We felt that the purpose of this Conference was to repair the situation created by an act which we maintain was illegal."[34] The difficulty was that the legal arguments had to be tailored in such a way as to prove that Egypt had a duty to permit the Canal to be operated by an international body. The allies could not rely overmuch on the concessions themselves, since they had only twelve years to run. Freedom of passage through the Canal could not be indissolubly linked to its operation by the company, because the obligation to allow free passage would survive the expiration of the concession.

The London Conference ended on August 23. The Eighteen-Power proposals were as follows: they affirmed that there should be free navigation in accordance with the principles of the 1888 Convention, that the operation of the Canal should be insulated from the influence of politics of any nation, and that there should be respect for Egypt's sovereignty. They proposed that there should be a fair return to Egypt for the use of the Suez Canal, and also fair compensation to the Suez Canal Company, with canal tolls as low as to be consistent with the above requirements. To achieve these ends there was to be a new Convention which would establish a Suez Canal Board to have the responsibility of operating, maintaining and developing the Canal. The Board would make reports to the United Nations. It would be composed of Egypt and other states chosen in a manner to be agreed upon by the states party to the Convention, with regard to use, pattern of trade, and geographical distribution.[35]

The Four-Power proposals placed greater emphasis on the recognition of Egypt's sovereign rights and on the recognition of the Canal as an integral part of Egypt. But since it was a waterway of international

---

[32] *Id.* at pp. 233–34.
[33] *H. L. Deb.*, Vol. 199, Col. 706, September 12, 1956.
[34] *Suez Canal Problem*, p. 234.
[35] *Id.* at p. 289–90.

importance, the interests of the users must receive due recognition. To this end they proposed a consultative body of user interests charged with advisory, consultative and liaison functions which would act in association with the Egyptian managing corporation.[36]

This divergence of views went to the substance of the problem. Egypt was denying none of the obligations under the 1888 Convention, at least in principle, apart from the special case of Israel. The Eighteen Powers wanted international operation of the Canal, and the Four Powers were proposing mere international supervision.

A mission led by Prime Minister Robert Menzies of Australia was despatched by the Eighteen Powers to put their proposals to Nasser. Menzies wrote to Nasser that the Powers had not attempted to arrive at any joint opinion as to the validity of the nationalization of the Suez Canal Company.[37] There were discussions in Cairo from September 3 to September 9, but the proposals of the so-called Suez Committee were unacceptable to President Nasser. The Egyptian government reaffirmed its adherence to the principle of free passage guaranteed by the Constantinople Convention, and stated its view that the way for the Canal to be insulated from politics was by reaffirmation or renewal of the 1888 Convention.[38]

After the abortive Menzies' mission the next stage was the establishment of the equally unsuccessful Suez Canal Users' Association (SCUA). By the beginning of September, Eden was apparently ready to take the question of the canal to the Security Council. But Dulles abandoned the idea of a new Convention with Egypt, and proposed instead that the principal users of the Canal should join together to operate the waterway; the SCUA was to hire pilots and collect dues. But Eden and Dulles were not of one mind: Eden envisaged the SCUA as a means of exerting pressure on Nasser, who could be met by force if he resisted; Dulles, however, made it clear almost at once that he was opposed to any attempt at concerted boycotting, to Eden's dismay. Eden has said that at first he was cool to the idea of the SCUA and was doubtful of its legal basis.[39] By this he presumably meant that he at once thought of it as an instrument of coercion. Because of this lack of unity of conception, the SCUA never became an effective weapon of any kind; it was formally established after a sec-

---

[36] *Id*. at pp. 288–89.
[37] *Id*. at p. 309.
[38] *Id*. at pp. 317–22.
[39] *Full Circle*, p. 516.

ond London conference on September 21. The association was denounced by Nasser as a threat of force.

The scene for debate then moved to the United Nations. On September 12 the representatives of Britain and France wrote to the President of the Security Council that the unilateral action of Egypt in attempting to bring to an end the system of international operation of the Canal confirmed by the 1888 Convention might endanger free and open passage through the Suez Canal. Egypt replied on September 17 that the nationalization had been effected in the exercise of its sovereign rights, and that the proposed SCUA was incompatible with the dignity and sovereign rights of Egypt. On September 23 Britain and France requested a meeting of the Security Council to consider the situation created by the unilateral action of Egypt; the Egyptian government countered with a request for the Security Council to consider the action by Britain and France which, Egypt alleged, constituted a danger to international peace and security.

The Security Council met on September 26 and voted unanimously to consider the British and French complaint. Britain and France abstained on the proposal to hear the Egyptian complaint, which was carried by seven votes, including that of the United States. The proceedings took place between October 5 and 13. What Britain and France hoped to gain by recourse to the Security Council is not clear. They would press for nothing less than full acceptance of the Eighteen-Power proposal for the establishment of a Suez Canal Board. This was unacceptable to Egypt, and the Soviet Union had made it clear at the London Conference that it supported Egypt in rejecting proposals for international operation of the Canal.

In the debates, the legal arguments were once again rehearsed. The British case was put by Foreign Secretary Selwyn Lloyd. Relying on the name of the company as the *Universal* Suez Canal Company and on the fact that it had an international character in terms of ownership, capital, and personnel, he argued for the existence of international rights in the operation of the Canal. In addition to the familiar arguments based on this international character, he made greater use of the reference in the preamble of the 1888 Convention to completing the system under which the Canal had been placed:

As a matter of accepted legal principle, if one instrument is entered into expressly in order to "complete the system" established by a previous instrument, it must be a necessary basis of the later instrument, and implicit in it, that the system will continue, at any rate for the period for which that system was originally established.[40]

This was close to Dulles' view that the Convention incorporated the concession by reference.[41] Further, Selwyn Lloyd relied on a little known international instrument — a declaration made by Turkey in 1873. After an International Commission meeting in Constantinople which considered questions of tolls in relation to measurement of tonnage, Turkey declared

that no modification, for the future, of the conditions for the passage through the canal shall be permitted, whether in regard to the navigation toll or the dues for towage, anchorage, pilotage, etc., except with the consent of the Sublime Porte, *which will not take any decision on this subject without previously coming to an understanding with the principal Powers interested therein* [emphasis added].[42]

This declaration made its first appearance in the Suez dispute of 1956 in a letter to the London *Times* by Lord McNair on September 10.[43] But little reliance could be placed on it. First, there was the difficulty of whether Egypt, as a successor state, would be bound by it in the absence of acceptance. Second, the declaration was limited to conditions of passage in terms of tolls and charges. Third, no use had been made of the procedure for over eighty years, and the declaration had probably ceased to be operative. The only use that the British Foreign Secretary could make of it was to attempt to show that user states had some legal interest not only in passage but also in the conditions of operation of the Canal. He concluded

Under the system of the Convention and the concessions, and the Turkish declaration of 1873 . . . the interests of the user countries were safeguarded not only in respect of passage but in respect of operation also, without which passage could not take place. . . . This was the fundamental reason why the 1888 Convention assumed, and based itself upon the assumption of, operation by the Company for the period of its concession.[44]

The French shared the view that the existence of the company constituted an essential element of the guarantees established by the 1888

[40] United Nations, Security Council, *Official Records* (11th year) [hereafter cited as SCOR], 735th Mtg., pp. 5–6.

[41] SCOR, 738th Mtg., p. 8.

[42] See *Suez Canal — Documents,* p. 45.

[43] *The Times* (London), September 10, 1956, p. 9.

[44] SCOR, 735th Mtg., p. 6.

Convention, but placed greater emphasis on the international character of the company as reflected in its ownership and management.

The Egyptian reply to the legal arguments represented the epitome of its view of the law. In reply to the charge that the action of the Egyptian government was "unilateral," her representative pointed out that an act of sovereignty such as nationalization could not be anything but unilateral. The United Nations General Assembly had recognized the right of nationalization. The company was Egyptian, and this had been admitted by the British before the Egyptian Mixed Courts. The term "Universal" indicated the character of the company's activity rather than its legal status. The 1888 Convention did not alter the juridical character of the company. It was the system of free navigation that the Convention completed.[45]

On October 13 the British and French draft resolution was put to the vote.[46] The first part of the draft proposed that the operation of the Canal should be insulated from the politics of any one nation, that questions of tolls and charges should be decided by agreement between Egypt and the users, and that a fair proportion of the dues should be allotted to development. It reaffirmed the need for free and open transit, and for respect of Egypt's sovereignty. On all of these points there was general agreement. The second part of the draft resolution called for implementation of the Eighteen-Power proposals on the international operation of the Canal. The first part was adopted unanimously, but the Soviet Union and Yugoslavia voted against the second part, which was thus not adopted because of the negative vote of a permanent member of the Security Council. This was hardly surprising, for it was entirely consistent with the Soviet Union's attitude at the London conference.

The proceedings in the Security Council mark the halfway stage in the Suez crisis. Stalemate had been reached. The United States, on the one hand, and Britain and France, on the other, were not at one as to the best means to secure international operation of the Canal. Although the United States had been behind the plans for the Suez Canal Board and the Suez Canal Users' Association, the signs were that its enthusiasm for international control of the Canal was on the wane. Suez for the United States had none of the historical, emotional, economic, and strategic connections that it had for Britain and France.

[45] SCOR, 736th Mtg., pp. 1–8.
[46] U.N. Doc. S/3671.

International law had not played a conspicuous part in the diplomacy. Britain and France were taken aback by the nationalization. The development of their legal arguments shows their realization that they would not be able to secure the restoration of the Suez Canal Company, and would have to press for an alternative international operating authority by negotiation. Their quandary was this: even if they could show that the nationalization of the company was illegal, the concession had in any case only twelve years more to run. Therefore they were required to establish that there was an international duty on Egypt to permit the Canal to be operated by some kind of international authority. This they were not able to do. Instead they were forced to use their view of the illegality of the nationalization as a weapon to persuade Egypt to negotiate a new treaty accepting international operation. The legal arguments of the United States show how intent its government was on separating the issue of Suez from that of Panama. It relied very much less on the international character of the waterway and its economic and strategic importance than on the particular treaty provisions governing its operation.

Selwyn Lloyd had said in the Security Council, "the real issue in this matter is the sanctity of treaties and respect for international obligations."[47] "Our duty is clear," said Dulles, "it is to seek by peaceful means a settlement in accordance with the principles of justice and international law."[48] The stage was set for the next act, which would throw greater light on the role of international law at Suez.

II

Armed Intervention. Against the background of the dispute over the nationalization of the Suez Canal Company loomed the danger that force might be used at any time. Immediately after the decree of nationalization, Egyptian assets abroad were frozen. On August 2 Eden announced to the House of Commons that troop movements were taking place in the Mediterranean and that British reservists were being recalled.[49] The avowed purpose was to strengthen the British position in that area to deal with any situation that might arise.

Eden's attitude from the first was that there must be readiness to use force in the last resort. He has testified that one of the reasons for not using forceful means to settle the dispute was, in his phrase, the

[47] SCOR, 735th Mtg., p. 8.
[48] SCOR, 738th Mtg., p. 6.
[49] *H. C. Deb.*, Vol. 557, Col. 1606, August 2, 1966.

political one, that Britain was bound as a signatory of the United Nations Charter to seek redress by peaceful means.[50] On August 3 Dulles warned that there were "some people" who urged immediate forcible action, but this, he explained, was contrary to the principles of the United Nations Charter and would undoubtedly lead to widespread violence endangering the peace of the world.[51]

When, on September 12, Eden explained his conception of the Suez Canal Users' Association to the House of Commons, he said that in the event of the Egyptian government not cooperating with the SCUA, "Her Majesty's Government and others concerned will be free to take such steps . . . as seem to be required . . . either through the United Nations, *or by other means, for the assertion of their rights.*"[52] The Labour opposition party interpreted these remarks as a threat of force and denounced them. On the same day in the House of Lords' debate on the Suez Canal, Lord McNair, former President of the International Court of Justice, while agreeing that the British government was justified in pressing for international control of the Canal, voiced his disquiet at the massing and display of armed force in the Mediterranean. While he was of the opinion that a reasonable amount of force could be used to protect nationals and their property, it seemed to him, as a lawyer, that the Pact of Paris and the United Nations Charter both threw grave doubt on the legality of the display of force by the government. He concluded, "I attach so much importance to the maintenance by this country of its leadership as an exponent of the rule of law that I feel I should be failing in my duty as a Member of your Lordships' House if I did not present these remarks for your consideration."[53]

In reply, the Lord Chancellor and principal Law Officer of the Crown, Viscount Kilmuir, admitted that he did "not want to get involved in theoretical arguments on International Law."[54] He then went on to make a plea, in effect, for the right of self-help in international relations. He emphasized that the Pact of Paris outlawed war as an instrument of *national* policy. If the Charter was intended to save succeeding generations from the scourge of war, it was also intended to establish conditions for the maintenance of treaty obliga-

[50] *Full Circle*, p. 479.
[51] *Suez Canal Problem*, p. 40.
[52] *H. C. Deb.*, Vol. 558, Col. 11, September 12, 1956 (emphasis added).
[53] *H. L. Deb.*, Vol. 199, Col. 663, September 12, 1956.
[54] *Id*. at Col. 718.

tions. These aims were interdependent. The United Nations might be blocked by the veto. He asked:

Is it not plain that in such circumstances [where a treaty regulates the status of an international waterway and is violated] States which are party to the agreement, in the fulfilment of their international obligations, have not only the right but a positive duty to take such steps as may be necessary to compel the delinquent to fulfil his international obligations? . . . [T]he United Nations, should our action under Article 33 not be successful, should take that view of international obligation which does not forget the duties of life.[55]

It should have been clear from the start that the United States was not willing to risk war over the Suez Canal; her interest in the Middle East lay in stability and the prevention of Soviet influence. Dulles was the initiator of the schemes to achieve international control of the Canal. "We do not intend to shoot our way through,"[56] he said in a press conference explaining his conception of the Suez Canal Users' Association. Eden hoped, however, that if the United States would not support him in military action should this become necessary, it would at least remain neutral and not actively oppose the use of force.

Although the British government was especially worried that Egypt might sever England's economic and strategic lifeline, the Suez Canal, Britain had not been strong in its support of the only country to whose shipping the Canal was closed, Israel. After the Arab-Israeli war and the General Armistice Agreements of July, 1949, Egypt had continued to exercise the right of visit and search against Israeli ships and cargo and to deny Israel the use of the Canal.

In 1951 Israel complained to the Security Council concerning the restrictions imposed by Egypt on passage through the Canal. Israel relied on the Armistice Agreement with Egypt and the United Nations Charter to allege that Egypt had no right to block the Canal to Israeli shipping. The Armistice Agreement of February, 1949 provided that the parties would respect "the injunction of the Security Council against resort to military force in the settlement of the Palestine question";[57] the parties undertook to refrain from any "aggressive action by the armed forces . . . of either Party . . . against the people or the armed forces of the other,"[58] and to abstain from "any warlike or

[55] *Id.* at Col. 722.
[56] *Suez Canal Problem*, p. 341.
[57] Article I (1).
[58] Article I (2).

hostile act against the military or paramilitary forces of the other Party."[59] Israel claimed that the Egyptian action was in violation of the Armistice Agreement and of her obligation under general international law to permit free passage through the Canal.[60] The United Nations Charter had created a "new world of international relations" in which there were no longer any traditional rights of war, and so Egypt could not claim to exercise belligerent rights.[61]

The Egyptian view of the law was that a technical state of war survived the Armistice Agreement, and that she was therefore entitled to exercise her belligerent rights in interfering with Israeli shipping.[62] Furthermore, Egypt relied on Article X of the Constantinople Convention of 1888, which allows measures to be taken "to assure . . . the defense of Egypt and the maintenance of public order," to justify her action against Israel. In the Security Council her delegate referred to the right of self-preservation in terms of national survival.[63]

In September, 1951, the Security Council adopted a draft resolution proposed by France, Britain and the United States. The terms of the resolution were that neither party could reasonably assert that it was still a belligerent, and that the interference with Israeli ships and cargo bound to or from Israeli ports was inconsistent with the Armistice Agreement, and could not be justified on the grounds either of the right of visit and search or of self-defense. The Council did not pass on the controversial question of whether a state of war remains a possible legal relation since the ratification of the United Nations Charter.[64]

The Egyptian government has maintained since, that the resolution is a "political" one which she is entitled to disregard. Some support for this view is provided by the remarks of the British representative in the Security Council debate, who said,

these legal issues are no doubt debatable, but I still do not consider that it is necessary for the Security Council to go into them. It is at least questionable whether the Security Council is really qualified to undertake the detailed legal study and analysis which would certainly be required if the Council were to attempt to make a legal finding. Nor do we feel . . . that

[59] Article II (2).
[60] SCOR (6th year), 549th Mtg., pp. 2–11.
[61] Id. at pp. 11–12.
[62] Id. at p. 23.
[63] Id. at p. 21.
[64] See, generally, Nathan Feinberg, The Legality of a "State of War" after the Cessation of Hostilities (Jerusalem: The Magnes Press, 1961).

it would be profitable to make such an attempt, since the view which the Council takes on this question should depend, in our opinion, on the actual situation as it exists rather than on any legal technicalities.[65]

Other representatives, including those of France, the United States, and India, did not share the view of Britain that international law had little relevance.[66]

The distinction between "legal" and "political" resolutions is itself a political one. It does not affect the validity of the recommendation of the Security Council which was ignored by Egypt. In 1954 a similar proposed resolution was vetoed by the Soviet Union, which had abstained on the 1951 vote. Incidents involving Israeli cargoes on foreign ships continued to occur. In 1954 an Israeli ship, the "Bat Galim," was seized at the southern entrance of the Suez Canal and later confiscated.

Arab-Israeli relations were fast deteriorating. Israel was repeatedly condemned by the Security Council for incursions into neighboring territories in violation of the Armistice Agreements. Border incidents led to reprisals, and reprisals to counter-reprisals. In 1955 there was a large paratroop raid by Israel in the Gaza strip; that same year Egyptian *fedayeen* raids into Israel began, in a pattern of hit-and-run guerrilla sabotage that is a familiar feature of modern conflict. In September, Egypt negotiated an arms deal with Czechoslovakia. The balance of power in the Middle East had been disturbed.

France's links with Israel were becoming stronger because France was not as interested as Britain in cultivating the friendship of the Arab world. Since 1954 the French had been engaged in the war against the Algerian rebels, and Nasser was aiding and encouraging the rising Algerian nationalism. By 1956 France had become a firm ally of Israel.

The events of mid-October 1956 are still shrouded in mystery. On October 13 the allies' proposal for international control of the Suez Canal was vetoed by the Soviet Union. On October 16 the French captured an Egyptian ship, the "Athos," which they alleged was carrying arms for the rebels in Algeria. From that date on, Britain and France were at pains to keep the United States in the dark as to their Middle East policy. On October 24 came the announcement of the establishment of a joint Egyptian-Syrian-Jordanian command, and the next day Israel mobilized.

---

[65] SCOR (6th year), 552nd Mtg., p. 2.
[66] France, *id.* at p. 5, United States, *id.* at p. 10, India, 553rd Mtg. at p. 30.

It may be many years before it is established beyond a shadow of a doubt whether there was "collusion." Recent revelations by some of the French ministers involved, especially by Christian Pineau, who was Foreign Minister then, form the basis of the following account:[67] by the early part of October the British had become parties to a Franco-Israeli plan to strike at Egypt; the plan was cemented on October 23 at a meeting in Sèvres, a quiet suburb of Paris; at that meeting the French leaders were joined by the British Foreign Secretary and the Israeli Prime Minister, and together they hammered out a secret treaty, which they swore never to publish; the "treaty"[68] provided for an attack by Israel on Egypt, and a subsequent Anglo-French landing to "protect" the Canal. The interests of the principal actors, as well as the course of prior and subsequent events, strengthen the presumption that Pineau's account is to be believed.[69]

On October 29, 1956, Israeli forces crossed the armistice lines to attack Egyptian territory, with the avowed purpose of ridding Israel of the danger from the Egyptian *fedayeen* raiders based in the Gaza area. The United States at once informed the Security Council that the Israelis had advanced, and requested an urgent meeting of the Council, which met at 11 A.M. on October 30. The United States' representative Henry Cabot Lodge expressed the shock of his government that the Israeli attack had occurred so soon after President Eisenhower had appealed to Israel not to undertake any military action against its neighbors. Relying on the responsibility of the United Nations to maintain the armistice agreements and of the Security Council to maintain international peace and security, he proposed that a breach of the peace be determined and that Israel be ordered to withdraw behind the armistice lines.[70] The Soviet representative drew attention to reports that the terms of an Anglo-French ultimatum had been made public while the Council was meeting.[71]

---

[67] See Terence Robertson, *Crisis: The Inside Story of the Suez Conspiracy* (London: Hutchinson, 1965), pp. 108–63; Peter Calvocoressi, "Some Evidence of Collusion," in *Suez Ten Years After,* ed. Anthony Moncrieff (London: the B.B.C., 1967), pp. 83–107.

[68] Whatever the arguments on *jus cogens,* there could hardly be a clearer example of an illegal treaty, if indeed it existed.

[69] Anthony Nutting, who resigned on November 3, 1956, from a junior government post (Minister of State at the Foreign Office) has only recently broken a long public silence to confirm what he calls "a squalid piece of collusion." Anthony Nutting, *No End of a Lesson* (London: Constable, 1967), pp. 100–107.

[70] SCOR (11th year), 748th Mtg., p. 2.

[71] *Id.* at pp. 5–6.

Soon after 4 P.M. Greenwich mean time, the governments of the United Kingdom and France addressed urgent communications to Israel and Egypt. Taking note of the outbreak of hostilities between Israel and Egypt and the threat which this caused to the freedom of navigation through the Suez Canal, they requested Israel to cease fire and withdraw her forces ten miles east of the Canal. They asked Egypt to cease fire and, in addition, to withdraw her forces from the vicinity of the Canal and accept the temporary occupation by Anglo-French forces of key positions along the Canal. Britain and France requested a reply within twelve hours. If at the expiration of that time one or both governments had not undertaken to comply, "United Kingdom and French forces will intervene in whatever strength may be necessary to secure compliance."

The terms of the announcement had apparently been agreed some days in advance of the Israeli attack. The alleged purpose was to separate the belligerents and guarantee freedom of transit through the Canal. But when the ultimatum was issued Israeli forces had not yet reached the Canal, and it seemed unlikely that Egypt would withdraw *west* of the Canal. It had been Israel which had penetrated deep into Egyptian territory.

When the Security Council met on the afternoon of October 30, the text of the ultimatum was before it. The United States reserved its position on the legality of the ultimatum and pressed for a cease-fire. Its draft resolution noted that the armed forces of Israel had penetrated deep into Egyptian territory in violation of the General Armistice Agreement with Egypt. The operative paragraphs read:

1. *Calls upon* Israel and Egypt immediately to cease fire;
2. *Calls upon* Israel immediately to withdraw its armed forces behind the established armistice lines;
3. *Calls upon* all Members
   (a) To refrain from the use of force or threat of force in the area in any manner inconsistent with the purposes of the United Nations;
   (b) To assist the United Nations in ensuring the integrity of the armistice agreements;
   (c) To refrain from giving any military, economic or financial assistance to Israel so long as it has not complied with this resolution.[72]

The resolution failed to carry because of the negative votes of two permanent members of the Security Council: Britain, exercising the

[72] U.N. Doc. S/3710.

power of veto for the first time, and France. A Soviet draft resolution also calling for a cease-fire was vetoed later the same night. Britain and France explained their negative votes on the ground that the proposals would not be effective to stop the fighting and safeguard the Canal.[73]

The stated purpose of the Israeli advance was to eliminate the *fedayeen* bases. Israel's defense of her action was based on the familiar provision of Article 51 of the United Nations Charter that "nothing in the present Charter shall impair the inherent right of individual or collective self-defense if an armed attack occurs against a Member of the United Nations." The legal defense was based on two lines of argument. First, Israel argued that the Egyptian raids amounted to an actual armed attack within Article 51. "Can anyone say that this long and uninterrupted series of encroachments did not constitute in its totality the essence and the reality of an armed attack?" her representative asked.[74] Second, in pointing to evidence that there was to be renewed activity by Egypt against Israeli territory, and in stating that the purpose of the intervention was to eliminate the *fedayeen* bases, Israel in effect was arguing for an interpretation of Article 51 which allowed the right of preventive or anticipatory self-defense. There had been *fedayeen* raids, there were likely to be more, therefore she was entitled to eliminate the danger from the bases in the Gaza area.

Even when Israeli troops had all but reached the Canal, Israel was still justifying her action as intended against the *fedayeen* bases. She declared:

We are not satisfied with a justification of our actions in pure terms of national expediency. There is perhaps no Member of [the United Nations] more sensitive to all the currents of international opinion. . . . [W]e have been forced to interpret Article 51 of the Charter as furnishing both a legal and a moral basis for such defensive action.[75]

The action in occupying most of the Sinai Peninsula, however, was out of all proportion to the danger that Israel faced, even if she were right in her interpretation of Article 51 as allowing anticipatory action. Furthermore, it is difficult to resist the conclusion that the action was undertaken in concert with France to deliver a crushing blow to the prestige of Nasser.

[73] SCOR, 749th meeting, pp. 29–30.
[74] United Nations General Assembly Records [hereafter cited as GAOR], 1st Emergency Special Session, 562nd Mtg., p. 23.
[75] *Ibid.*

The declared motives of the Anglo-French intervention were to halt the hostilities between Israel and Egypt and to safeguard the Suez Canal for international shipping; it was left to Britain to attempt to justify the action in terms of international law. While France kept silent, British spokesmen were required to run through a variety of legal arguments, some strong on the law but weak on the facts, others weak in both respects. Britain had to contend with two vital provisions of the United Nations Charter: the obligation under Article 2(3) that "All Members shall settle their international disputes by peaceful means in such a manner that international peace and security, and justice, are not endangered" and the prohibition in Article 2(4) that "All Members shall refrain in their international relations from the threat or use of force against the territorial integrity or political independence of any state, or in any other manner inconsistent with the Purposes of the United Nations."

When Eden announced the terms of the Anglo-French ultimatum to the House of Commons he said that there was "nothing . . . in the [United Nations] Charter which abrogates the right of a Government to take such steps as are essential to protect the lives of their citizens and vital rights." He quickly corrected his reference to vital rights to "vital international rights."[76] These propositions became the twin pillars of the British legal justification — the former, protection of nationals, largely for home consumption, and the other, protection of international rights, for the international arena. In effect, although this was hardly made explicit, they represented a wide view of the effect of Article 51 and a restrictive view of the obligation to use peaceful means to settle international disputes and refrain from the use of force in international relations.

The first argument, self-defense in protection of nationals and their property, was pursued for the most part in the House of Commons and in the House of Lords:

Self-defence undoubtedly includes a situation where the lives of the state's nationals abroad are in imminent danger. . . . Article 51 of the Charter recognises the right of self-defence, and it would be a travesty of the Charter to say that no intervention can take place until our nationals are actually being attacked and perhaps killed.[77]

Foreign Secretary Selwyn Lloyd then went on to explain the requirements of this particular right of self-defense in terms remarkably sim-

[76] *H. C. Deb.*, Vol. 558, Col. 1277, October 30, 1956.
[77] *Id.* at Cols. 1565–1566.

ilar to the views of Waldock:[78] first, there must be an imminent threat of injury to a state's nationals; second, there must be a failure or inability of the territorial sovereign to protect them; third, the measures of protection must be strictly confined to the object of protecting the nationals from injury.

This statement reveals an interpretation of Article 51 which goes beyond its literal wording in two respects: first, the danger to nationals is either regarded as an armed attack justifying the use of force in their defense or is not regarded as an armed attack but is justified under the theory of "inherent right" not limited to, but merely including, armed attack; second, for the British Foreign Secretary the words "if an armed attack occurs" are not exhaustive and do not preclude the use of force in preventive self-defense. The Lord Chancellor, Viscount Kilmuir, elaborated the argument when he argued that Article 51 was concerned with external aggression and that it was therefore natural for its terms to be related to armed attack. He, too, thought it would be a "travesty of the purpose of the Charter to compel a defending State to allow its opponent to deliver the first fatal blow."[79]

The next stage in the argument was to relate the defense of nationals to the defense of their property in order to justify the plan to occupy the Canal zone. This Viscount Kilmuir linked to the doctrine of vital interests. "If really valuable and internationally important foreign property is in danger of irreparable injury, through the breakdown of order, entry by a foreign State for the sole purpose of securing the safety of that property is excusable."[80] It is noteworthy that as the arguments progressed further away from self-defense and Article 51, they moved closer to traditional ideas of vital interests and hegemonial intervention. "If the interests concerned are sufficiently vital and if the damage which threatens them is sufficiently great, then . . . action to protect our interests is also justified," the Foreign Secretary said.[81]

The legal arguments were in reality a reversal of the fact pattern. They developed from notions of the protection of nationals to notions of the protection of their property. British shipping might be endan

---

[78] See Sir Humphrey Waldock, "The Regulation of the Use of Force by Individual States in International Law," 81 Hague *Recueil des Cours* (1952), 451, 467.

[79] *H. L. Deb.*, Vol. 199, Cols. 1350–52, November 1, 1956.

[80] *Id.* at Col. 1349.

[81] *H. C. Deb.*, Vol. 558, Col. 1566, October 31, 1956.

gered, and the installations of the Canal might be damaged and dis-
rupt the economic life of Western Europe, but British lives were endangered by the Anglo-French intervention more than they were
the occasion for it. The Lord Chancellor in September had spoken of
the right of self-help, and the indications now are that self-help was
the basis of the Anglo-French threat and the eventual use of force.

In the international forum, the United Nations, the British arguments took on a different shape. There was little mention of protection of nationals[82] and none of Article 51, perhaps because they would
not stand the scrutiny of an international organization. In the Security
Council the British representative, joined by the French, argued that
the Security Council could take no constructive action to contribute
to the objectives of halting the fighting between Israel and Egypt
and safeguarding free passage through the Canal. He accused the
Soviet Union of a persistent abuse of the power of veto.[83] Since the
Security Council could have provided no adequate remedy, Britain
and France had been compelled to act independently of the United
Nations.

This was the "police action" argument: The Security Council was
depicted as a policeman with his hands tied behind his back, who,
frustrated by the veto, could not act immediately.[84] Therefore, in the
phrase of the French, Britain and France were acting on behalf of
the United Nations.[85] Vital national rights were being translated into
international rights, and the legal basis of the justification for this is
unclear. Two strands appear to run through it. The first is that the
United Nations Charter intended the Security Council to be an effective
instrument of coercion, but since it had proved its ineffectiveness, states
could revert to their former rights of self-help under customary international law. This would be a form of the potentially anarchical principle
of *rebus sic stantibus.* The second possible line would be that the
Charter only forbids the use of force inconsistent with the purposes of
the United Nations. Some support to the view that this lay behind some
of the British legal justifications is the suggestion by the British representative in the General Assembly that the action was undertaken for
the restoration of order in the interests of many nations.[86]

Whatever the interpretation of Articles 2(4) and 51, there could be

[82] See SCOR, 749th Mtg., p. 24.
[83] *Id.* at pp. 4–5.
[84] *H. C. Deb.*, Vol. 558, Col. 1377, October 30, 1956.
[85] GAOR, 563rd Mtg., p. 73.
[86] GAOR, 561st Mtg., p. 7.

no escaping the fact that on this occasion it had been Britain and France who had frustrated the working of the Security Council. It was because Israel could rely on the veto power of Britain and France that she could penetrate so deep into Egyptian territory. Israel complied promptly with the Anglo-French "ultimatum" to her; if she had not been acting in concert with France and Britain, then presumably she would have obeyed a unanimous resolution of the Council that she withdraw.

The 1950 Uniting for Peace Resolution[87] of the General Assembly, moreover, had recognized that "failure of the Security Council to discharge its responsibilities on behalf of all the Member States . . . does not relieve Member States of their obligations . . . under the Charter to maintain international peace and security." That resolution provided that if the Security Council failed to exercise its primary responsibility for the maintenance of peace, an emergency session of the General Assembly might be called if requested by the Security Council on the vote of any seven members, or by a majority of the Members of the United Nations.

At the meeting of the Security Council on October 31, 1956, after two vetoes had been cast by Britain and France, a Yugoslav draft called for an emergency session of the General Assembly as provided for in the Uniting for Peace Resolution, "*Taking into account* that the lack of unanimity of its permanent members at the 749th and 750th meetings of the Security Council has prevented it from exercising its primary responsibility for the maintenance of international peace and security."[88] The British delegate objected on the grounds that the Security Council had not voted on the substance of the agenda, the letter from Egypt charging aggression, and that the veto had been cast because the United States' and Soviet draft resolutions would not have been an effective method for maintaining international peace and security. Nevertheless, the resolution was carried over the dissenting votes of Britain and France, with the United States and the Soviet Union voting together to call an emergency session of the General Assembly.

When the General Assembly met on November 1, 1956, Anglo-French air attacks on Egypt had begun and the Suez Canal had been blocked by sunk and scuttled ships; thus the alleged objective

[87] Resolution 377A (V), November 3, 1950.
[88] SCOR, 751st Mtg., pp. 13–14.

of safeguarding passage through the Canal had already failed. Israeli forces were in occupation of most of the Sinai Peninsula. The mood of the General Assembly was one of anger. Secretary Dulles began by saying, "I doubt that any representative ever spoke from this rostrum with as heavy a heart as I have brought here tonight."[89] He then referred to the Egyptian violation of the 1888 Convention with regard to Israeli shipping, the heavy rearmament of Egypt, her abrupt seizure of the Suez Canal Company, but continued,

We have, however, come to the conclusion that these provocations — serious as they were — cannot justify the resort to armed force. . . . If . . . we were to agree that the existence in the world of injustices which this Organization has so far been unable to cure means that the principle of the renunciation of force should no longer be respected, that whenever a nation feels that it has been subjected to injustice it should have the right to resort to force in an attempt to correct that injustice, then I fear that we should be tearing this Charter into shreds. . . . [T]he violent armed attack by three Members of the United Nations upon a fourth cannot be treated as anything but a grave error inconsistent with the principles and purposes of the Charter; an error which, if persisted in, would gravely undermine this Organization and its Charter.[90]

The United States' draft resolution noted the deep penetration of Israeli forces into Egyptian territory in violation of the General Armistice Agreement, that armed forces of Britain and France were conducting military operations against Egypt, and that traffic through the Suez Canal had been interrupted. It urged that all parties involved in hostilities agree to an immediate cease-fire and halt the introduction of forces into the area.[91] The resolution was adopted overwhelmingly, only Australia and New Zealand joining Britain, France and Israel in voting against it. The first call for a cease-fire was made by the General Assembly in the early hours of November 2.

On the following day Secretary-General Dag Hammarskjöld reported that military action was still continuing, but that Britain and France had declared that although their police action remained necessary, they would halt their military action if a United Nations' force were introduced into the area pending a settlement of the Arab-Israeli problem. On November 1, Anthony Eden had said in the House of Commons that the British government would be pleased if

[89] GAOR, 561st Mtg., p. 10.
[90] *Id.* at pp. 10–11.
[91] Resolution 997 (ES-1), November 1, 1956.

the United Nations were willing to take over the physical task of maintaining peace in the area.[92] How seriously this remark was meant is not clear, but in face of the overwhelming opposition by the United Nations to the armed intervention it gave the opportunity to save as much face as was possible under the circumstances.

On November 4 the General Assembly called once again for a cease-fire. On the same day it adopted a Canadian proposal which requested "as a matter of priority, the Secretary-General to submit to it within forty-eight hours a plan for the setting up, with the consent of the nations concerned, of an emergency international United Nations Force to secure and supervise the cessation of hostilities."[93] In his subsequent report the Secretary-General emphasized that he would try to develop a plan under which, as a matter of principle, the permanent members of the Security Council would be excluded from the U.N. force. Eden, however, had declared that if there was to be such a force Britain would want to be part of it.

Resolution 1000 (ES-1) was adopted by the General Assembly on November 5. The operative part read:

The General Assembly:
1. *Establishes* a United Nations Command for an emergency international Force to secure and supervise the cessation of hostilities in accordance with all the terms of General Assembly Resolution 997 (ES-1) of 2 November 1956;
2. *Appoints,* on an emergency basis, the Chief of Staff of the United Nations Truce Supervision Organization, Major-General E. L. M. Burns, as Chief of the Command;
3. *Authorizes* the Chief of Command immediately to recruit, from the observer corps of the United Nations Truce Supervision Organization, a limited number of officers who shall be nationals of countries other than those having permanent membership in the Security Council, and further authorizes him, in consultation with the Secretary-General, to undertake the recruitment directly, from various Member States other than the permanent members of the Security Council, of the additional number of officers needed.

On November 5–6 Port Said was occupied by the Anglo-French forces following an airborne assault, and the Soviet Union made thinly veiled threats of nuclear retaliation on November 5. The Brit-

---

[92] *H. C. Deb.,* Vol. 558, Col. 1649, November 1, 1956.
[93] Resolution 998 (ES-1), November 4, 1956.

ish and the French had intended to take the whole Canal, but the mounting pressure in the United Nations and the fact that there was almost no support for the intervention foredoomed the operation. Furthermore, economic pressure was increasing and a run on the British pound had developed, with potentially disastrous results unless the United States would come to Britain's aid with a loan. On November 6 Eden agreed to a cease-fire.

The seeds of another dispute were soon to be sown. The Soviet Union had voted for the emergency session of the General Assembly under the Uniting for Peace resolution, but it had abstained on the resolutions establishing the U.N. force. It took the now familiar view that the United Nations Charter gave only the Security Council the power to set up international forces, as provided in Chapter VII of the Charter. At the time of the Suez Crisis the General Assembly, in accordance with its usual habits, did not make explicit which articles of the Charter the creation of the force was based on. It was to be six years more before the crisis over the financing of U.N. peacekeeping operations fully developed.

Once the fighting had come to a halt it was to be only a matter of time before the Anglo-French reversal was complete. On November 7 the General Assembly again called upon the United Kingdom and France to withdraw all their forces from Egyptian territory. France reported a partial withdrawal by November 21, but as late as November 23 there had been no significant withdrawal of British forces. Britain declared that her forces would be withdrawn as soon as the United Nations Emergency Force (UNEF) was in a position to insure that hostilities would not be resumed. The General Assembly called for compliance with its resolutions in the following terms:

The General Assembly;
1. *Notes with regret* that, according to the communications received by the Secretary-General, two-thirds of the French forces remain, all the United Kingdom forces remain . . . and no Israel forces have been withdrawn behind the armistice line although a considerable time has elapsed since the adoption of the relevant General Assembly resolutions;
2. *Reiterates* its call to France, Israel and the United Kingdom of Great Britain and Northern Ireland to comply forthwith with resolutions 997 (ES-1) and 1002 (ES-1) of 2 and 7 November 1956.[94]

[94] Resolution 1120 (XI), November 24, 1956.

The Anglo-French forces could not hold their position indefinitely. As the strength of the United Nations Emergency Force grew it was able to take up positions between the Israeli and Egyptian lines. UNEF assumed control of Port Said on December 22, 1956, and it was only then, nearly two months after the initial intervention, that the British and French finally completed their withdrawal.

Israel's withdrawal took considerably longer. By late January, 1957, Israel still held the Gaza strip and an area along the Gulf of Aqaba, the Sharm-el-Sheikh area. Israel was seeking a guarantee that the Egyptian blockade of the Gulf would not be restored. The Secretary-General reported that the United Nations would not allow a change of status resulting from military action contrary to the Charter.[95] After further calls by the General Assembly for Israel's withdrawal in January and February 1957, Israeli troops finally withdrew at the beginning of March on the assumption that UNEF would prevent any further encroachments into Israeli territory from the Gaza strip and any exercise of belligerent rights in the Gulf of Aqaba.

By the middle of April, the Suez Canal had been cleared, under U.N. auspices, with the participation of Anglo-French salvage vessels. On April 24, the government of Egypt made a formal declaration on the Suez Canal and the arrangements for its operation.[96] It reaffirmed its policy and purpose to respect the terms of the Constantinople Convention of 1888 and to abide by the United Nations Charter. There would continue to be free navigation, and tolls would continue to be levied in accordance with an agreement with the Suez Canal Company of 1936. The Canal would be operated by the Suez Canal Authority established by the nationalization decree of July 26, 1956. Egypt declared its intention to accept the compulsory jurisdiction of the International Court of Justice in disputes over the 1888 Convention, which it did by a unilateral declaration dated July 18, 1957.

By agreements made in 1958 between the United Arab Republic, as successor state to Egypt, and the shareholders of the Suez Canal Company and the Company itself,[97] arrangements were made for compensation of over eight million dollars to be paid over five years. External assets were to be left to the Company. In 1959 the British government agreed to remove restrictions on Egyptian assets within

---

[95] U.N. Doc. A/3512.

[96] Text in Elihu Lauterpacht, *The Suez Canal Settlement — A Selection of Documents* (London: Stevens and Sons, 1960), pp. 35–38.

[97] *Id.* at pp. 3–33.

its territory.[98] The governments of the United Arab Republic and
the United Kingdom agreed to waive all claims arising out of the
damage to, and clearance of, the Canal.[99]

The Suez adventure ended in utter failure for Britain and France. A
series of political misjudgments culminated in an indecisive military
intervention. Largely because they lacked confidence in the United
States as an ally (with some justification), they decided to go it alone;
but not only did they misjudge the American reaction, they also failed
to anticipate that this intervention would produce a rare case of joint
action by the United States and the Soviet Union. The result, inevitably,
was that the military objective failed, and with it the political objectives. At the end of 1956, the Canal was blocked, Eden was a broken
man, and Nasser's prestige, far from being struck a fatal blow, was
higher than it had ever been.

III

The Suez Canal in Retrospect. The Suez crisis demonstrates how
international law may be used in a situation of political conflict, and
what the limitations of its efficacy as a means of controlling the behavior of the participant states are. All the interests at stake at Suez
were deeply affected by the nature of the relationship between the
two superpowers, the United States and the Soviet Union. The con-
vergence of interests of these two powers, rather than the strength of
the international legal order account for the final outcome of the Suez
episode.

The crisis can be divided into two phases: nationalization and intervention.

During the initial nationalization, international law served as a vehicle for maintaining a dialogue of confrontation. It also was used to
buttress the Western contention that Egypt had an international obligation to permit international operation of the Canal. In short, international law in the early phases of the crisis served not as a medium
for the solution of the conflict but as a means to reestablish the Western position.

However modest the role of law in the early phases of the Suez
crisis, it proved even less meaningful as a constraint on state behavior
in the more crucial stage of intervention. If Israel could establish at

---

[98] *Id.* at p. 48.
[99] *Id.* at pp. 58–60.

least a rudimentary legal basis for its invasion of the Sinai peninsula under Article 51 of the U.N. Charter, as it could with more justification in the Arab-Israel war of June, 1967, France and Great Britain could not. The military venture failed for one very simple and overriding reason — it ran athwart the joint position of the United States and the Soviet Union. However much the American and Soviet condemnations of the intervention were framed in terms of the U.N. Charter and general principles of international law, subsequent actions by both powers show that law yields to policy where the two conflict. The acid test of the precedence of international legal norms comes when fundamental interests risk being undermined by adherence to such norms and where a state with the capacity to act otherwise yields to the mandate of those norms. It is sufficient to point to the Hungarian crisis of 1956, the Cuban missile crisis of 1962, the Dominican intervention of 1965, and the current Vietnam hostilities to dispel any notion that either the Soviet or the American response to the Suez intervention represents anything more than the calculation of cost, risk, and interest couched in the language of the law.

It was at the very height of the Suez Canal crisis that the Soviet Union intervened by force in Hungary to suppress and reverse a successful anti-communist revolution. Strong individual national protests, especially by the United States, and various U.N. resolutions condemning this intervention did not prevail against the overwhelming power and assertion of national interest of the Soviet Union in that part of the world.

The legality of the U.S. "quarantine" which led to the interception of Soviet ships carrying missiles and selected army units into Cuban territory has been much debated.[100] Whatever the legal merits of the dispute, President Kennedy made it quite clear that the United States felt compelled to act in accordance with her vital national interest. As Dean Acheson, an advisor to the government, put it in the missile crisis debate, "the survival of states is not a matter of law," although accepted legal principles "influenced the United States in choosing a course of action consistent with ethical restraint." Even though the restrained response of the United States to the Soviet provocation found far more general international support than had the Anglo-French-Israel intervention in the Suez crisis — because the threat to

---

[100] See, among many other discussions, *The Proceedings of the American Society of International Law*, 75th Annual Meeting, Washington, D.C. (April 25–27, 1963), pp. 1–18.

the national security of the United States posed by the Soviet action was far more obvious than that to the national security of Britain, France and Israel posed by the nationalization of the Suez Canal Company — the justification put forward by the United States was clearly at variance with the argument of international law emphasized so strongly by the same country during the Suez Canal crisis.

National interest and considerations of power politics prevailed far more obviously over arguments of international law in the case of the U.S. intervention in the Dominican Republic. The original justification put forward by President Lyndon B. Johnson, Secretary of State Dean Rusk, and other U.S. authorities was like that originally stressed by Britain to justify armed intervention in the Suez Canal: the protection of lives, security, and property of nationals. But this soon gave way to a far more sweeping argument, made particularly in President Johnson's speech of May 2, 1965, to the effect that "the American nations could not and would not tolerate another Communist government in the Western Hemisphere." This could clearly not be reconciled with the unconditional prohibitions of unilateral intervention contained not only in Article 2 (4) and (7) of the U.N. Charter, but also in Articles 15 and 17 of the Charter of the Organization of American States (OAS). Although various attempts were made subsequently to justify the intervention in terms of the OAS Charter, the reason for intervention was clearly political, and international law had to take a back seat. The vindication put forward by the legal advisor of the Department of State, in an address to the American Foreign Law Association of June 9, 1965, was in fact strikingly parallel to the language used by the British Lord Chancellor, Viscount Kilmuir, as quoted in this study,[101] to justify British intervention in the Suez case:

It does not seem to me that law and other human institutions should be treated as abstract imperatives which must be followed for the sake of obeisance to some supernatural power or for the sake of some supposed symmetry that is enjoined upon the human race by external forces. Rather, it seems to me that law and other institutions of society should be seen as deliberate and hopefully rational efforts to order the lives of human communities — from small to great — in such a way as to permit realization by all members of a community of the full range of whatever creative powers they may possess. . . .

. . . We recognized that, regardless of any fundamentalist view of inter-

[101] See text at note 54 *supra*.

national law, the situation then existing required us to take action to remove the threat and at the same time to avoid nuclear war. In the tradition of the common law we did not pursue some particular legal analysis or code, but instead sought a practical and satisfactory solution to a pressing problem.

The massive armed intervention by the United States in the Vietnamese conflict has been justified — by the government and a substantial number of American international lawyers — by invocation of the right of individual and collective self-defense, permitted by Article 51 of the U.N. Charter, in conjunction with certain provisions of the Southeast Asia Treaty (SEATO). Obviously, the United States' intervention — which began almost immediately after the Geneva Accords of 1954, which had divided Vietnam into two separate zones with the object of eventual reunification — had a political objective: the purpose was the erection of an anti-communist bastion through the establishment and support of a separate South Vietnamese state. U.S. action was essentially unilateral; it has never been backed either by a U.N. resolution or by a resolution of the Council of SEATO — two of whose seven members are strongly opposed to the intervention. Legal justification was an afterthought, developed in response to growing criticism.

The lesson to be drawn from a comparison of these events and actions is that international law is, in times of crises, still not the controlling factor in the use of force. Britain, France and Israel behaved in ways very similar to those of the Soviet Union and the United States in situations which closely affected their national interest — the main difference was one not of law but of power. Britain, France and Israel were compelled to withdraw because the United States and the Soviet Union put their weight behind the United Nations, though they were helped by the sentiment of the majority of the smaller nations. But the U.S.S.R. and the United States got away with their unilateral actions because their power could not be effectively challenged — at least not in regions within their immediate spheres of influence: Hungary in the case of the Soviet Union, Cuba and the Dominican Republic in the case of the United States. The most that can be said, in the case of Vietnam, is that the divisions of world opinion, and doubts about the legality of the intervention have imposed some restraint upon the scale of operations.

Such limited restraint also operates in the Middle Eastern crisis of 1967. Here the two superpowers are in sharp conflict but have a common interest in preventing the hostilities from escalating to the point of direct confrontation between the United States and the Soviet Union. Although the United Nations is unable to obtain sufficient agreement for action, either in the Security Council or the General Assembly, the fear of overwhelming condemnation for unequivocal aggression, coupled with the interest of both superpowers in confining the conflict, serves as a limited restraint on the naked use of force by either side. But this is a long way from the regulation or solution of the conflict by U.N. action, or by judicial decisions.

Nearly half a century after the first attempt made to impose the restraints of international law through a permanent organization on the unilateral use of force, it has to be admitted that international law, at least in situations of vital clashes of national interest, is still used essentially as a point of argument. It has been twisted this way or that way to bolster political action, and no state has hitherto found it difficult to contradict its own line of action or reasoning when it believed that national interest required such contradiction. Seen by itself, and in insulation from other international crises of our time, the solution of the Suez Canal crisis would give the illusion that the cause of international law and collective security had triumphed over the unilateral use of force. The history of the subsequent decade makes such a conclusion highly doubtful. The battle for the supremacy of international law over national sovereignty remains to be won.

RICHARD A. FALK

Confrontation Diplomacy: Indonesia's Campaign to Crush Malaysia

I

In a Security Council debate provoked by a Malaysian complaint of Indonesian armed aggression Sudjarwo, the Indonesian representative, made the following comment:

When Indonesia proclaimed its independence from Dutch colonial rule in 1945, asserting its own sovereignty, was not Indonesia — according to that international law — legally tied to the Netherlands as a colony, possessing legal existence only under Dutch sovereignty? What would have happened if we had had to abide by the application of legal arguments under that international law? The Indonesian Revolution would have been strangled and smothered.[1]

This candid repudiation of traditional international law as it related to the Indonesian struggle for independence summarizes Indonesia's attitude toward respect for international law, especially to the extent that such respect might appear to hamper President Sukarno's militant championship of a new political order for Asia. This militancy

I wish to thank Robert Cocks and Nelson Rosenbaum for their valuable research assistance in the preparation of this chapter. It is also my pleasure to thank Priscilla Bryan for typing successive drafts of the manuscript quickly and accurately, subject to a time-pressure not of her making.
[1] United Nations Security Council, Official Records [hereafter cited as SCOR], 1144th Mtg., September 9, 1964, para. 86.

was most dramatically expressed by the adoption of a Crush Malaysia campaign in the period from September, 1963 when the Malaysian Federation came into existence to June, 1966 when the anti-Sukarno turn of Indonesian domestic politics led to an abrupt normalization of relations with Malaysia.

From one important point of view Indonesia's policy of "Confrontation" toward Malaysia was a self-consciously blatant violation of fundamental rules of international law. President Sukarno's avowed objective was "to crush Malaysia" and the means used included military action overtly undertaken against a Member of the United Nations. The Charter of the United Nations in Article 2(4) expresses the basic constraint of international law upon the use of force by one state against another: "All Members shall refrain in their international relations from the threat or use of force against the territorial integrity or political independence of any state. . . ." Article 51 permits limited uses of force for self-defense against an armed attack, but Indonesia never contended that it was acting in self-defense, nor was there any substantial evidence of prior Malaysian aggression against Indonesia.

On the basis of the above situation it hardly seems worthwhile to consider the role of international law in the relations between Indonesia and Malaysia during the period of Confrontation. It hardly seems worthwhile because Indonesia seems clearly guilty of violating international law and Malaysia seems entirely innocent. However, closer scrutiny discloses several reasons for abandoning this first impression. First of all, the basic policies upheld by international law with respect to the use of force can rarely be disposed of merely by considering the relationship between legal rules abstracted from the international environment and challenged national behavior. The legal basis for Indonesia's approach to Confrontation rests upon a certain conception of political equilibrium and regional autonomy in the post-colonial world that has received diverse and quite widespread backing in the period since World War II. It is not necessary to claim that Indonesia's espousal of Confrontation was a consequence of its reinterpretation of international law, but merely that it is possible to make arguments in favor of Indonesia's contentions that conform to certain ideas about the evolving nature of international legal order, ideas that antedate the Charter and that find resonances in the work of an international lawyer as renowned as Emmerich de Vattel and in the practice of a country as strongly opposed to Indonesia's Confrontation as was the

United States.[2] Therefore, my first point is that it may be valuable, precisely because it is not fashionable, to consider the kind of basis that does exist in international law, even as it is most traditionally conceived, for the legally discredited and politically discarded espousal of Confrontation.

Indonesia's claims against Malaysia might also have found expression in an argument for a new international legal order. Sudjarwo in the statement quoted at the outset refrained from doing this, but it could have been done on Indonesia's behalf, and it might be useful to put Indonesia's case in as good a legal posture as possible, if only to disclose the ease with which a plausible legal argument can be developed to defend action that appears to be so clearly a violation of international law.

But more important than restating the legal issues provoked by the Indonesian use of force against Malaysia in terms wider than as a dispute about compliance with Charter rules, the Confrontation gives us an opportunity to examine the ways in which international law forms an integral aspect of the diplomatic process, even when its legal rules of restraint are ignored by one of the parties to a dispute. Indonesia's objections to the formation of Malaysia were expressed in legal terms and Malaysia's response depended heavily on being able to use its strong position in international law to rally political support to offset its military weakness.[3] More and more international lawyers are growing aware that international law may provide the participants to a dispute with an agreed instrument of communication.[4] The role of international law as an integral part of the process of international communication is especially prominent with regard to the formulation of claims and responses and with regard to the expression of third-party and community expectations as to the nature of a reasonable outcome of the dispute.[5] Malaysian Confrontation will illustrate such

[2] Emmerich de Vattel, *The Law of Nations,* esp. Bk. II, Chap. 1 (Fenwick translation of 1758 edition, Carnegie Classics, 1916).

[3] George Modelski reports that as of 1962 Indonesia was spending $1,301,000,-000 on defense whereas Malaysia was spending only $42,000,000 (the Malaysian figure refers only to Malayan expenditures, but these were controlling). Modelski, "Indonesia and Her Neighbors," Policy Memorandum No. 30, Center of International Studies, Princeton University, p. 4, October 29, 1964.

[4] E.g., William Coplin, *The Functions of International Law* (Chicago: Rand McNally, 1966), pp. 168–71.

[5] This approach is exhibited to excellent analytic advantage in Myres S. McDougal and William Burke, *The Public Order of the Oceans* (New Haven: Yale University Press, 1962).

an interaction. Each side invoked legal norms to communicate with its adversary and to mobilize effective political support for its position within international society.

Confrontation also provides an instructive example of the form that an international dispute takes in the contemporary world when the protagonists are both newly independent Asian states, the one adopting an essentially conservative orientation at home and abroad and the other pursuing revisionist policies that seek a partial reconstituting of the international legal order. Malaysia's security, and even her survival appeared to depend upon mobilizing support external to Asia, whereas Indonesia sought to discourage this external support by a combination of ideological, diplomatic, economic, and military means. Neither side was altogether successful, but it is clear that the political variables affecting the course of Confrontation were themselves partly a consequence of the extent to which Indonesia and Malaysia presented their legal cases in convincing terms. We learn from a study of Confrontation, then, something about the styles of communication used by adversaries seeking to legitimate their respective claims and implementing acts in various international arenas. These arenas include not only those traditional for diplomacy, but the newer regional and global ones, including the *ad hoc* arenas constituted by periodic meetings of the non-aligned states of Asia and Africa. One of the interesting facets of the Indonesian campaign for external support was its effort, partly successful, to isolate Malaysia in the Third World, even to the extent of seeking its formal exclusion from the meetings of Afro-Asian states.[6]

International law in the wider sense also provided the protagonists and third-party mediators with various alternatives to Confrontation as a basis for revising the relations between Malaysia and Indonesia. Hovering ambiguously in the background throughout the dispute was an aspiration to attain subregional and ethnic harmony by implementing the loosely formulated idea of a confederation, called Maphilindo — to join together in friendship and cooperation the national destinies of Malaysia, Indonesia, and the Philippines.[7] This contra-

[6] Indonesia was successful in excluding Malaysia from formal participation in the 1964 Meeting of the Heads of State of Non-Aligned Countries that took place in Cairo. Compare the parallel efforts of the Arab nations to exclude Israel. The United States has sought successfully, in similar vein, to exclude Castro's Cuba from participation in the inter-American system.

[7] These subregional movements preceded and followed upon the Malaysian Confrontation, taking the form of proposals for an Association of South

puntal diplomatic melody was given credible expression by recourse to legal conceptions and procedures that might resolve the underlying political conflicts provoked by Indonesia's reaction to the formation of Malaysia on a basis that would not make it appear that either side was acquiescing in the demands of the other or backing down. The forms and procedures of international law provided thus a way to transform the antagonisms of Confrontation into the harmonies of Maphilindo. And in fact the end of Confrontation, which principally resulted from the drastic reorientation of Indonesian foreign policy after the bloody counter-coup of 1965–66, was signaled and symbolized by the formalities associated with the reestablishment of diplomatic relations between the two countries, and by the Indonesian resumption of active membership in the United Nations.

In sum, then, a legal study of the Confrontation staged by Indonesia against Malaysia offers insight into the use of international law to communicate diplomatic positions and to mobilize or undermine support for these positions in various international arenas. We do not learn much about the static dimensions of international law that are constituted by a framework of rules and a set procedure for their impartial interpretation and application. Such rules and procedures were *invoked* against Indonesia, but to no significant effect, except perhaps to induce its withdrawal from the United Nations in January of 1965. One point is obviously that Confrontation was a conscious and unambiguous repudiation of the restraints of international law, but a deeper point, one that has eluded students and critics of the subject for centuries, is that the failure of international law as a restraint system is not equivalent to the failure of international law. The dynamics of Confrontation are so suggestive for the international lawyer precisely because the relevance of international law is so clear, despite the refusal of Indonesia to be restrained by its rules.

II

This relevance of international law to Confrontation becomes clearer by a selective narration of the main phases of the dispute between Indonesia and Malaysia. We must begin, first, with a consideration of the decision to create a single sovereign state out of the separate political entities of Malaya, Singapore, Sarawak, and Sabah. Indo-

---

East Asia (ASA), a loose confederation working together on common problems, especially in the area of security.

nesia's reponse to the creation of Malaysia in 1963 was to initiate the policy of Confrontation. The second phase, then, of the narrative is to describe the acts and events that together constitute the Confrontation. Third, and briefly, a description of the termination of Confrontation in 1966 as a result of the shift of the domestic balance of power in Indonesia to the army.

The Malaysian Federation. Malaya became independent of British colonial rule in 1957.[8] It appears that Britain did not contemplate the inclusion of its Borneo territories of Sabah and Sarawak in a single sovereign state until 1961, partly because these territories were very backward compared to Malaya and Singapore. The first public statement proposing Malaysia was made on May 27, 1961 by the Prime Minister of Malaya, Tengku Abdul Rahman, in a speech made in Singapore to the Foreign Correspondents Association: "Malaya today as a nation realizes that she cannot stand alone and in isolation. Sooner or later she should have an understanding with Britain and the people of the territories of Singapore, North Borneo, Brunei and Sarawak."[9] Underlying this impulse toward federation were two sets of factors, one ethnic and the other geopolitical. The large Chinese populations in these political units would almost certainly come to dominate their political destinies unless kept in a subordinate position by means of some artificial scheme designed to assure Malay domination disproportionate to numbers, talents, or resources. Malay racism, then, gave some of the impetus to the idea of creating Malaysia under the banner of Malay nationalism, quite a deception if one recognizes that there are more Chinese than Malays in Malaysia.[10] There were also geopolitical factors present. The acquisition of Chinese political control in Singapore and the Borneo territories would also lead, it was thought, to an eventual allegiance to the policies of

[8] For the Malayan background of Malaysia, see R. S. Milne, *Government and Politics in Malaysia* (Boston: Houghton Mifflin, 1967), pp. 1–48.

[9] Quoted in "Malaysia – in Brief" (Department of Information Malaysia, 1963), at p. 120; this pamphlet contains the official Malaysian perspectives on development up through the creation of Malaysia.

[10] "On Malaysia Day, the Malays totalled 40 percent of the Malaysia population, the Chinese 43 percent, Indians and Pakistanis 9 percent, and the indigenous tribes of Borneo and other races 8 percent." Harry Miller, *A Short History of Malaysia* (New York: Praeger, 1966), p. 15; the Malays became the dominant group after the withdrawal of Singapore from the Federation in August, 1965. According to the 1961 census the total population of Malaysia (excluding Singapore) is about 8.3 million; of the 1.7 million living in Singapore, 1.3 are ethnic Chinese.

mainland China. Therefore, the creation of Malaysia was designed, at once, to thwart the extension of Chinese Communist influence in Asia by means of internal takeovers and to provide a viable political unit of anti-Communist commitment to thwart the expansionist policies of China and Indonesia, Peking's then friend and ally.[11]

There are indications that as of 1961 the politically sensitive leadership of the Borneo territories would have preferred either to remain somewhat longer under British rule or to achieve independence as a Borneo federation rather than being absorbed as a subordinate unit of Malaysia.[12] In 1962 a conservative bi-national commission (Malaya and Britain) headed by Lord Cobbold concluded that the populations of the Borneo territories desired to join Malaysia provided certain safeguards were granted their particular interests and some federal monies were diverted to hasten their economic development.[13] There was a disagreement among the members of the Commission about when Malaysia should be established. The two British members favored a transition period of three to seven years before merger, but the two Malayan members of the Commission argued that Malaysia should be brought into being within twelve months; to delay longer would lead to racial conflict and "expose these territories and their peoples to dangerously disruptive influences both internally and from the outside."[14] The British government was persuaded to accept the Malayan view on timing, and it was announced that Malaysia would come into being as of August 31, 1963.

George Kahin speculates that it was the urgency of proceeding with the merger of Malaya and Singapore that accounted for the British willingness to encourage the merger of the Borneo territories before they could be prepared for a greater measure of self-government.[15] Until the middle of 1961, Tengku Abdul Rahman opposed the merger of Malaya and Singapore, evidently fearing that adding Chi-

---

[11] For a perceptive account of the motivation to establish the Malaysian Federation, especially on the part of the British, see George Modelski, "Indonesia and the Malaysia Issue," *The Year Book of World Affairs 1964* (London: Stevens and Sons), pp. 128–49.

[12] For an analysis along these lines see George McT. Kahin, "Malaysia and Indonesia," *Pacific Affairs*, XXXVII (1964), 254–56.

[13] An account of the operation of the Cobbold Commission is contained in Milne, *op. cit.*, pp. 64–68; for a view critical of the Cobbold Commission see Kahin, *op. cit.*, p. 256.

[14] Kahin, *op. cit.*, p. 256.

[15] *Id.* at pp. 256–57.

nese-dominated Singapore to Malaya would upset the ethnic balance sufficiently (44 percent Chinese, 42 percent Malay) to vest political control in the Chinese. As well, the Tengku's political power depended on support it received from conservative Chinese groups in Malaya; this support might be withdrawn once the more radical socialist Chinese leaders of Singapore's political life were allowed to compete for power in a merged political unit. Singapore was run by the socialist Lee Kuan Kew, an advocate of union with Malaya to achieve economic advantages, whose leadership seemed endangered by the rise of a pro-Communist opposition. The negotiation of merger was a delicate matter, as it depended on a trade-off of political influence for economic gain, a trade-off that later led to racial strife and secession in 1965.[16] The 1963 formula gave Singapore considerable local control over education and labor affairs, but involved underrepresentation in Malaysian political affairs as measured on a per capita basis and as compared to the other sub-parts of Malaysia.[17]

The Indonesian response to projected Federation is difficult to reconstruct and appears to reflect the interplay of a series of domestic and foreign considerations. The first major public Indonesian reaction was a friendly one by Subandrio, then Foreign Minister, in the General Assembly of the United Nations, in November, 1961:

We [the Republic of Indonesia] are not only disclaiming the territories outside the former Netherlands East Indies, though they are of the same islands, but — more than that — when Malaya told us of her intentions to merge with the three British Crown Colonies of Sarawak, Brunei and British North Borneo as one Federation, we told them that we have no objections and that we wish them success with this merger so that everyone may live in peace and freedom. For the sake of clarification, I may tell this Assembly that three quarters of the island of Borneo (Kalimantan) is Indonesian territory, while the remainder constitutes the three aforementioned British Crown Colonies.

Naturally, ethnologically and geographically speaking, this British part is closer to Indonesia than, let us say, to Malaya. But we still told Malaya

[16] There is a useful description in Milne, *op. cit.*, pp. 49–73 (see pp. 73–74 for further sources).

[17] For a positive assessment of the operation of Malaysia as a multi-racial community see George Modelski, "Indonesia and Her Neighbors," Policy Memorandum No. 30, Center of International Studies, Princeton University, October 29, 1964, pp. 14–15.

that we have no objections to such a merger based upon the will for freedom of the peoples concerned.[18]

Indonesia was at the time preoccupied with securing a successful termination of its long campaign to acquire control over West Irian and quite evidently did not want to jeopardize its imminent victory by fostering the impression that West Irian was merely the first of a series of demands in Southeast Asia.[19] Therefore, Subandrio's reassurance vis-à-vis Malaysia must be understood in terms of the earlier instance of Confrontation — West Irian. West Irian, however, was safely in Indonesian hands by January 1, 1963 (or more than nine months before Malaysia came into being), and the basic settlement favorable to Indonesia had been reached several months earlier. Therefore, from August, 1962 on, Indonesian statesmen were free to respond to the prospect of Malaysia without impairing their efforts to obtain West Irian.[20]

Several factors seem to have inclined Indonesia toward Confrontation. First of all, there was the recollection of the role played by Malaya in promoting the 1958–60 uprisings against Sukarno. These uprisings were centered on the ethnically Malay island of Sumatra and were partly financed and guided by the United Kingdom and the United States.[21] It is hardly reasonable to suppose that the prospect of a strong Malaysia with a permanent British military presence in Southeast Asia was welcome news in Djakarta, especially given the mandate to use British military power based in Malay for purposes wider than Malaysian security. For instance, Article VI of the 1963 Defense Agreement between Malaysia and the United Kingdom af-

[18] Quoted in "A Survey on the Controversial Problem of the Establishment of the Federation of Malaysia," Information Division, Embassy of Indonesia, Washington, D.C., p. 2 (no date given).

[19] The United Nations was expected to administer West Irian for a transitional period from October, 1962 to January, 1963 when Indonesian Administration began four months ahead of schedule. For a critical view of Indonesia's campaign to obtain control over West Irian see Modelski, *op. cit.*, note 17, at pp. 6–12.

[20] The negotiations between Indonesia and Malaysia led to a settlement of the West Irian Question as of August 15, 1962. Ellsworth Bunker, acting as private citizen and representative of U.N. Secretary-General U Thant, tended his good offices to the parties and his presence seems to have helped produce an agreement.

[21] For a popular, yet impressive, account of foreign participation (including the U.S. Central Intelligence Agency) in these Indonesian uprisings, see William Stevenson, *Birds' Nests in Their Beards* (Boston: Houghton Mifflin, 1964).

firms the British right to maintain its base facilities in Singapore and use them "as that Government may consider necessary for the purpose of assisting in the defense of Malaysia and for Commonwealth defense and for the preservation of peace in South-East Asia."[22] So the creation of Malaysia maintained in existence a situation in which Western powers hostile to the Sukarno leadership in Indonesia could continue to threaten, if not actively engage in, covert military activity, a threat that had already been carried out during the 1958–60 period at great cost to Indonesia.[23] The Indonesian reaction to this kind of Western presence must be compared with the reaction of the United States to the establishment of a Soviet military presence in Cuba after Castro's accession to power in 1960, a comparison not lost to Indonesian leaders.

A second important factor was the revolt in the Sultanate of Brunei in December, 1962. Brunei was the one territory in North Borneo that refused to join Malaysia, partly because it was rich due to oil resources and partly because its Sultan would not accept a protocol position inferior to the Tengku of Malaya. At the time of the revolt Brunei was a British Crown Colony that was operated on a semi-feudalistic basis. The revolt was evidently led by A. H. Azahari, then in exile in the Philippines. The objective of the revolt was to promote the cause of the Borneo Federation as an independent sovereign state. British and Gurkha troops and Malayan police sent from Singapore were used to crush the revolt, and the Malayan government accused Indonesia of playing a leading role in instigating its outbreak.[24] The Indonesian government denied any role in the Brunei uprising, although it praised its anti-colonial character and called upon Malaya to cease its unfriendly attitude toward Indonesia. The Brunei uprising, however, resulted in raising the issue of self-determination for the Borneo territories. This issue led to ever more clearcut opposition by Indonesia to the proposed Malaysian Federation. This opposition was partially seconded by the Philippines through the revival of a historic claim to the ownership of the Borneo territory of Sabah.[25]

[22] For other relevant provisions in defense agreements affecting Malaysia, see A. G. Mezerik, ed., "Malaysia-Indonesia Conflict," International Review Service (1965), Appendix H, pp. 109–10.

[23] This fact was much stressed in the Indonesian official presentations of their reasons for opposing Malaysia as it was constituted — e.g., Sudjarwo's presentation in the Security Council of Indonesia's argument in response to a Malaysian complaint about aggression in September, 1964, esp. SCOR, 1149th Mtg., September 14, 1964, para. 12–30.

[24] Cf. Milne, op. cit., pp. 185–87.

[25] Ibid., pp. 187–88; cf. articles by Lorenzo Sumulong, Jovito R. Salonga,

On January 20, 1963 Subandrio made an official declaration: "We cannot but adopt a policy of confrontation toward Malaya because at present they represent themselves as accomplices of neo-colonialist and neo-imperialist forces pursuing a policy hostile toward Indonesia." Throughout early 1963 hostile incidents occurred with increasing frequency, and accusations were made that Indonesia was aiding dissident groups in the Borneo territories to fight against federation with Malaya. Domestic influences in Indonesia intensified Confrontation. The Communist party was quick to grasp the Malaysian project as a popular anti-colonialist issue and was responsible for the earliest Indonesian opposition to the federation. The Indonesian army was eager to appear as nationalistic as the Communists on Malaysia and was sensitive to the security hazards that would be created by the long common, porous "jungle-infested" border between Malaysia and Indonesia in Borneo. The West Irian campaign was a vivid model of a successful use of confrontation diplomacy that combined ideological truculence with military intimidation to achieve an expansionist goal of foreign policy and, at the same time, develop the image of an Indonesia on the move as a leading member of the Afro-Asian world.[26]

These, then, were the elements of the international dispute that developed between Indonesia and Malaya about the proposed federation of Malaysia. This dispute can be expressed as a series of legal issues:

1. The applicability of the principle of self-determination to the Borneo territories;
2. The incompatibility of a colonial military presence in Malaysia with regional security and with regional autonomy;
3. The danger to Indonesian security arising from a permanent Western extra-regional military presence in contiguous territory.

Such legal issues are not conventional ones in international law. But the relevance of regional consensus to the competing rights and duties of states has been an evolving theme of the efforts to secure order

---

Arturo A. Alafraz, and Juan M. Arreglado in *Philippine International Law Journal*, II (January–June 1963), 6–28, 78–104. (There is also a useful documentary supplement on pp. 216–339.)

[26] Cf. Modelski, *op. cit.*, note 17, pp. 6–12; also Arnold Brackman, *Southeast Asia's Second Front – The Power Struggle in the Malay Archipelago* (New York: Praeger, 1966), pp. 91–114.

in both Latin America and Africa, and it is the status of such a regional consensus that underlies Indonesian claims if these claims are considered in a legal setting.[27] In the formulation of its claims to oppose the creation of Malaysia, Indonesia relied upon arguments that tended to discredit the legitimacy of Malaya's position. First, Indonesia tried to create the impression that Malaya was a tool of British influence and therefore lacking real national independence. Such an argument amounted to both questioning Malaya's sovereign status and contending that the United Kingdom was exercising covert colonial rulership. In addition, Indonesia argued that there had been no fair test made of the will of the populations in the Borneo territories, and that federation was in violation of the principle of self-determination.

Throughout the dispute the dominant theme of conflict was set off against a subordinate theme of cooperation based upon joint action. In the background of Indonesian diplomacy was a vague project to sponsor a loose confederation of Malaya, Indonesia, and the Philippines — an objective basis for which was the common interest in controlling the influence of the Chinese overseas populations in these countries and the creation of a security bulwark against expansion by China. The disposition toward cooperation culminated in the Manila Conference held in August, 1963 that included a Maphilindo proposal, an aspect of which was a procedure for settling the dispute over the imminent creation of Malaysia.

The framework for a peaceful resolution of the dispute was set forth in the Manila Accord of 31 July 1963, the outcome of a meeting among the Foreign Ministers of the three countries. Paragraphs 10 and 11 of the Manila Accord outline the basic approach:

10. The Ministers reaffirmed their countries' adherence to the principle of self-determination, for the peoples of non-self-governing territories. In this context, Indonesia and the Philippines stated they would welcome the formation of Malaysia provided the support of the people of the Borneo territories is ascertained by an independent and impartial authority, the Secretary-General of the United Nations or his representative.

11. The Federation of Malaya expressed appreciation for this attitude

[27] Comparable assertions of a regional consensus have been relied upon in other parts of the world as a legitimizing influence and as a basis for objection to extra-regional intervention in regional affairs. This kind of objection underlay the African reaction to Operation Stanleyville in December, 1964. For an account see Richard A. Falk, *Legal Order in a Violent World* (Princeton: Princeton University Press, 1968).

of Indonesia and the Philippines and undertook to consult the British Government and the Governments of the Borneo territories with a view to inviting the Secretary-General of the United Nations or his representative to take the necessary steps in order to ascertain the wishes of the people of those territories.[28]

In paragraph 12 of the Manila Accord, the Philippines reserved the right to pursue its territorial claims against North Borneo "in accordance with international law and the principle of the pacific settlement of disputes" and enumerated "negotiation, conciliation, arbitration, or judicial settlement as well as other peaceful means of the parties' own approach" as suitable, and proposed settlement "in conformity with the Charter of the United Nations and the Bandung Declaration."[29] The Manila Accord thus embodies an approach to the settlement of an international dispute dangerous to international peace that relies upon a series of universally accepted postulates of international law:

1. The suitability of the principle of self-determination to resolve a dispute about the federation of internationally distinct political units;

2. Recourse to the machinery of the United Nations to obtain an authoritative decision as to whether the principle of self-determination had been truly implemented;

3. Recourse to traditional methods of peaceful settlement to resolve a territorial dispute.

In effect, the Malaysian question had been narrowed by the Manila Accord to challenging the authoritativeness of the prior efforts, principally by the Cobbald Commission, to apply the principle of self-determination to the Borneo territories.[30] The Philippine claim to Sabah was dealt with by an agreement to find some peaceful means to obtain an impartial judgment as to its merits, but without any specification of time or form that this judgment should take.

---

[28] For the full text, see Mezerik, *op. cit.*, Appendix E, pp. 100–102.

[29] *Ibid.*

[30] In Paragraph 11 of the Joint Statement at Manila the three parties agreed to resolve the problem of the post-colonial military presence of the colonial power in the following vague, but apparently conciliatory, fashion: "The three Heads of Government further agreed that foreign bases — temporary in nature — should not be allowed to be used directly or indirectly to subvert the national independence of any of the three countries. In accordance with the principle enunciated in the Bandung Declaration, the three countries will abstain from the use of arrangements of collective defence to serve the particular interests of any of the big powers." Mezerik, *op. cit.*, p. 104.

At a meeting of the three Heads of Government held immediately thereafter, the Accords approved by the Foreign Ministers were endorsed in the Manila Summit Statement and Declaration of August 3, 1963. The main operative section of the Manila Statement called for "a fresh approach" to the dispute over the establishment of Malaysia. The fresh approach consisted of an elaboration of paragraphs 10 and 11 of the Manila Accord by adding a reference to the specification of self-determination "within the context of General Assembly Resolution 1541 (XV), Principle IX." The Secretary-General of the United Nations was advised to examine the basis for the creation of Malaysia by "taking into consideration":

(I) The recent election in Sabah (North Borneo) and Sarawak but nevertheless further examining, verifying and satisfying himself as to whether
    (a) Malaysia was a major issue, if not the main issue;
    (b) Electoral registers were properly compiled;
    (c) Elections were free and there was no coercion; and
    (d) Votes were properly polled and properly counted; and

(II) The wishes of those who, being qualified to vote, would have exercised their right of self-determination in the recent elections had it not been for their detention for political activities, imprisonment for political offense or absence from Sabah (North Borneo) or Sarawak.[31]

In addition, in paragraph 7 of the Statement the three governments stated that they "deem it desirable to send observers to witness the carrying out of the task to be undertaken by the working teams," presumably constituted by the representatives of the Secretary-General. In formal terms this mode of approach appeared to involve an optional recourse of global institutions to resolve an intra-regional dispute in terms of an agreed frame of reference. As such, it illustrates a new kind of settlement procedure in which a multi-national confer-

---

[31] The text of Principle IX of General Assembly Resolution 1541 (XV) is as follows:

PRINCIPLE IX

Integration should have come about in the following circumstances:

a) The integrating territory should have attained an advanced stage of self-government with free political institutions, so that its peoples would have the capacity to make a responsible choice through informed and democratic processes;

b) The integration should be the result of the freely expressed wishes of the territory's peoples acting with full knowledge of the change in their status, their wishes having been expressed through informed and democratic processes, impartially conducted and based on universal adult suffrage. The United Nations could, when it deems it necessary, supervise these processes.

ence selects the chief executive of the United Nations to provide an authoritative determination of facts to resolve an international dispute.[32]

However, the Manila Statement and its accompanying Declaration also indicate some commitment to the underlying principles of regional autonomy and the importance of eliminating colonial powers from the life of Asian states. In Paragraph 9 it was affirmed "that initial steps should be taken toward the establishment of Maphilindo by holding frequent and regular consultations at all levels to be known as Mushawarah Maphilindo"; furthermore "it is agreed that each country shall set up a national secretariat for Maphilindo affairs and as a first step the respective national secretariats will consult together with a view to coordinating and cooperating with each other in the study on the setting up of the necessary machinery for Maphilindo." But more directly in Paragraph 10 "The three Heads of Government emphasized that the responsibility for the preservation of the national independence of the three countries and of the peace and security in their region lies primarily in the hands of the governments and peoples concerned, and that the three governments undertake to have close consultations [Mushawarah] among themselves on these matters." And, finally, in Paragraph 11 the leaders of the three countries "agreed that foreign bases — temporary in nature — should not be allowed to be used directly or indirectly to subvert the national independence of any of the three countries. In accordance with the principle enunciated in the Bandung Declaration the three countries will abstain from the use of arrangements of collective defense to serve the particular interests of any of the big powers." The language of the Declaration is permeated by "the spirit of Afro-Asian solidarity forged in the Bandung Conference of 1955."[33] Such a regionalization of the political affairs of these countries goes a long way toward eliminating any reasonable basis for regarding Malaysia as a neo-colonialist project. One may question whether Prime Minister Rahman of Malaysia subscribed with any sincerity to such a radical Afro-Asian stance; it would not appear compatible with the basic orientation adopted by his country in making its gradual and conciliatory transition from colonial to independent status, without any basic alteration

---

[32] The obvious analogue is the role played by the Pope in the late medieval period in Western international relations.

[33] Mezerik, *op. cit.*, p. 104.

of socio-economic structure and without any repudiation of the British role in Malayan affairs. With regard to President Sukarno one may doubt whether he desired to settle so amicably an external dispute that was useful to deflect Communist opposition at home and to glorify his Afro-Asian leadership abroad; one may wonder whether Sukarno was willing to cast aside so graciously the mantle of West Irian in a historical period that he was fond of calling "the era of Confrontation."[34] Despite these questions, the Manila framework taken on its own terms appears to be a viable compromise that takes account of the basic interests of each of the participating states. As such, it illustrates the flexible use of the concepts and forms of international law to clarify an agreed framework of an ensuing peaceful settlement.[35]

The events subsequent to the Manila meeting are complex and their interpretation difficult. U Thant promptly accepted the request contained in the Manila Statement and appointed a nine-member U.N. mission to ascertain whether the peoples of Sabah and Sarawak sought federation. The mission was scheduled to arrive in the Borneo area on August 16, 1963 and complete its work in about four weeks. In the period after Manila, guerrilla activities were reported in the Borneo territories, there were clashes between guerrilla troops and Gurkha army units under British command, and there were fairly reliable contentions made that the guerrilla operations were based in and guided by Indonesia. Anti-Malaysia demonstrations greeted the U.N. mission on its arrival in Sarawak and a vigorous dispute arose as to the size and nature of the observer teams from both the Philippines and Indonesia.[36] Sukarno repeated on a nationwide radio broadcast as late as August 28 that "We will bow our heads [and] obey" if the mission found that the peoples of Borneo wanted to join Malaysia.

Malaya's announcement on August 29 that Malaysia would be formed on September 16, 1963 was a decisive occurrence.[37] Such an

---

[34] Compare President Sukarno's speech, "One cannot escape history," delivered at the closing ceremonies of the Manila Conference and reprinted in George Modelski, ed., *The New Emerging Forces — Documents on the Ideology of Indonesian Foreign Policy*, Documents and Data Paper No. 2, Institute of Advanced Studies, Australian National University (1963), pp. 77–80.

[35] Compare the assessment of George Kahin who accompanied Sukarno to and from the Manila Conference and was in close contact with the Indonesian Delegation at this time. Kahin, *op. cit.*, p. 269, esp. footnote 18.

[36] For an anti-Indonesian interpretation of these events see Brackman, *op. cit.*, supra note 26, pp. 193–97.

[37] See the official Indonesian account of the extent to which the Manila Settlement was undermined by Malaya's announcement, in "A Survey on the Contro-

announcement, coming while the U.N. mission was engaged in its work, seemed to take for granted an outcome favorable to Malaya and, thereby to presuppose the outcome of the issue left open by the Manila compromise. Indonesia immediately sent a protest calling the announcement "a reckless and premature decision" that is "a unilateral act contravening the letter and spirit of the Manila Summit agreements."[38] The Tengku's statement can only be regarded as a betrayal of the Manila approach to the creation of Malaysia and can only have been expected to lead Indonesia to revive its Confrontation diplomacy.[39] It is indeed strange that the timing of Malaysia's creation had not been taken up at Manila, as the original plan called for a date of August 31, obviously too soon for the United Nations to carry out its mission with any care. In his "Final Conclusions" U Thant stated that Malaya's announcement "led to misunderstanding, confusion, and even resentment among other parties to the Manila Agreement."[40] And in the Aide-Memoire attached by the official observers of the Philippines to the U.N. Malaysia mission was a stronger condemnation: "The announcement made while the survey was going on that Malaysia would be launched on September 16, 1963, had the effect of rendering the mission of the United Nations Malaysia Team virtually meaningless."[41] At face value, the Manila solution was tantamount to an acquiescence by both Indonesia and the Philippines in the inclusion of the Borneo territories in the projected union of Malaysia. For instance, George Kahin, who attended the conference at Manila and had known the Indonesian leaders since 1948, has written that "both leaders [Sukarno and Macapagal] expected the U.N. to find in favor

---

versial Problem of the Establishment of the Federation of Malaysia," Information Division, Embassy of Indonesia, Washington, D.C., p. 4 (no date given). The description of these events concludes as follows: "Thus the confidence of Indonesia and Philippines in the honesty and loyalty of Malaya as a party to the Manila agreement has been greatly damaged. Whoever might have provoked Malaya into such disloyal behaviour, the fact remains that the Philippines and Indonesia face the bitter and bare reality of an undermining of the Manila Agreement."

[38] Mezerik, *op. cit.*, p. 76.

[39] Compare the statement of the Deputy Prime Minister of Malaysia, Tun Abdul Razak, made on January 13, 1964 to discover Malaysia's view of these controversial events. Text in *ibid.*, p. 112.

[40] United Nations Malaysia Mission Report (Kuala Lumpur: reproduced by the Department of Information, Malaysia, 1963), p. ii.

[41] Text of the Aide-Memoire is reprinted in "A Survey," *supra* note 37, pp. 14–15; the quoted statement is contained in numbered paragraph 17 on p. 15.

of Malaysia — and had privately so advised U Thant."[42] Recourse to the Secretary-General was evidently devised to save face for all concerned.

The Secretary-General's Report issued on September 14, 1963 came as an anticlimax. It did, in fact, confirm the expectation that the great majority of the inhabitants of Sabah and Sarawak favored joining Malaysia. The Aide-Memoire of the Philippine observers criticized the mission for its failure to carry out its mandate from the Manila conference. In a rather persuasive analysis, the Philippine observers complain that the U.N. mission, although fair and impartial to the extent of its inquiry, did not have the time or manpower available to truly apply the intentions at Manila to use "a fresh approach" by way of Principle IX of the annex to G.A. Resolution 1541 (XV).[43] The comparable Aide-Memoire of the Indonesian observers was more extreme in its condemnation of the findings of the U.N. report, arguing that it provided no basis for concluding that merger of the Borneo territories with Malaysia was an application of the principle of self-determination.

One wonders why U Thant did not impose terms on the carrying out of the mission so that it would be less vulnerable to persuasive criticism, especially insisting that no plans for the creation of Malaysia be created until the report had been made public and that the U.N. team be allowed the time and resources to investigate the situation in sufficient depth to attach confidence to its results. Perhaps the three states asked only that the United Nations ratify a political solution reached at Manila, instead of the states making an independent assessment. But given the inflamed background, the continuation of Indonesia-supported rebel activities in the Borneo territories, and the precarious basis of Singapore's relation to Malaysia, it was unwise not to safeguard the authoritativeness of the U.N. role to a far greater extent. As it was, the United Nations carried out its role in such an unconvincing fashion that there was created a plausible, if not fully persuasive, basis for Indonesia's later hostility and temporary withdrawal from that organization.

Malaysia came into being on schedule on September 16, 1963. Both Indonesia and the Philippines withheld diplomatic recognition from the new entity, and Indonesia went further by breaking diplomatic

[42] Kahin, op. cit., p. 269.
[43] Compare Aide-Memoire from the Observers of the Philippines to the U.N. Malaysia Mission in Sarawak and Sabah, reprinted in "A Survey," supra note 37, pp. 14–16.

relations with Kuala Lumpur and by staging mass demonstrations outside the British and Malayan Embassies in Djakarta. Further incidents took place in Indonesia, especially directed against Britain's role in promoting and securing Malaysia, to signify the intensification of Confrontation to heights well above those attained during the months preceding Manila. On September 18 the British Embassy in Djakarta was burned by an angry mob, eliciting a protest from the United States and a mildly conciliatory statement of explanation from Indonesia. But the line was drawn, and within a few days Indonesia ended all trade relations with Malaysia, thereby eliminating the extensive trade with Singapore upon which Indonesia depended heavily for foreign exchange.

The months that followed September, 1963 witnessed a continuation of the Confrontation with the Western powers indicating their support of Malaysia's independence and integrity. This support was symbolized by collective security gestures by the United Kingdom, Australia, and New Zealand and by the U.S. move of sending part of the Seventh Fleet into the Indian Ocean. The United States refused to continue economic aid to Indonesia in reaction to the stepped-up military dimension of Confrontation, mainly taking the form of guerrilla operations and terrorist raids across the Borneo frontiers. The Soviet Union and China endorsed Confrontation and the Soviet Union agreed to meet Indonesia's needs for military equipment.

In December, 1963 the Maphilindo theme, somewhat surprisingly, suddenly recurs amid the cacophonies of Confrontation. President Diosdado Macapagal of the Philippines proposed another tripartite meeting to overcome the Malaysian problem and Sukarno actually proposed that a second survey be conducted by the United Nations, provided it include interviewing imprisoned leaders as a basis for Indonesian acceptance of Malaysia.[44] In effect, the architects of the Manila compromise appeared prepared to try the same formula for resolution and scheduled a bilateral meeting in Manila from January 7 to 11. Despite all the relevant events since June, 1963, Presidents Sukarno and Macapagal declared themselves "loyal adherents to the Manila Agreements" and affirmed that their just concluded talks "were held in the spirit of Mushawarah as the fundamental method of Maphilindo."[45] Their Joint Statement went so far as to say that "the two Presidents considered it essential to strengthen Maphilindo as a living

[44] Cf. Chronology of Dispute in Mezerik, *op. cit.*, p. 79.
[45] For full text of Joint Statement see *ibid.*, pp. 110–12.

reality, in the firm belief that within its framework constructive and equitable solutions could be found for many of the serious problems of the region, including those arising from the formation of the 'Federation of Malaysia,' the promotion of regional security, and the development of regional economic cooperation." Calling for a return "to the spirit and principles of the Manila Agreements" the Joint Statement said that the two Presidents "cherish the hope that a tripartite Mushawarah could be convened to resolve existing differences among the three signatories." Sukarno in Paragraph 5 of the Joint Statement explains "the Indonesia policy of confrontation" as follows:

It is not a policy of aggression, much less of territorial expansion. Its main purpose is to oppose neocolonialist policy of an outside power which, by distorting the procedures laid down in the Manila Agreements for the ascertainment of the wishes of the peoples concerned regarding the establishment of "Malaysia," is bent on wrecking Maphilindo. This divide and rule policy, backed by predominant military force, can only be checked by a firm defensive policy of confrontation, lest the national independence and security of the countries of this region succumb to foreign domination.[46]

Sukarno's statement emphasizes the anti-British character of Confrontation, but the return to regional harmony appears to be conditioned on the unrelated validation of the popular will in Borneo with regard to joining Malaysia and, somewhat, on Malaysia's willingness to identify openly with Maphilindo as a central aspect for its future security. Throughout the period of Confrontation it is difficult to assess the extent to which Sukarno was seeking to eliminate the British colonial presence from Southeast Asia. It is also plausible to contend that Sukarno was merely using this British presence as a convenient pretext on which to build moral validity for a neo-colonialist policy of Indonesian expansionism being pursued at Malaysia's expense.[47]

Deputy Prime Minister of Malaysia Razak denied the implication of the Joint Statement that Malaysia had failed to live up to the Manila Agreements.[48] As to the Second Tripartite Summit proposed in

[46] *Ibid.*, p. 111.

[47] For a detailed interpretation along these lines see Brackman, *op. cit., supra,* note 26, pp. 242–43; Kahin's interpretation is much more sympathetic with Indonesia's contentions.

[48] Razak's Statement is reprinted in Mezerik, *op. cit.*, pp. 112–13; his reply is to three charges contained in the Joint Statement issued by Indonesia and the Philippines:

1. Premature announcement of the date of Federation;
2. Refusal by Malaysia to deal with the Philippine claim to Sabah in the manner established by the Manila Agreements;

the Joint Statement, he asked a series of rhetorical questions that amounted to preconditions:

1. Does this meeting mean that the two countries recognize Malaysia as an Independent Sovereign State?
2. Does it mean that Indonesia agrees to withdraw her policy of confrontation so that the meeting could be held in an atmosphere of peace and good will?
3. Does it mean that Indonesia is prepared to withdraw her troops massed along the borders of Sarawak and Sabah?
4. Does it mean that Indonesia agrees to withdraw her troops now engaged in operations deep in Malaysian territory of Sabah and Sarawak?
5. If so, would Indonesia agree to accept a neutral nation acceptable to Malaysia and Indonesia to act as a referee to ensure that all the terms of the truce are strictly and scrupulously carried out?

Mr. Razak concludes the statement of reply by saying that "If we could be assured of all those points nothing would make us happier than to attend such a conference anywhere and at any time."[49] These requests for assurances appeared tantamount to a demand that Indonesia renounce Confrontation prior to the next summit and that the reality of this renunciation be validated by a neutral nation. Malaysia was, in effect, insisting that Indonesia's use of force in violation of the United Nations Charter cease prior to a negotiation of "the dispute"; such an insistence is consistent with a rule-oriented approach to international law, as Indonesia's basis for Confrontation, whatever it is, cannot be vindicated as a form of self-defense. Some international lawyers have argued, however, that until the international legal order is in a position to assure states that their just claims will find assured methods of satisfaction, it is impossible to take the Charter prohibitions on the use of force literally.[50] If states retain discretion to use force to pursue just claims, then it is necessary to test whether Indonesia has had a reasonable basis for contending that its claim is just. An argument on behalf of Indonesia's claims might take the following form:

1. Malaysia was created in violation of the Manila Agreements because (a) Malaya undermined the settlement by its premature an-

---

3. Decision by Malaysia to break diplomatic relations with the Philippines and Malaysia.

[49] *Ibid.*, p. 114.

[50] Julius Stone, *Aggression and World Order: A Critique of United Nations Theories of Aggression* (Berkeley: University of California Press, 1958).

nouncement, and (b) the U.N. mission team did not conduct a survey that established the wishes of the inhabitants of Sabah and Sarawak;

2. The military presence of Great Britain in Malaysia posed a threat to the regional security of Southeast Asia;[51]

3. The proposals for Mushawarah Maphilindo amounted to efforts in good faith to find a prior peaceful settlement for the disputes between Indonesia and the Philippines and Malaysia.[52]

An adversary presentation of Confrontation could then be based on the rules and procedures of international law. It is also helpful to realize that the assertion of claims by Indonesia and the Philippines and counter-claims by Malaysia is part of the interaction process by which international disputes are resolved, community expectations as to a reasonable settlement are formed, and degrees of legitimacy and illegitimacy are attached to the opposing positions by the responses made by third-party states and by international institutions.[53]

A few days after the Manila meeting of Sukarno and Macapagal, President Lyndon B. Johnson asked Robert F. Kennedy, then Attorney General, to bring about an end to the Malaysian conflict. Presumably recalling the successful role played by the third-party intervention of the United States in the last stages of the West Irian dispute, the American hope was evidently to explore whether this second instance of Confrontation diplomacy could not also be ended through the good offices of the United States.[54] Kennedy's mission did meet with an immediate, if limited and temporary success — as on January 23, 1964 during Kennedy's visit to Djakarta, Sukarno announced Indonesian adherence to a cease-fire in Malaysia, although he did assert that the "Crush Malaysia" policy would continue, even if its tactics

---

[51] The United States has insisted upon the same line of argument in opposing the extension of Communist influence to the Western Hemisphere in the period since World War II, as well as in opposing the extension of Fascist and Nazi influence during the period of World War II. For an account see Richard A. Falk, "The United States and the Doctrine of Nonintervention in the Internal Affairs of Independent States," *Harvard Law Journal,* V (1959), 163–81.

[52] Compare, e.g., Article 33(1) of the United Nations Charter: "The parties to any dispute, the continuance of which is likely to endanger the maintenance of international peace and security, shall, first of all, seek a solution by negotiation, enquiry, mediation, conciliation, arbitration, judicial settlement, resort to regional agencies or arrangements, or other peaceful means of their own choice."

[53] For an account of this process see the studies contained in Myres S. McDougal, *et al., Studies in World Public Order* (New Haven: Yale University Press, 1960).

[54] See Brackman, *op. cit., supra* note 26, pp. 101–14, 214–17.

might change. Kennedy also affirmed the basic Indonesian insistence that Asian problems be solved by Asian countries, not by outsiders, and encouraged the reconvening of tripartite talks first at the ministerial and then at the summit level. In both respects the aftermath of Kennedy's January visit appeared to confirm the value of his visit: a cease-fire of sorts was proclaimed and maintained in the Borneo territories and tripartite meetings were arranged for Bangkok in early February. Asian diplomacy involving Cambodia and Thailand, as well as the three protagonists, sought to establish a political climate suitable for a second summit. Rahman demanded Indonesian withdrawal as well as a cease-fire, but Sukarno refused to withdraw Indonesian guerrillas from Malaysian territories unless British troops were simultaneously withdrawn.[55]

The Maphilindo theme is again accented in the Joint Communiqué of the Bangkok Ministerial Meeting issued on February 11, 1964. Once again the text of the document is couched in the phraseology of Mushawarah Maphilindo, and once again the Manila Agreements are made the baseline for a settlement of the underlying dispute.[56] The Communiqué confirmed the cease-fire originally proclaimed during the Kennedy mission with regard to fighting in Sabah and Sarawak. A new component added by the Bangkok meetings was bringing in Thailand as a mediating state, evidently in response to Malaysia's request for a neutral state, a request contained in its January 13 reply to the Joint Statement of Sukarno and Macapagal issued two days earlier in Manila.[57] The Bangkok Communiqué indicated in Paragraph 6 that the three states "agreed to invite the Secretary-General of the United Nations to designate Thailand to supervise the cease-fire." Inviting the Secretary-General to designate Thailand is a striking acknowledgement of the legitimizing role of the United Nations, an acknowledgement that is not common in multilateral negotiations and is not characteristic in Great-Power approaches to peaceful settlement.[58] As Malaysia did not include this feature in its original sug-

---

[55] See Mezerik, *op. cit.*, pp. 44–45.

[56] For text of the Bangkok Communiqué, see *ibid.*, pp. 114–15.

[57] To select Thailand as the third-party intermediary bears some witness to Indonesia's conciliatory attitude at this juncture. After all, Thailand was of all Asian states the most pro-Western in orientation, a member of SEATO, and generally opposed to the foreign policy and domestic programs associated with Indonesia.

[58] See Inis L. Claude, Jr., "Collective Legitimization as a Political Function of the United Nations," *International Organization*, XX (1966), 367–79.

gestion of neutral supervision it would seem reasonable to attribute its appearance at Bangkok to Indonesian diplomacy.

The use of formal documents to establish expectations of the parties at the end of a multilateral meeting was a characteristic feature of the diplomacy that involved the dispute about Malaysia.[59] The Manila Agreements acquired an aura of legitimacy that was sustained despite their failure to deal with the provoking cause of Confrontation — the British presence. Such an ascriptive legitimacy illustrates the ways in which international norms — stable expectations about permissible outcomes — are established in the course of the diplomatic interaction. Also, despite the enlarging and overt intervention of Indonesian armed forces in Sabah and Sarawak over the period from September, 1963 to February, 1964, a considerable ideological basis for peaceful settlement evolved. The tripartite settings resulted in an affirmation of Mushawarah Maphilindo, in both its aspects — the meeting together and the search for solidarity, in the midst of an armed struggle reinforced by shrill invective.

On the formal level Indonesia appeared to be quite reasonable in seeking an ordered solution to its dispute with Malaysia. In deeds, however, there appeared to be little clear evidence of an Indonesian disposition to end Confrontation, although it is not clear that Malaysia ever offered Indonesia anything in exchange, even of a face-saving variety. Malaysia insisted that a cease-fire could only be implemented by arranging the withdrawal of Indonesian troops, regulars and irregulars, whereas Indonesia contended that a cease-fire did not imply withdrawal and that it was not willing to withdraw until an overall political solution was reached. In the interim Indonesia claimed the right to re-equip its troops and to have them hold their positions within Malaysian territory.

President Macapagal, sensing the redeterioration of the situation, sought to mediate once again by a state visit to Sukarno in Djakarta. On February 28, 1964 a Joint Communiqué was issued by the two leaders that reaffirmed Indonesia's adherence to (a) the cease-fire and (b) "reiterated their faith in the wisdom of solving Asian problems by Asians themselves in an Asian fashion and trust that the con-

[59] This basis for a negotiated settlement was not characteristic of the West Irian dispute in which Indonesia's claim was posited in the form of a unilateral demand to receive satisfaction.

structive and brotherly Mushawarah is inherent in the Asian way of finding solutions to common problems." The Joint Communiqué also called for a "summit Mushawarah" that would seek "a peaceful settlement of the problems of the region, without pre-condition, at a place and date still to be determined."[60]

In the succeeding months two opposed developments took place. First, the guerrilla fighting in Sabah and Sarawak resumed, and the rhetoric of the "Crush Malaysia" campaign was intensified. Second, diplomatic efforts to implement the cease-fire by searching for a way to secure the withdrawal of Indonesian troops from Malaysian territory and by seeking agreement on the pre-conditions for a second tripartite summit were continued. Thailand played a role of intermediary in this effort, and in June, 1964 a provisional agreement was reached on withdrawal checkpoints on both sides of the Indonesian border. Some withdrawals of Indonesian troops were actually verified by Thai observers.[61] On this basis, a summit was scheduled for June 20, 1964 in Tokyo, preceded by two days of meetings at the ministerial level. Shortly beforehand, the Malaysian posture of Rahman and his party toward Indonesia had been confirmed by its victory at a major election.

The Tokyo meeting failed to bring the dispute to an end, quickly stumbling over the familiar negotiating obstacles. Rahman insisted that all Indonesian troops be withdrawn within four weeks, withdrawal being an absolute pre-condition for a discussion of other elements in "the dispute." President Macapagal proposed a four-member Afro-Asian Conciliation Commission to be constituted by the appointment of one member each by Indonesia, Malaysia, and the Philippines, the fourth member being chosen by the unanimous agreement of the other three. The Tokyo summit meeting endorsed the idea of the Afro-Asian Conciliation Commission in its Final Communiqué. The Commission was called upon "to study the existing problems between the three countries and to submit recommendations for their solution."[62] Sukarno gave strong assurances that he was favorable to this approach and that Indonesia would abide by any recommendations made by the Commission. Malaysia, too, in its draft commu-

---

[60] Cf. Mezerik, *op. cit.*, p. 45.
[61] *Ibid.*, p. 46.
[62] For text of Tokyo Communiqué see *ibid.*, p. 115.

niqué that was rejected by Indonesia because of its insistence on prior withdrawal, "agreed . . . in principle" to the establishment of the Commission "for the purpose of normalizing relations" among the three countries.[63]

The Tokyo meeting appeared to harden the adverse positions of the disputants. Both sides sought to intensify their campaign to secure international support of an economic, ideological, and diplomatic variety. Malaysia turned increasingly toward the West, Indonesia toward the Communist powers. The Confrontation became gradually transformed into an Asian phase of the global struggle going on between the forces of Communism and anti-Communism. The United States especially abandoned its earlier pretense of neutrality to take the side of Malaysia. Indonesia received during the early months of 1964 increasing military assistance from the Soviet Union in the form of modern equipment. The guerrilla war in Malaysian territory was gradually expanded in scale and scope, with overflight and terrorist incidents being reported on the Malayan peninsula, as well as in Sabah and Sarawak. Rahman visited the United States in late July to rally greater support for Malaysia. On August 17 Malaysia reported to the United Nations about armed incursions into Malayan territory by Indonesian irregulars. Subandrio denied such allegations as "mere fabrications." But on September 2 an Indonesian aircraft flying over Malaya was observed dropping a band of about thirty armed paratroopers, who were subsequently captured.

At this point Malaysia requested an urgent meeting of the Security Council to consider its allegations of Indonesian aggression. The ensuing Security Council debate in September was the high point of the efforts of each side to mobilize support for its position by arguing in favor of the legitimacy of its claims. Just prior to the Security Council debates, severe rioting took place in Singapore resulting in thirteen deaths and in the arrest of 800.[64] This rioting was provoked by racial tensions in Singapore and seemed largely independent of the dispute with Indonesia, although it did show the world some of the fragility of the Malaysian Federation.

The Security Council Debate. The Security Council debate was directed at the Malaysian complaint about a specific act of Indonesian aggression, the paratroop landing in Malaya on September 1–2,

---

[63] For text of rejected Malaysian communiqué see *ibid.*, pp. 116–17.
[64] *Ibid.*, p. 91.

1964.[65] This "blatant and inexcusable aggression against a peaceful neighbor" was the basis for requesting this "urgent meeting" of the Security Council. Underlying the Malaysian complaint was its contention that the whole Indonesian policy of Confrontation was a disturbance of international peace, especially insofar as it included the sponsorship of guerrilla activities being carried on within Malaysian territory.

The various positions taken in the Security Council during the discussions of the Malaysian complaint witnessed a sharp clash between Western-oriented conceptions of world order and the most militant post-colonial Afro-Asian conceptions. The representatives of Indonesia and Malaysia made long statements in the Security Council that recapitulated the dispute since its inception in 1963. The non-Communist Members of the Security Council, including Bolivia, Brazil, Ivory Coast, and Morocco opposed Indonesia; only the Soviet Union and Czechoslovakia favored the Indonesian interpretation of the dispute. The United States and the United Kingdom were most vigorous in their verbal denunciations of Indonesia's position, not only with regard to the specific allegation of aggression that was before the Council, but more generally, in denouncing Indonesia's overall espousal of Confrontation. The consequence of the debate in the Security Council was to give the impression that Indonesia's position was rejected by the majority of the organized international community, including the non-aligned and Afro-Asian portions of it.

International law entered prominently into the discussion. Supporters of the Malaysian complaint rested their case on the rather clear-cut incompatibility between an unrepudiated recourse to force by Indonesia and the requirements of the Charter. Indonesia and its Communist supporters brushed aside the specific allegation of aggression and concentrated upon developing an argument on the merits of Indonesia's Confrontation policy. Indonesia's argument was essentially that Malaysia was a neo-colonialist creation fabricated to perpetuate British influence in the area. Indonesia reinforced this argument by reference to its desire for a peaceful settlement, first in the form of its early friendship with Malaya in the pre-Malaysia period, then by its willingness to work toward a peaceful accommoda-

---

[65] Consideration by the Security Council was initiated by a complaint contained in a letter of September 3, 1964 from the Permanent Representative of Malaysia at the United Nations to the President of the Security Council. Document S/5930.

tion with Malaysia within the Manila framework, and finally, by its continuing adherence to Maphilindo as the way out, an adherence manifested most recently by Sukarno's declaration that Indonesia was prepared to accept any recommendations made by the Afro-Asian Conciliation Commission that had been proposed at the Tokyo summit meeting.

In the Security Council the decisive issue from the perspective of international law was whether Indonesia's line of argumentation had any relevance. There is no entirely satisfactory way to resolve this issue. It is possible to construe the 9–2 vote in favor of the Norwegian Resolution as a repudiation of Indonesia's line of contention; more legalistically, it is possible to maintain that the Soviet Union's negative vote was a veto that prevented the Security Council from reaching any conclusion, as formally the Council took no action on Malaysia's complaint and the Norwegian Resolution was not adopted.[66]

Alternatively, one might examine the argumentation itself and seek to determine the relative persuasiveness of the contending positions. Adlai Stevenson, the Representative of the United States in the Security Council at the time, referred to Indonesia's position as "a new and dangerous doctrine of international law outside the Charter of the United Nations." He referred to the large number of active international disputes and pointed out that "If other nations involved in these disputes were to take the law into their own hands, drop armed forces on the territory of their neighbors, the precarious peace of our inflammable world would soon go up in smoke."[67] Stevenson relied heavily on the clear incompatibility between the Charter obligation to settle disputes peacefully and Indonesia's use of force against Malaysia for purposes other than self-defense.

Sudjarwo replied on behalf of Indonesia that this condemnation of Indonesia's position "is rather strange when it comes from the representative of the United States," and asked whether Stevenson had "forgotten occurrences, to mention only recent events, such as the 'Bay of Pigs' and 'Tonkin' affair?" The Indonesian representative analogized recourse to force by the United States in its dispute with Cuba to the Indonesian claim to use force against Malaysia. Sudjarwo contended, furthermore, that it is not *the fact* that force is used that

[66] The Resolution introduced by Norway is Document S/5973; text reproduced by Mezerik, *op. cit.*, pp. 117–18.

[67] SCOR, 1145th Mtg., para. 24, p. 5.

determines its legal status, but rather the acceptability of *the justification* for its use. In this instance such a justification, according to Sudjarwo, depended on a fair examination of the British colonial record, consisting of exploitation and dominance, and of the use of the territory of Malaysia to molest the independence of Indonesia. Indonesia argued that the United States had used its great influence in the past to keep complaints about American uses of force from being considered by the Security Council, but with respect to Indonesia the United States was adopting a sanctimonious attitude about the literal character of Charter commitments.

There is no question that the United States has claimed for itself considerable discretion to use force within the territory of foreign states in situations other than self-defense. The military intervention of the United States in the Dominican Republic in 1965 provides a clear example. In replying to critics of this undertaking, the Legal Adviser to the Secretary of State, Leonard Meeker, chided those who argued that such action was illegal with taking a fundamentalist attitude toward international law, and urged a greater appreciation of the need to reconcile the constraints of law with the realities of international conflict.[68]

Assuming that the United States has used force outside the Charter limits, how does such use affect the status of Indonesia's position vis-à-vis Malaysia? Even if such a demonstration of American practice in analogous situations would establish the proposition that the United States was being hypocritical about its condemnation of Indonesia, or that it was claiming for itself a discretionary right to use force that it was unwilling to grant Indonesia, why should such a double standard deprive Malaysia of the protection of the Charter?

This last question seems to depict the underlying issue for international legal order. It points toward the "legislative" status of international practice inconsistent with rules incorporated in documents such as the United Nations Charter.[69] Not every violation of a rule is a legislative revision of it, but if the violations are frequent enough or if

---

[68] Leonard Meeker, "The Dominican Situation in the Perspective of International Law," *Department of State Bulletin,* LIII (1965), 60–65.

[69] For explanation see Richard A. Falk, "On the Quasi-Legislative Competence of the General Assembly," *American Journal of International Law,* LX (1966), 782–91; in general, see Oscar Schachter, "The Relation of Law, Politics, and Action in the United Nations," Hague Academy of International Law, *Recueil des Cours,* CIX (1963), 169–256.

their commission is vindicated or even acquiesced in by a consensus of the members of international society then a legislative claim seems to be established. In this respect the opposition of the Latin American and other non-Western Members of the Security Council to Indonesia's position is of some significance and should be contrasted with the response to the Portuguese complaint about India's use of force against Goa in 1961.[70] India's claim to use force rested upon the illegitimacy of maintaining colonial title to a territorial enclave, whereas Indonesia's claim rested upon the illegitimacy of a neo-colonialist political unit that had the characteristics of a sovereign state, including Membership in the United Nations.

Therefore, it would seem possible to conclude that although some of Indonesia's main opponents in the Security Council had less than clean hands on the matter of Charter compliance, nevertheless there was insufficient support for Indonesia's case to give it much legislative status as a precedent looking toward the expansion of the occasions upon which it is legally permissible to use force. It should be appreciated, however, that in addition to the patterns of American practice (and supporting justification), both the Communist and the Afro-Asian groupings claim the right to use force to support in the first instance "wars of national liberation"[71] and in the second instance, force against the states in Southern Africa that are either colonialist or racist in character. Given these broad claims to establish exceptions to the Charter system of constraints, it is at least arguable that there is no effective international law applicable to uses of force by one state against another, especially if the force used is of an unconventional variety that does not involve "war" in the traditional sense. "Confrontation" is a species, at worst, of "indirect aggression," and it is arguable that this form of international violence, including military responses to it by third powers, presently eludes legal control.[72]

---

[70] For the Goa debate see SCOR, Mtgs. 987–88, December 18–19, 1961; an interpretation of these events is offered in Richard A. Falk, "The New States and International Legal Order," Hague Academy of International Law, *Recueil des Cours*, Vol. CXVIII (1965).

[71] There is, of course, considerable ambiguity surrounding the idea of "support" and concerning the identification of what constitutes "a war of national liberation." — also, what levels of support are forbidden by international law and what kinds of support provoke countervailing geopolitical pressures.

[72] For an argument to the effect see Richard A. Falk, "Janus Tormented: The International Law of Internal War," in J. N. Rosenau, ed., *International Aspects of Civil Strife* (Princeton: Princeton University Press, 1964), pp. 185–248.

Undoubtedly Indonesia's failure to receive more support in the Security Council contributed to Sukarno's subsequent decision to withdraw from the United Nations. The debate produced only the relatively mild Norwegian Resolution of censure. A Resolution cannot be adopted officially if any Permanent Member of the Security Council casts a negative vote; as the Soviet Union did vote against the Norwegian Resolution it was not officially adopted. The Resolution although using fairly indirect language, in effect, endorsed the Malaysian position rather completely. It "*deplores* the incident" that gave rise to the Malaysian complaint and "*Calls upon* the parties to refrain from all threat or use of force and to respect the territorial integrity and political independence of each other, and thus to create a conducive atmosphere for the continuation of their talks." Only "thereupon" does it call for an implementation of the Tokyo arrangement to create an Afro-Asian Conciliation Commission entrusted with recommending a solution.

This Resolution supported by nine-elevenths of the Security Council closely resembles the Malaysian view on "preconditions"[73] — namely, (1) acknowledging the validity of Malaysia as a political entity endowed with the attributes of sovereignty and (2) termination of the military aspects of "Confrontation" prior to talks on a settlement, including apparently both cease-fire and withdrawal. After satisfying these preconditions the issues that constituted the dispute remained: (1) self-determination for the Borneo territories; (2) consideration of the Philippines' claim to Sabah; and (3) agreement on the nature, size, and duration of the British military presence in Malaysia. However, it is hard to imagine how Indonesia, or the Philippines, could exert much leverage, especially as the voting rules of the Commission proposed at Tokyo were never laid down, and its mandate was, at best, only to make recommendations.

From the perspective of international law the outcome of the debates in the Security Council were quite ambiguous. Certainly a consensus repudiated Indonesia and supported Malaysia, despite the absence of formal action. The Indonesian reaction to such a repudiation was to turn against the United Nations and to attack the Organization as a hostile environment for a new state eager to carry on the struggle against the forces of reaction and neo-colonialism. A second reaction

[73] See, e.g., the Malaysian reply to the Philippine-Indonesian Joint Communiqué of January 11, 1964; text reprinted in Mezerik, *op. cit.*, pp. 112–13.

by Indonesia was to move closer in alignment with China and the Soviet Union. And a third reaction was once again to step up the pace of guerrilla activity both in the Borneo territories and on the Malayan mainland, as well as virtually to abandon the conciliation motif.

Withdrawal from the United Nations. Indonesia's disenchantment with the United Nations was a partial consequence of its diplomacy of Confrontation. This disenchantment began, it would appear, in September, 1963 when the Secretary-General issued his Report confirming the wishes of the inhabitants of Sabah and Sarawak to join Malaysia. Sukarno subsequently suggested a second survey by the United Nations to resolve the self-determination issue. There was, then, an inclination by Indonesia early in the dispute to treat the Secretary-General, acting on behalf of the United Nations, as an impartial and authoritative decision-maker capable of resolving the controversy. It hardly seems plausible that a nation would refer these issues to the United Nations unless there had been some disposition to act in accordance with its recommendations. And it is the case, as the reaction of the Philippines bears out, that the Secretary-General did not conduct the survey of Sabah and Sarawak in a manner that would allow confidence to attach to its results, especially in view of his rather weak reaction to Malaya's premature announcement of the date on which Malaysia was to be formed. Such an experience might cause Indonesia to feel that its original confidence in the United Nations had been unwarranted.

Indonesia also resented the rapid acceptance of Malaysia as a Member of the United Nations on September 17, 1963, an acceptance that took place at a time when Indonesia questioned the legitimacy of the Federation. Such an acceptance can easily be contrasted with the long-sustained exclusion of mainland China from the organization. A contrast of this sort, especially given Indonesia's sensitivity about its status in the world, confirmed the view that the United Nations was controlled by the reactionary forces in the world.

The more general conditioning factor was the Western control of the United Nations, especially the Security Council. This was expressed forcibly during the debate on Goa in 1961, but became more relevant for Indonesia during the September, 1964 debates. If Sukarno believed that international society was the scene of a sharp struggle between OLDEFO (Old Emerging Forces) and NEFO (New Emerging Forces), then it was reasonable for him to believe that the United Nations was in the control of OLDEFO and a parallel structure was needed to establish greater legitimacy for the claims of NEFO.

The event immediately precipitating withdrawal was the selection of Malaysia on December 30, 1964 to be a Member of the Security Council. This development provoked Sukarno to say in the course of a speech on the following day that if Malaysia was seated in the Security Council, then Indonesia would quit the organization. Malaysia was seated on January 1, 1965 and Indonesia formally withdrew a few days later.

Subandrio in his letter of withdrawal addressed to the Secretary-General refers to the Indonesian decision as "a revolutionary one," but one that "could well entail a beneficial effect for the speedy solution of the problem of 'Malaysia' itself."[74] Two sets of important questions were posed for the international legal order by Indonesia's withdrawal: (1) the relation of the United Nations to a non-member and (2) the possibility of a rival international organization purporting to be an independent and equivalent source of authority vis-à-vis the world community.[75]

Article 2(6) of the Charter claims control over non-member states to the extent necessary to maintain international peace and security. There is, thus, a legal basis for a continuing role for the United Nations subsequent to withdrawal, especially in a context disturbing to international peace. As a practical matter, however, the authority of the United Nations seems to depend heavily at this stage upon a voluntary attitude of deference toward its views by states in dispute. Indonesia's withdrawal seemed to symbolize its refusal to accord the organization any further deference; the United Nations has not attempted to exert much influence on the behavior of mainland China, its principal non-Member.

With China excluded and Indonesia withdrawn, there did exist a real danger that the position of the United Nations as a center of international legal authority would be undermined. China and Indonesia threatened to establish a rival organization, a threat that was not carried out because no other states were willing to abandon the

---

[74] Letter dated January 20, 1965 addressed to the Secretary-General, U.N. Document A/5857. Text in *ibid.*, pp. 120–22.

[75] For a general discussion see Richard A. Falk, "The Authority of the United Nations to Control Non-Members," *Rutgers Law Review*, XIX (1965), 591–645.

United Nations as of early 1965. The other kind of danger to the position of the United Nations was to remind disenchanted Members, especially states like Portugal and South Africa, of their withdrawal option and its bargaining potential.[76] Such a timely withdrawal by these states, although stimulated by reasoning opposite to that provoking Indonesia's decision, might have undermined the authority of the United Nations to speak with the legal voice of the organized community of mankind. In this regard, it is relevant to recall that the failures of the League of Nations were accented by a series of withdrawals by disenchanted Members.[77]

The point brought home by Indonesia's withdrawal is that whatever legitimacy is enjoyed by the United Nations derives largely from the voluntary participation in its activities by almost all states, including especially the enterprise of community conciliation that such participation implies. Universality or quasi-universality is the keystone of a voluntary association of sovereign states; the loss of this keystone may well endanger the entire structure of authority that it supports. In effect, Indonesia's withdrawal, although short-lived, did serve to reveal the fragile foundation of United Nations' authority and should, perhaps, prompt a renewed effort to approximate more closely the ideals of universal membership.

Furthermore, the option of withdrawal clarifies the limits of U.N. authority in normal circumstances, as it emphasizes the costs to the organization of completely alienating a state that has any substantial political role in international society. These limits may not apply if the state in question is as isolated as Portugal and South Africa appear to be; Indonesia, it should be recalled, received overt support throughout Confrontation from the Communist powers and sympathy from several militant anti-Western new states (e.g., Cambodia).[78] Besides, such pro-Western states as Thailand and the Philippines were careful to refrain from taking sides. Indonesia, then, was not nearly so isolated in the international system as it appeared to be in the Security Council debates.

[76] The authority of the United Nations rests, in part, on its global and quasi-universal character. States under pressure could threaten withdrawal and by this threat possibly inhibit the United Nations as the implementation of the threat would almost certainly weaken the organization.

[77] For a brief account see Francis P. Walters, A History of the League of Nations (London: Oxford Press, 1952), esp. Chaps. 27 and 33.

[78] Indonesia's influence was also illustrated by the success of her efforts to exclude Malaysia from formal or active informal participation in Afro-Asian affairs during the period of the dispute.

It is interesting to note that the local and small-scale violence between Indonesia and Malaysia provoked an authority crisis of first magnitude in the world community.

Termination of Confrontation. The drift of Confrontation into a full-scale cold war conflict was abruptly halted by the drastic political changes that ensued in Indonesia after the abortive coup of September 1–October 1, 1965.[79] After domestic political control shifted from Sukarno to General Suharto in the aftermath of the countercoup and widescale purge resulting in the death of anywhere from 300,000–1,200,000 Indonesians, there was a notable determination by the Indonesian government to detach itself from the Communist orbits of influence and seek friendly relations with the West — no better way to signal this shift could be found than to repudiate the militant approach of Sukarno on the Malaysian class of issues and to resume participation in the affairs of the United Nations. In the hectic weeks immediately following the coup, there were ritualistic reaffirmations of the Confrontation policy, but once the domestic situation in Indonesia calmed down it was evident that the era of Confrontation diplomacy was at an end, temporarily at least.

On June 1, 1966, normalization was negotiated at Bangkok in a simple bilateral document drawn up at a meeting on the Ministerial level.[80] The Bangkok Accord, as the document is known, was officially ratified and brought into force by the two countries on August 11, 1966. The Bangkok Accord involves an element of reciprocal obligation. In Article 1, Malaysia "agrees to afford the people of Sabah and Sarawak who are directly involved, an opportunity to reaffirm, as soon as practicable, in a free and democratic manner through General Elections, their previous decision about their status in Malaysia." Article 2 looks toward the exchange of diplomatic representatives and entails Indonesian acknowledgement of the legitimacy of Malaysia as a sovereign state. And Article 3 affirms that "hostile acts between the two countries shall cease forthwith."[81] The political implementation of the Bangkok Accord seems fully successful and there are indications of renewed interest in working out subregional cooperation of the Ma-

[79] For a preliminary assessment see Brackman, *op. cit., supra* note 26, pp. 284–99.
[80] For an analysis see Michael Leifer, "Indonesia and Malaysia: The Changing Face of Confrontation," *The World Today* (September, 1966), pp. 395–405.
[81] Compare issues of *News and Views* for background and relevant texts including the Bangkok Accord, during the period between May 1, 1966 and August 30, 1966, issues No. 136–95.

lay peoples on security and economic matters. It is worth noting that the settlement of the dispute did not involve an explicit renunciation of Indonesian demands, but rather contained a formula that accorded them nominal deference.— namely, the agreement to ascertain the wishes of the inhabitants of Sabah and Sarawak.

Indonesia's return to the United Nations followed a parallel path. The appointment of Adam Malik as Foreign Minister in March, 1966 appears to have been the decisive act. As late as May, 1966, however, Sukarno reiterated his view that Indonesia should remain outside the United Nations unless certain changes were made in its structure. But Malik was increasingly definite about his intention to return to the United Nations and by August, Sukarno, too, supported the move to return, a move acted on shortly thereafter.

Indonesia's return to the United Nations thereby ended the crisis of authority provoked by its withdrawal a year and a half earlier. Such a return to the established structures of international authority was avowedly part of the effort of the new Indonesian leadership to pursue a more conservative foreign policy, a foreign policy that would be compatible with the receipt of economic aid from the West. It was evident that Confrontation had been a costly diplomatic adventure for Indonesia. Not only were there the military costs associated with supporting the guerrilla effort within Malaysian territory, but foreign trade with Singapore, a major source of Indonesian foreign exchange, had been terminated and Western economic assistance ended. These economic sacrifices associated with Confrontation were abetted by Indonesia's failure to achieve significant economic growth and by an inflation of runaway proportions.

Conclusions. In several respects, international law was relevant to the course of the Malaysia-Indonesia dispute:

1. *Stable Expectations.* At each stage of the dispute the parties sought to formulate an agreed statement that contained the results of their efforts to reach a settlement. Departures from these agreed statements were later perceived as "violations" by the aggrieved party. The consequence of this pattern is to inject a law element into an encounter between states. Without this law element the encounter would more easily degenerate into unmitigated conflict resolvable only by the clash of wills and arms; with this law element there is a braking mechanism that allows the disputing parties a certain flexibility to accelerate, decelerate, or even halt the conflict.

This process can be illustrated by reference to the Manila Conference held in 1963. That Conference led to the Manila Accords which proposed a reassessment of the wishes of the inhabitants of the Borneo territories to be carried out under the auspices of the Secretary-General to assure that their inclusion in the Federation was consistent with the principle of self-determination. In an accompanying Statement the disputing states affirmed their commitment to regional solidarity and to an Asian solution for Asian problems. Of course, a series of subsequent events undermined the Manila solution, but nevertheless the framework for settlement established at Manila remained the basis for efforts at conciliation up to and including the termination of the dispute at Bangkok in 1966. In a quite different setting, the Geneva Accords of 1954 have been invoked by all parties to the conflict in South Vietnam as containing the guidelines upon which a restoration of peace could be based. The extent of departure from the Manila Accords by each side is a matter of interpretation, but the reference back to those guidelines created a legal structure to which adversary diplomacy might revert from time to time.

2. *Political Mobilization.* Recourse to legal arguments by the adversary states in various international arenas was designed to mobilize support and neutralize opposition. Malaysia's greatest success, of course, was to complain about being the victim of unprovoked and illegal uses of force by Indonesia; such an argument was appealing to the Western powers and it went a long way to neutralize opposition from the non-aligned states to the neo-colonialist elements in the Malaysian context. The highwater mark of Malaysian diplomacy in this latter regard was its success in acquiring support from all nine non-Communist Members of the Security Council, including the Ivory Coast and Morocco, during the debates of September 1964. Indonesia, in contrast, relied upon arguments about the illegitimacy of neo-colonial regimes bolstered by a continuing military and economic role by the ex-colonial power to rally support for itself in the Communist world and to solicit sympathy throughout the Afro-Asian world. The highwater mark of Indonesian diplomacy in this latter regard was the exclusion of Malaysia from the 1964 Cairo Meeting of the Non-Aligned, although Malaysia possessed all of the qualifications needed to participate, including the wish to do so.

In general, the rhetoric of international law was used as an instrument of diplomatic persuasion by the participants in the dispute to demonstrate either the unreasonableness of the other side or to demonstrate the underlying justice of one's own cause. The effect on behavior is difficult to measure, but it is not implausible to contend that the weakness of Indonesia's case against Malaysia in legal terms had an effect on the relative failure of Indonesia to be successful in political terms. In this regard, Indonesia's success in the West Irian Case was in part at least explicable by the fact that its confrontation diplomacy, including threats and uses of military force in violation of the Charter, was based upon a legal case plausible enough to attract support from independent jurists.[82]

3. *Signaling Intentions.* International law provides actors with symbols by which they can communicate intentions, including demands for rectification. Indonesia and the Philippines withheld recognition from Malaysia to signal their intention to regard the Federation as an "illegitimate" entity. The United Kingdom signaled its intention to remain a military presence in South East Asia by undertaking broad security functions as specified in the 1957 Agreement with Malaya and as renewed and extended in 1963. Malaysia's insistence on "preconditions" to settlement — withdrawal of Indonesian troops — conveyed its intention to refuse negotiations until Indonesia ceased to rely upon military intimidation; the norm of aggression was invoked to clarify the basis of Malaysia's refusal "to settle" the dispute so long as Confrontation diplomacy continued in its unabated form.

4. *Supranationalism.* Throughout the period of Confrontation there were repeated efforts to refer the dispute to a supranational forum. The original effort to avert a crisis at Manila in 1963 was highly supranational in character, inviting third-party intervention by the Secretary-General on the self-determination issue and looking toward a political settlement by means of creating a Maphilindo framework. Later on at Bangkok, Thailand was called upon to verify the agreed withdrawal of Indonesian troops from the Borneo territory. The Tokyo summit meeting recommended the establishment of a four-power Asian Conciliation Commission. Malaysia had recourse to the Security Council to complain about Indonesia's armed intervention in Malaya. These main efforts to rely upon the supranational resources of international society to resolve a predominantly bilateral dispute are an interesting reflection of new trends in crisis diplomacy, although the actual settlement was achieved by traditional nation-to-nation diplomacy.

[82] E.g., B. V. A. Röling, *Nieuw Guinea als Wereld probleem* [New Guinea World Problem] (Assen, The Netherlands: Van Gorcum, 1958).

The essence of legal order is the impartial determination of conflicting claims that arise between parties to a dispute. International legal order is basically decentralized, the extent of impartiality injected into a settlement of a dispute being a reflection of whatever adjustment is reached through the interaction of claims and counter-claims. Unless the parties are reasonably protective of each other's interests — not common in adversary settings — the tendency is for any kind of serious dispute to be resolved by ultimate reference to the relative power that each actually or potentially can bring to bear. As such, conflict resolution works to the grave disadvantage of the weaker party; the outcome of "legal" interaction is not sharply separable from the outcome reached by the application of naked force. To the extent, however, that supranational decision-makers are introduced into the context of dispute, there is à greater tendency to determine the dispute by reference to considerations other than the relative power of the disputants. This equalizing impact is, in effect, a consequence of the third-party resolution of an international dispute. When conciliatory, Indonesia stressed the role of third-party settlement procedure, whereas when antagonistic, insisted upon sovereign prerogatives to proceed against Malaysia in whatever manner as it deemed warranted.

5. *Regionalism.* Indonesia's insistence, one supported even by the adverse Norwegian Resolution in the Security Council and by Robert Kennedy's efforts to mediate the dispute, was that the proper mode of settlement was by Asian countries in brotherly concert. This claim of regional autonomy has important implications for the structure of world order and is paralleled by analogous claims made by the Organization of African Unity in response to Operation Stanleyville and by the Organization of American States in response to several hemispheric disputes. Such support for the regionalization of international disputes suggests an effort to insulate Afro-Asian instabilities from Great-Power interventions. If some kind of strong tradition of regional autonomy were to emerge with the support of both Great Powers and the Afro-Asian states, an improvement in the quality of world order might result.

In terms of traditional conceptions of international law, the growth of a regional competence to influence what is permitted and what is prohibited national conduct is a very significant development. A regional basis for legitimizing and delegitimizing national action establishes a community-based international law to complement the traditional sovereignty-based international law. Furthermore, the insistence on a primary regional jurisdiction to control the settlement of disputes between members of a region is a significant attempt in the Asian (or African) context to safeguard independence from the Great Powers in the post-colonial context. As law evolves out of the expectations of the community of its subjects, it is most interesting and significant to take full account of the stress upon the legitimacy of regional settlement procedures and the illegitimacy of recourse to extra-regional actors throughout the period of Confrontation. Indonesia's emphasis on the "neo-colonial" impact of Britain's military presence in Malaysia seemed to draw some strength from the appeal to the principle of regional autonomy.

The Indonesia-Malaysia dispute, in short, is quite susceptible to analysis from the perspective of international law. In fact, it is a revealing instance of diplomatic and legal interaction that is distinctively Asian in character. International lawyers may tend to underestimate the interest of this dispute either because their perception of it was slanted against Indonesia by the Western presentation of the argument, or because the new regime in Djakarta so quickly abandoned the Indonesian position. A closer scrutiny suggests that Indonesia had a credible, if somewhat novel, legal argument to support its claims vis-à-vis Malaysia, and that the argument is an extreme example of the sort of revisionist outlook that is becoming more and more explicit in the attitudes and behavior of the Afro-Asian group of states.[83]

[83] Cf. Final Act of the United Nations Conference on Trade and Development, E/Conf. 46/L.28, 16 June 1964.

Appendix

THE MANILA ACCORD. JUNE 1963. REPORT AND RECOMMENDATIONS OF THE CONFERENCE OF FOREIGN MINISTERS OF THE FEDERATION OF MALAYA, THE REPUBLIC OF INDONESIA AND THE REPUBLIC OF THE PHILIPPINES TO THEIR RESPECTIVE HEADS OF GOVERNMENT. PUBLISHED BY GOVERNMENT PRESS, KUALA LUMPUR IN "MALAYA/INDONESIA RELATIONS 1957–63" AND BY THE INDONESIAN EMBASSY IN LONDON IN "THE PROBLEM OF MALAYSIA."

1. The Governments of the Federation of Malaya, the Republic of Indonesia and the Republic of the Philippines, prompted by their keen and common desire to have a general exchange of views on current problems concerning stability, security, economic development and social progress of the three countries and of the region and upon the initiative of President Diosdado Macapagal, agreed that a Conference of Ministers of the three countries be held in Manila on 7th June 1963, for the purpose of achieving common understanding and close fraternal co-operation among themselves. Accordingly, Tun Abdul Razak, Deputy Prime Minister of the Federation of Malaya; Dr. Subandrio, Deputy First Minister/Minister for Foreign Affairs of the Republic of Indonesia; and Honourable Emmanuel Pelaez, Vice-President of the Philippines and concurrently Secretary of Foreign Affairs, met in Manila from 7 to 11 June, 1963.

2. The deliberations were held in a frank manner and in a most cordial atmosphere in keeping with the spirit of friendship prevailing in the various meetings held between President Sukarno of the Republic of Indonesia, and Prime Minister Tengku Abdul Rahman Putra of the Federation of Malaya, and President Diosdado Macapagal. This Ministerial Conference was a manifestation of the determination of the nations in this region to achieve closer co-operation in the endeavour to chart their common future.

3. The Ministers were of one mind that the three countries share a primary responsibility for the maintenance of the stability and security of the area from subversion in any form or manifestation in order to preserve their respective national identities, and to ensure the peaceful development of their respective countries and of their region, in accordance with the ideals and aspirations of their peoples.

4. In the same spirit of common and constructive endeavour, they exchanged views on the proposed Confederation of nations of Malay origin, the proposed Federation of Malaysia, the Philippine claim to North Borneo and related problems.

THE MACAPAGAL PLAN

5. Recognising that it is in the common interest of their countries to maintain fraternal relations and to strengthen co-operation among their peoples who are bound together by ties of race and culture, the three Ministers agreed to intensify the joint and individual efforts of their countries to secure lasting peace, progress and prosperity for themselves and for their neighbours.

6. In this context, the three Ministers supported President Macapagal's plan envisaging the grouping of the three nations of Malay origin working together in closest harmony but without surrendering any portion of their sovereignty. This calls for the establishment of the necessary common organs.

7. The three Ministers agreed to take the initial steps towards this ultimate aim by establishing machinery for frequent and regular consultations. The details of such machinery will be further defined. This machinery will enable the three governments to hold regular consultations at all levels to deal with matters of mutual interest and concern consistent with the national, regional and international responsibilities or obligations of each country without prejudice to its sovereignty and independence. The Ministers agreed that their countries will endeavour to achieve close understanding and co-operation in dealing with common problems relating to security, stability, economic, social and cultural development.

8. In order to accelerate the process of growth towards the ultimate establishment of President Macapagal's plan, the Ministers agreed that each country shall set up its own National Secretariat. Pending the establishment of a Central Secretariat for the consultative machinery, the National Secretaries should co-ordinate and co-operate with each other in the fulfilment of their tasks.

9. The Ministers further agreed to recommend that Heads of Government and Foreign Ministers meet at least once a year for the purpose of consultations on matters of importance and common concern.

MALAYSIA AND NORTH BORNEO

10. The Ministers reaffirmed their countries' adherence to the principle of self-determination for the peoples of non-self-governing territories. In this context, Indonesia and the Philippines stated that they would wel-

come the formation of Malaysia provided the support of the people of the Borneo territories is ascertained by an independent and impartial authority, the Secretary-General of the United Nations or his representative.

11. The Federation of Malaya expressed appreciation for this attitude of Indonesia and the Philippines and undertook to consult the British Government and the Governments of the Borneo territories with a view to inviting the Secretary-General of the United Nations or his representative to take the necessary steps in order to ascertain the wishes of the peoples of those territories.

12. The Philippines made it clear that its position on the inclusion of North Borneo in the Federation of Malaysia is subject to the final outcome of the Philippine claim to North Borneo. The Ministers took note of the Philippine claim and the right of the Philippines to continue to pursue it in accordance with international law and the principle of the pacific settlement of disputes. They agreed that the inclusion of North Borneo in the Federation of Malaysia would not prejudice either the claim or any right thereunder. Moreover in the context of their close association, the three countries agreed to exert their best endeavours to bring the claim to a just and expeditious solution by peaceful means, such as negotiation, conciliation, arbitration, or judicial settlement as well as other peaceful means of the parties' own choice, in comformity with the Charter of the United Nations and the Bandung Declaration.

13. In particular, considering the close historical ties between the peoples of the Philippines and North Borneo as well as their geographical propinquity, the Ministers agreed that in the event of North Borneo joining the proposed Federation of Malaysia the Government of the latter and the Government of the Philippines should maintain and promote the harmony and the friendly relations subsisting in their region to ensure the security and stability of the area.

MEETING OF HEADS OF GOVERNMENT

14. The Ministers agreed to recommend that a Meeting of their respective Heads of Government be held in Manila not later than the end of July 1963.

15. The Ministers expressed satisfaction over the atmosphere of brotherliness and cordiality which pervaded their meeting and considered it as a confirmation of their close fraternal ties and as a happy augury for the success of future consultations among their leaders.

16. The Ministers agreed to place on record their profound appreciation of and gratitude for the statesmanlike efforts of President Macapagal whose courage, vision and inspiration not only facilitated the holding of this historic meeting but also contributed towards the achievement for the

first time of a unity of purpose and a sense of common dedication among the peoples of Malaya, Indonesia and the Philippines.

THE MANILA DECLARATION. AUGUST 1963.

The President of the Republic of Indonesia, the President of the Philippines and the Prime Minister of the Federation of Malaya, assembled in a Summit Conference in Manila from 30 July to August 5, 1963, following the Meeting of their Foreign Ministers held in Manila from June 7 to 11, 1963:

Conscious of the historic significance of their coming together for the first time as leaders of sovereign States that have emerged after long struggles from colonial status to independence:

Desiring to achieve better understanding and closer co-operation in their endeavour to chart their common future:

Inspired also by the spirit of Asian-African solidarity forged in the Bandung Conference of 1955:

Convinced that their countries, which are bound together by close historical ties of race and culture, share a primary responsibility for the maintenance of the stability and security of the area from subversion in any form or manifestation in order to preserve their respective national identities and to ensure the peaceful development of their respective countries and their region in accordance with the ideals and aspirations of their peoples: and

Determined to intensify the joint and individual efforts of their countries to secure lasting peace, progress and prosperity for themselves and their neighbours in a world dedicated to freedom and justice:

DO HEREBY DECLARE:

First, that they reaffirm their adherence to the principle of equal rights and self-determination of peoples as enunciated in the United Nations Charter and the Bandung Declaration:

Second, that they are determined, in the common interest of their countries, to maintain fraternal relations, to strengthen co-operation among their peoples in the economic, social and cultural fields in order to promote economic progress and social well-being in the region, and to put an end to the exploitation of man by man and of one nation by another:

Third, that the three nations shall combine their efforts in the common struggle against colonialism and imperialism in all their forms and manifestations and for the eradication of the vestiges thereof in the region in particular and the world in general:

Fourth, that the three nations, as new emerging forces in the region, shall co-operate in building a new and better world based on national freedom, social justice and lasting peace: and

Fifth, that in the context of the joint endeavours of the three nations to achieve the foregoing objectives, they have agreed to take initial steps towards the establishment of Maphilindo by holding frequent and regular consultations at all levels to be known as Mushawarah Maphilindo.

MANILA
August 5, 1963

> SUKARNO,
> *President of the Republic of Indonesia*
>
> DIOSDADO MACAPAGAL,
> *President of the Philippines*
>
> TENGKU ABDUL RAHMAN PUTRA AL-HAJ,
> *Prime Minister of the Federation of Malaya*

EXTRACT FROM THE FINAL CONCLUSIONS OF THE SECRETARY-GENERAL, UNITED NATIONS ORGANIZATION. (UNITED NATIONS SPECIAL RELEASE SPL/84 DATED 16 SEPTEMBER 1963.)

The basic assessment which I was asked to make has broader implications than the specific questions enumerated in the request addressed to me by the three governments. As previously mentioned, I was asked to ascertain, prior to the establishment of the Federation of Malaysia, the wishes of the people of Sabah (North Borneo) and Sarawak within the context of the General Assembly Resolution 1541 (XV), Principle IX of the Annex, by a fresh approach, which in the opinion of the Secretary-General, is necessary to ensure complete compliance with the principle of self-determination within the requirements embodied in Principle IX. . . .

I have given consideration to the circumstances in which the proposals for the Federation of Malaysia have been developed and discussed, and the possibility that people progressing through stages of self-government may be less able to consider in an entirely free context the implications of such changes in their status, than a society which has already experienced full self-government and determination of its own affairs. I have also been aware that the peoples of these territories are still striving for a more adequate level of educational development.

Having reflected fully on these considerations, and taking into account the framework within which the Mission's work was performed, I have come to the conclusion that the majority of the peoples of Sabah (North Borneo) and of Sarawak have given serious and thoughtful consideration to their future and to the implications for them of participation in a Federation of Malaysia. I believe that the majority of them have concluded that they wish to bring their dependent status to an end and to realise their independence through freely-chosen association with other peoples in their region with whom they feel the ties of ethnic association, heritage, language, religion, culture, economic relationship, and ideals and objectives. Not all these considerations are present in equal weight in all minds, but it is my conclusion that the majority of the peoples of these two territories have taken them into account and wish to engage with the peoples of the Federation of Malaya and Singapore, in an enlarged Federation of Malaysia through which they can strive together to realise the fulfilment of their destiny. . . .

Bearing in mind the fundamental agreement of the three participating governments in the Manila meetings, and the statement by the Republic of Indonesia and the Republic of the Philippines that they would welcome the formation of Malaysia provided that the support of the people of the territories was ascertained by me and that, in my opinion, complete compliance with the principle of self-determination within the requirements of the General Assembly Resolution 1541 (XV), Principle IX of the Annex, was ensured, my conclusions based on the findings of the Mission are that on both of these counts there is no doubt about the wishes of a sizeable majority of the peoples of these territories to join in the Federation of Malaysia.

In reaching my conclusions I have taken account of the concern expressed with regard to political factors resulting from the constitutional status of the territories and about influences from the outside area on promotion of the proposed Federation. Giving these considerations their due weight, in relation to the responsibilities and obligations established in Article 73 and General Assembly Resolution 1541 (XV) in respect of these territories, I am satisfied that the conclusions set forth above take cognisance of, and are in accordance with, requirements set forth in the request addressed to me on 5 August 1963 by the Foreign Ministers of the Republic of Indonesia, the Federation of Malaya and the Republic of the Philippines. . . .

From the beginning of this year, I have been observing the rising tension in South-East Asia on account of differences of opinion among the countries most directly interested in the Malaysia issue. It was in the hope that some form of United Nations involvement might help to reduce tension that I agreed to respond positively to the request made by the three Manila powers. I would hope that the exercise in which my colleagues and I have been involved in this regard will have this effect, and that the coming into being of Malaysia will not prove to be a continuing source of friction and tension in the area.

The emergence of dependent territories by a process of self-determination to the status of self-government, either as independent sovereign states or as autonomous components of larger units, has always been one of the purposes of the Charter and the objectives of the United Nations.

Whatever the origins of the proposal of Malaysia may have been, it seems to me in the light of actual events, including the present exercise, that we have witnessed in Sarawak and North Borneo the same process leading to self-government. I fervently hope that the people of these territories will achieve progress and prosperity, and find their fulfilment as component states of Malaysia.

*I - show legality of U.S is illegality
of USSR*

*II legality used as justification for
action*

*III legal norms so broad that can
be interpreted freely.*

WILLIAM P. GERBERDING

International Law
and the Cuban
Missile Crisis

In the first and dominant section of this three-part study of the Cuban missile crisis, the uses which the participants made of alleged international legal norms are evaluated in terms of their plausibility and utility. The second attempts to determine what role legal considerations actually played in the decisions and actions of a major participant, the United States. Finally, some observations — growing in part out of the study of this episode — are proffered regarding the efficacy of alleged legal norms in international politics.

Because much of what follows is interpretive and analytical, it seems especially appropriate that I state at the outset at least some of my views on the missile crisis and, more generally, on the role and status of international law in international politics. If the perspectives that inform the essay are clear, some misunderstandings may be prevented. I regard President John F. Kennedy's handling of the missile crisis as one of the great successes of United States foreign policy, and do not agree with those who believe his actions were not forceful enough or with those who believe they were too bellicose. As for the legal status of the blockade (or "quarantine," as it was euphemistically called), this seems to me to be a question that is at once unanswerable in any definitive and persuasive manner and also of comparatively little significance. Therefore, as indicated above, the primary focus here is on the uses to which alleged international legal norms were put in this political-strategic confrontation.

175

Furthermore, I am convinced that international legal norms, if defined in any meaningful and substantive manner, had very little, if any, influence on the policies of the involved powers, that this is unavoidable in a confrontation perceived by the involved governments as involving the vital interests of their nations, and that — at least on the United States' side — this is the way it should be. These positions are today both common and arguable among observers of international politics, and the Cuban missile crisis presents an excellent, though admittedly not conclusive, event by which to retest and reappraise them.

I

A survey of the major pronouncements and activities of the various nations during the Cuban missile crisis might give an unsophisticated observer the impression that a lively concern for the norms of international law was a major factor in setting the character of the confrontation. According to each government's self-assessment, unswerving allegiance to the dictates of the United Nations Charter and the "well-recognized principles of international law" characterized the behavior of each participant. It is perhaps a tribute to the malleability of the Charter and the obscure nature of international law in general that most of these claims were simultaneously plausible. And it is unquestionably a tribute to the creativity and suppleness of mind of legal apologists the world over that so much learned argumentation about the legal status of the actions of the involved powers was concocted and promulgated so quickly during those tense and dramatic days.

The United States, not unexpectedly, was conspicuously concerned with wrapping its policies in the mantle of legal rectitude and with demonstrating the illegality of its adversaries' activities. A starting point to catch the flavor and quality of this latter effort is President Kennedy's first public pronouncement about the crisis. His Monday, October 22, 1962, speech on television and radio was not as weighed down by legalisms as it might have been by a less straightforward President, but they were present and they were treated with due solemnity. Early in the speech, after announcing the presence of the missile sites and describing their characteristics, President Kennedy said that "this urgent transformation of Cuba into an important strategic base . . . constitutes an explicit threat to the peace and security

legal basis for action

of all the Americas, in flagrant and deliberate defiance of the Rio Pact of 1947, the traditions of this nation and Hemisphere, the Joint Resolution of the 87th Congress, the Charter of the United Nations, and my own public warnings to the Soviets on September 4 and 13.

This rather random array of phenomena which the Soviets had allegedly defied contained at least two with apparent legal significance. The first was the Rio Pact of 1947. More formally known as the "Inter-American Treaty of Reciprocal Assistance," this document is designed — in the words of the preamble — *inter alia* "to provide for effective reciprocal assistance to meet armed attacks against any American State" and "to deal with threats of aggression against any of them. . . ." Article 6 of the treaty declares that

> . . . if the inviolability or the integrity of the territory or the sovereignty or political independence of any American State should be affected by an aggression which is not an armed attack . . . or by any other fact or situation that might endanger the peace of America, the Organ of Consultation shall meet immediately in order to agree on . . . the measures which should be taken for the common defense and for the maintenance of the peace and security of the Continent.

In the opinion of all the American states except Cuba, the Soviet installation of missile sites in Cuba certainly did constitute a "threat of aggression" and it did endanger "the peace and security of the Continent." In that sense, the charge that the Soviets had defied the Rio Pact was valid enough. But were the Soviets legally bound not to defy a treaty to which they were not signators? The point at which a multilateral agreement acquires authoritative legal status for nonsignatory states is, quite obviously, a debatable matter. But governments engaged in public pronouncements regarding alleged legal claims and charges are not likely to display either much candor or much willingness to apply their own legal criteria to their own behavior. The uses to which the alleged norms of international behavior are put are highly selective and always self-serving.

Although not using language that explicitly appealed to alleged legal norms, Adlai E. Stevenson, United States Ambassador to the United Nations, came quite close to it while discussing Western Hemispheric traditions in his opening speech to the Security Council of the United Nations on the crisis. He was endeavoring to distinguish between U.S. overseas missiles and Soviet missiles in Cuba.

For a hundred and fifty years the nations of the Americas have labored painfully to construct a hemisphere of independent and co-operating countries, free from foreign threats. An international system far older than the United Nations — the inter-American system — has been erected on this principle. The principle of the territorial integrity of the Western hemisphere has been woven into the history, the life and the thought of all the people of the Americas. In striking at that principle, the Soviet Union is striking at the strongest and most enduring strain in the policy of this hemisphere. It is disrupting the convictions and aspirations of a century and a half.[1]

If this denunciation of Soviet policy had any legal status at all, it was derived more from a very special Western Hemispheric view of the world than from any clear-cut legal "principles" or norms.

President Kennedy also charged the Soviets with "flagrant and deliberate defiance of . . . the Charter of the United Nations." This, of course, is the favorite charge on all sides in such disputes. The United Nations Charter is to international disputants what the flag and motherhood are to old-fashioned domestic political orators, i.e., something to be valued or protected above all else against the depredations of the lawless and immoral adversaries. All nations aver their unshakeable determination to adhere to the Charter, and by their own public assessments, they are all brilliantly successful. In a similar spirit, most adversaries are publicly portrayed as despicable, or at least tragically misguided, defilers of that sacred document. And so it was in the Cuban missile crisis.

As was the case regarding the reference to the Rio Pact, the President did not make clear what it was in the Charter that the Soviets had allegedly defied. A few days later, however, Ambassador Stevenson was more specific. He told the Security Council that "no twisting of logic, no distortion of words can disguise the plain, obvious and compelling commonsense conclusion that the installation of nuclear weapons by stealth, the installation of weapons of mass destruction in Cuba poses a dangerous threat to peace, a threat which contravenes paragraph 4 of Article 2 of the Charter. . . ."[2]

Paragraph 4 of Article 2 of the Charter reads as follows: "All members shall refrain in their international relations from the threat or use of force against the territorial integrity or political independence of

---

[1] United Nations, Security Council, *Official Records,* Seventeenth Year, 1022nd Meeting, October 23, 1962, New York, S/PV. 1022, p. 13. [Cited hereafter as U.N., Security Council, 1022nd Meeting, October 23, 1962, S/PV. 1022.]

[2] United Nations, Security Council, *Official Records,* Seventeenth Year, 1025th Meeting, October 25, 1962, New York, S/PV. 1025, p. 5. [Cited hereafter as U.N., Security Council, 1025th Meeting, October 25, 1962, S/PV. 1025.]

any state, or in any other manner inconsistent with the Purposes of the United Nations." It is obvious that what constitutes a "threat . . . of force" — or, more loosely, a "threat to the peace" — in any given circumstance is not subject to clear and objective determination. The United States regarded its own overseas missile sites as preservers of the peace, while the overseas Soviet missiles in Cuba were regarded as a threat to the peace. This may or may not have been a sensible view of the matter, but it goes without saying that the Soviets and many others did not see the situation that way at all. Everyone may agree that a "threat to the peace" violates the Charter, but determining what in fact constitutes a "threat to the peace" is a judgment that is bound to be heavily conditioned by political circumstances.

In the draft resolution submitted by the United States, the Security Council would have called "as a provisional measure under Article 40 for the immediate dismantling and withdrawal from Cuba of all missiles and other offensive weapons. . . ."[3] Invoking Article 40 assumes that, under Article 39, the Security Council will determine that there exists a "threat to the peace, breach of the peace, or act of aggression. . . ." Then, under Article 40, "in order to prevent an aggravation of the situation, the Security Council may . . . call upon the parties concerned to comply with such provisional measures as it deems necessary or desirable." This kind of Charter-invoking is commonplace in the United Nations and is designed, however clumsily, to put one's own position in a favorable legal light while implicitly or explicitly doing the reverse for the adversary's position. Since it is understood by all concerned that such resolutions cannot be passed in the Security Council when directed at a permanent member with the veto power, they are perhaps the most conspicuous form of legal window-dressing.

Ambassador Stevenson raised still another issue regarding Soviet behavior that is at least faintly legal in character. In what some regard as his best U.N. address, Stevenson opened the debate over the crisis with a lengthy exposition and analysis of postwar Soviet foreign policy. The core of his argument was that the United States had striven determinedly to uphold and strengthen the "principles" of the Charter — he sometimes spoke of "the world of the Charter" and "the vision of San Francisco" — while the Soviet Union was doing just the op-

---

[3] U.N., Security Council, 1022nd Meeting, October 23, 1962, S/PV. 1022, p. 16. The resolution is United Nations document S/5182.

posite. After asking rhetorically what the world would have been like in 1962 if the Soviet Union had possessed the power and position enjoyed by the United States at the end of World War II, he reviewed the Soviet performance and concluded: "The record is clear: treaties, agreements, pledges and the morals of international relations were never an obstacle to the Soviet Union under Stalin." He then referred to the de-Stalinization campaign in the Soviet Union and declared that Soviet foreign policy had not yet been affected. The United States, on the other hand, had "sought loyally to support the United Nations, to be faithful to the world of the Charter, and to build an operating system that acts, and does not just talk, for peace." The installation of long-range missiles in Cuba by the Soviet Union was merely the latest in a long line of Soviet assaults on the Charter and must be dealt with accordingly.[4]   Stevenson's position

One does not have to disagree with this interpretation of history — and I happen to agree with it — in order to see that a person's response to these allegations of Charter-violation depends upon political, and not legal, perspectives. But given the presence in the Charter of this phrase proscribing "the threat or use of force," it is virtually inevitable that in any serious showdown each side will accuse the other of threatening the use of force — or threatening the peace — and therefore violating the United Nations Charter and therefore behaving in an illegal manner.

As indicated above, the United States did not, of course, confine itself to arguing that Soviet policies were *illegal*. Even more attention was devoted to the task of showing that United States policies were *legal*; indeed, those policies were put forward as evidence that "we remain committed to the principles of the United Nations, and we intend to defend them."[5]

The Kennedy Administration had been sensitive from early in the crisis to the desirability of making the best legal case possible for its actions. The President had been told about the presence of the missiles on Tuesday, October 16. He immediately called a meeting of his top advisers, the group that subsequently became known as the Executive Committee of the National Security Council or, more familiarly, "Ex Com." This group met secretly and often during the next

[4] *Ibid.*, pp. 2–17. The quoted passages are from pp. 8, 9, and 17.
[5] *Ibid.*, p. 10. Excerpted from Ambassador Stevenson's first speech to the Security Council during the crisis.

twelve days. On Thursday, October 18, a number of alternative courses of action were still being considered and a discussion of their legal status transpired. By evening of that day, the blockade option was apparently emerging as the preferred course of action, and Attorney General Robert Kennedy instructed his deputy, Nicholas Katzenbach, to draft a brief supporting the legality of such a move.[6] The Departments of State and Defense also put their legal experts to work drafting a blockade proclamation.[7] Llewellyn Thompson, who had recently completed his service as Ambassador to the Soviet Union and was serving as a Special Adviser to the President and the Secretary of State on Soviet Affairs, reportedly argued that the Russians were "impressed by legalities" and he therefore suggested that an endorsement by the Organization of American States might be taken seriously by the Soviet leaders.[8]

Sensitivity to presumed legal considerations was also apparently instrumental in President Kennedy's adoption of the word "quarantine" as a euphemism for blockade. On Thursday, October 18, in an Ex Com meeting, Leonard C. Meeker, a State Department legal adviser, suggested for the first time that the blockade should be called a defensive quarantine.[9] And on Saturday or Sunday, the President accepted this suggestion. His reasoning was apparently a mixture of concern for legal problems associated with the word "blockade" — especially the fact that traditionally a blockade had been regarded as legitimate only after a formal declaration of war by the blockading power — and the belief that the word "quarantine" simply sounded less bellicose.[10] And it was true that the blockade was partial, applying "only" to "offensive military equipment."

When the U.S. response to the discovery of the missiles was made public, the results of these preparations for putting the best legal face

[6] Elie Abel, *The Missile Crisis* (Philadelphia and New York: J. B. Lippincott, 1966), pp. 72–73, 82.
[7] Theodore C. Sorensen, *Kennedy* (New York: Harper and Row, 1965), pp. 691–92.
[8] Abel, *op. cit.*, p. 87.
[9] *Ibid.*, p. 73.
[10] Pierre Salinger, *With Kennedy* (Garden City, N.Y.: Doubleday, 1966), pp. 258–59, wherein Sunday is named as the day on which the word "quarantine" was chosen; and Sorensen, *op. cit.*, p. 694, wherein Saturday is indicated. See also Arthur M. Schlesinger, Jr., *A Thousand Days* (Boston: Houghton Mifflin, 1965), p. 807.

on our actions were readily apparent. Again, the first and most significant manifestation was the President's speech of Monday, October 22. In listing the "initial steps" being taken he said:

Fifth: We are calling tonight for an immediate meeting of the Organ of Consultation, under the Organization of American States, to consider this threat to hemispheric security and to invoke articles six and eight of the Rio Treaty in support of all necessary action. The United Nations Charter allows for regional security arrangements — and the nations of this Hemisphere decided long ago against the military presence of outside powers. . . .

From the outset, the men associated with Ex Com who bore the responsibility of preparing the legal case were of the opinion that an OAS [Organization of American States] resolution would carry considerable legal weight. According to the most extensive and apparently credible account of the crisis by journalist Elie Abel, Katzenbach and Meeker "agreed that an OAS resolution, if it could be passed, would provide solid legal support for the blockade."[11] Accordingly, the United States asked for a meeting of the OAS Council and it was convened on Tuesday morning, October 16. By a unanimous vote that same day — except for Uruguay, whose affirmative vote was delayed one day — it was resolved, *inter alia:*

2. To recommend that the member states, in accordance with Articles 6 and 8 of the Inter-American Treaty of Reciprocal Assistance, take all measures, individually and collectively, including the use of armed force, which they may deem necessary to ensure that the Government of Cuba cannot continue to receive from the Sino-Soviet powers military material and related supplies which may threaten the peace and security of the Continent and to prevent the missiles in Cuba with offensive capability from ever becoming an active threat to the peace and security of the Continent. . . .

The references to the Rio Treaty in this operative clause of the resolution are a mere hint of the extensive citing of documents in the rest of it. In the preamble, or "Whereas" paragraphs, the Rio Treaty was quoted extensively, as were selected resolutions of the OAS. And the resolution itself stated that the Security Council of the United Nations would be informed of the passage of the resolution "in accordance with Article 54 of the Charter of the United Nations. . . ." The document was conspicuously the product of a legal office.

As for the plausibility of these claims of legality, that depends on

<hr>

[11] Abel, *op. cit.,* p. 87.

one's view of the sources and nature of international law. The Rio Treaty unquestionably sanctions what was done. Article 6 was quoted in part above, and it explicitly sanctions "measures . . . for the maintenance of the peace and security of the Continent." Article 8, also cited in the resolution, specifically authorizes the "use of armed force" as one of the measures that may be agreed to. Therefore, if the Rio Treaty was valid and if the peace and security of the Continent were endangered, then the quarantine was legal. However, those are rather large "ifs," and the reasoning was surely not accepted by all and perhaps not even most of those persons around the world with any reasonable claim to being called international lawyers, to say nothing of the many and varied governments whose policies constitute the basic realities of international polities.

It is of some interest to note that, according to the Abel account, it was not until the morning of the President's speech that Abram Chayes, the Legal Adviser of the Department of State, suggested that the President base the blockade primarily upon the right of the OAS to take collective self-defense measures and not — as the speech then had it — on Article 51 of the Charter. The reasoning behind this proposal was apparently that Article 51 — which declares that "nothing in the present Charter shall impair the inherent right of individual or collective self-defense if an armed attack occurs against a Member of the United Nations, until the Security Council has taken the measures necessary to maintain international peace and security" — should not be invoked too readily lest it afford the Soviets a precedent which they might abuse in the future.[12]

If such reasoning was in fact employed, it was of dubious quality. In the first place, the Soviet Union is hardly likely to eschew a legal argument merely because it has never been employed by some other nation. One would, therefore, have to attach an entirely unwarranted value to the presence of precedent as a determiner of the strength and/or propaganda value of a legal argument in international affairs to avoid using such a Charter provision merely because the Soviets might misuse it later on. Secondly, if precedent really were so important, then the resort to the OAS collective defense argument is at least equally as susceptible to mischievous Soviet adaptation as Article 51. The Soviet Union, after all, is a member of a regional organization also, the Warsaw Pact. And it has frequently argued, for

[12] *Ibid.,* p. 115.

example, that the presence of Western troops in Berlin is a threat to the peace in Europe. Acting under a claimed requirement of collective self-defense, and citing the American arguments of October, 1962, what would be the legal status of a new Berlin blockade designed to force the West out?

Such an action is, to be sure, unlikely. But it is at least as worrisome legally — and, of course, much more so politically and strategically — as any promiscuous use the Soviets might conceivably have made of a U.S. invocation of Article 51 during the missile crisis.[13]

The United States did not rest its legal case exclusively on the endorsing action of the OAS, of course. President Kennedy's October 22 speech also included these words: "Sixth: Under the Charter of the United Nations, we are asking tonight that an emergency meeting of the Security Council be convoked without delay to take action against this latest Soviet threat to world peace." The alleged illegality of the Soviet action was discussed above. By contrast, the United States was portrayed as loyally upholding the "principles of the Charter"; indeed, to do less would have been to renege on a legal obligation. In Ambassador Stevenson's words during his opening address to the Security Council during the crisis:

The time has come for this Council to decide whether to make a serious attempt to bring peace to the world — or to let the United Nations stand idly by while the vast plan of piecemeal aggression unfolds, conducted in the hope that no single issue will seem consequential enough to mobilize the resistance of the free peoples. For my own Government, this question is not in doubt. We remain committed to the principles of the United Nations, and we intend to defend them.[14]

One could scarcely be more "legal" than that. It surely did not escape the attention of the American government that the Security Council was bound to be ineffectual (because of the Soviet veto) so long as Soviet policy remained unchanged. Therefore, these pro-

---

[13] Sorensen's account of the deletion of Article 51 does not delve into the reasons therefor. He does, however, say that the President "carefully chose his words for anyone citing" Article 51 (p. 699). And he then quotes from the President's speech this excerpt: "We no longer live in a world where only the actual firing of weapons represents a sufficient challenge to a nation's security to constitute maximum peril. Nuclear weapons are so destructive, and ballistic missiles are so swift, that any substantially increased possibility of their use or any sudden change in their deployment may well be regarded as a definite threat to peace."

[14] U.N., Security Council, 1022nd Meeting, October 23, 1962, S/PV. 1022, p. 10.

nouncements were merely "for the record," an attempt to legitimize the blockade. When Ambassador Stevenson continued by saying that "we are engaged today in a crucial test of those principles," the implied claim about who was supporting the sacred "principles of the Charter" and who, therefore, was pursuing legal policies was unmistakably clear.[15]

Stevenson also came at least close to legal issues in the course of his attempt to distinguish between U.S. overseas missiles and the Soviet missiles in Cuba. He told the Security Council that "in 1959, eighteen months after the boasts of Chairman Khrushchev had called the world's attention to the threat of Soviet long-range missiles, the North Atlantic Treaty Organization [Note the attempt to make the decision multilateral, therefore presumably more legitimate], without concealment or deceit — as a consequence of agreements freely negotiated and publicly declared — placed intermediate-range ballistic missiles in the NATO area."[16] Later on in the same speech, he stated again that the missile sites in NATO countries were a response to Soviet missile sites directed at those countries and these NATO states "had every right and necessity to respond. . . . These missiles were designed to deter a process of expansion already in progress."[17]

So it was that "the NATO nations" were in the "right" — legally, presumably — the Soviets in the wrong, and the blockade a legitimate response to "a process of expansion."

Despite these excursions into at least implicitly legal areas, Ambassador Stevenson's remarks were remarkably skimpy on the legal side. In fact, two days after his opening speech, he alluded to this by saying that he "would gladly expand on [the legal basis of] our position . . ., but . . . perhaps this is a matter for discussion which, in view of its complexity and length, could be more fruitfully delayed to a later time."[18] Thus was the Security Council spared a lengthy legalistic treatise.

But such documents were available and already on record. On October 23, the State Department circulated a legal brief on behalf of the legality of the blockade. This elaborate analysis began by saying that "the validity of the action in international law depends on af-

[15] *Ibid.*
[16] *Ibid.*, p. 9.
[17] *Ibid.*, p. 12.
[18] U.N., Security Council, 1025th Meeting, October 25, 1962, S/PV. 1025, p. 5.

firmative answers to two questions: 1) Was the action of the Organ of Consultation [of the OAS] authorized by the Rio Treaty; and 2) Is the action consistent with the provisions of the U.N. Charter . . . ?"[19] The resoundingly affirmative answers given to these questions were, of course, foreordained. The only interesting question is whether the State Department could have produced the opposite answers with equal skill and dispatch. Presumably, the answer is "yes."[20]

---

[19] The brief is printed in Henry M. Pachter, *Collision Course* (New York: Frederick A. Praeger, 1963), pp. 167–73. The quoted material is on p. 167. Pachter comments wryly about the brief that "the best that can be said of its arguments is that no one bothered to challenge them." *Ibid.*, p. 28.

[20] The blockade and the legal arguments made in its support naturally generated a great deal of verbal and written discussion in this country focused on whether international law was adhered to or violated. The most extensive and perhaps the most prestigious analysis of the legal aspects of the crisis appeared in *The American Journal of International Law*, LVII, No. 3 (July 1963), 515–604. This issue contains three articles and three "Editorial Comments" on the legality of the quarantine. Other scholarly discussions included the following: *Proceedings of the American Society of International Law* at its 57th Annual Meeting held at Washington, D.C., April 25–27, 1963, pp. 1–18; Lyman M. Tondel, Jr. (ed.), *The Inter-American Security System and the Cuban Crisis* (Dobbs Ferry, N.Y.: Oceana Publications, 1964); *International Journal* (Toronto), Vol. XVIII, No. 1 (Winter, 1962–1963); Larman C. Wilson, "International Law and the United States Cuban Quarantine of 1962," *Journal of Inter-American Studies*, VII, No. 4 (October, 1965), 485–92; and numerous articles in law reviews and journals.

In the last article cited in this list, Wilson came (p. 492) to the following conclusion after an exhaustive study of the scholarly debate: "Mr. [Quincy] Wright stands almost alone in questioning the legality of the quarantine action. . . ."

In the *Proceedings of the American Society of International Law* cited above, Professor Wright said (p. 9) that the United States quarantine was a "unilateral, forcible action, which cannot be reconciled with [the United States's] obligation under the United Nations Charter to settle its international disputes by peaceful means and to refrain from use or threat of force in international relations (Article 2, paragraphs 3, 4), except for individual or collective self-defense against armed attack (Article 51), under authority of the United Nations (Articles 24, 39), or on invitation of the state where the force is to be used (Article 2, paragraph 1)." Then, in an astonishing display of his highly legalistic mentality, Wright — the traditionalist's traditionalist — went on to say that the last-mentioned exception "may apply in respect to Cuba, because it had consented by the Rio and O.A.S. treaties to the use of sanctioning methods against itself if recommended by the Consultative Organ of the Organization of American States." On balance, however, he found the quarantine illegal.

Earlier in his article (p. 486), Wilson made the following observations which sum up the state of the argument very well:

Expressed opinion among North American lawyers (both national and international), jurists, and law professors has been almost unanimously favorable with regard to the legality of the "quarantine" action. In addition, most allies

Turning now to the legal arguments made by other governments, it becomes even more evident that there was no shortage of skillful lawyer-polemicists. All the disputants alluded to purported legal norms and all were, needless to say, by their own standards exemplary law-abiders. They stressed their concern for their own and the world's security but they all found their pursuit of these goals entirely legal, regardless of what activities might be required. And the alleged sins and transgressions of the law by the adversary nations were duly recorded, often with great indignation and sometimes even with skill.

While the United States had concentrated its legal fireworks on the alleged "threat to the peace" implicit in the establishment of missile sites in Cuba, the Soviet Union denounced the blockade as both intrinsically illegal and also a threat to the peace. And both governments, of course, charged the other side with doing violence to the U.N. Charter. The Soviets called for a Security Council meeting to consider "the violation of the Charter of the United Nations and the threat to peace by the United States of America."[21] And in a statement attached to this request for a meeting, they referred to "these unprecedented aggressive acts" and then launched into a vigorous condemnation of U.S. policy:

Insolently flouting the international rules of conduct for States and the principles of the Charter of the United Nations, the United States has arrogated to itself — and has so announced — the right to attack the vessels of other States on the high seas: in other words, to engage in piracy. . . .

Under the Charter of the United Nations, all countries, large or small, have the right to organize their lives in their own way, to take such meas-

---

of the United States rallied to its legal justification. One major criticism and objection, however, came from a "neutral" — Sweden. The government of Sweden maintained that the blockade of Cuba was in contravention of the "generally recognized principle of the freedom of the seas." In its note to United States Ambassador Graham J. Parsons, Sweden stated that "it is a well-recognized principle of international law that a nation's warships may not in peacetime take action against foreign ships in international waters." [Here he cites Wilfrid Fleisher, "Quarantine Is Protested by Sweden," *Washington Post,* October 26, 1962.]

And (p. 487):

The scholars of international law . . . rested their case on the cardinal tenet of self-defense and the compatibility of international and regional organizations.

[21] United Nations, Security Council, *Official Records,* Seventeenth Year, Supplement for October, November and December 1962, S/5186, Letter dated October 23, 1962 from the representative of the U.S.S.R. addressed to the President of the Security Council, p. 149.

ures as they consider necessary to protect their own security, and to rebuff aggressive forces encroaching on their freedom and independence. To ignore this is to undermine the very basis of existence of the United Nations, to bring jungle law into international practice, and to engender conflicts and wars without end.[22]

statement by Russia   *   *   *

As we know, United States statesmen like to talk about their adherence to the principles of international law and to dilate upon the need for law and order in the world. But in reality they evidently consider that the laws are written not for the United States, but for other States. The institution by the United States of a virtual blockade of Cuban shores is a provocative act, an unprecedented violation of international law, a challenge to all peace-loving peoples.[23]

Thus, did the government responsible for, *inter alia*, the Berlin blockade, the Sovietization of Eastern Europe, and the military liquidation of the Hungarian Revolution raise the banner of legality in international affairs. It must be said of the Soviets, however, that their legal preachments were mere appendages to declarations about matters that presumably concerned them a good deal more. These were, of course, liberal denunciations of United States policy toward Cuba — many of them, alas, being essentially valid — and grave pronouncements about the threat of war. The United States was "recklessly playing with fire" and "taking a step towards the unleashing of a world thermonuclear war." And there were broader issues raised as well. The U.S. policy of "positions of strength" was censured, and the world was informed once again that today "there is another force in the world which is no less powerful, and which takes the position that peoples should arrange their life as they please."

The Security Council met for the first time on Tuesday, October 23, 1962, at 4 P.M. and Ambassador Stevenson was the first speaker. The Soviet Ambassador, V. A. Zorin, repeated most of the allegations from the Soviet statement just summarized, and added a few other observations in response to Stevenson's remarks. He asserted that "Mr. Stevenson said practically nothing about any political, legal or moral grounds, deriving from the United Nations Charter, for the aggressive acts which the United States Government has committed during the past twenty-four hours against the small state of Cuba. This is, of course, not accidental, since there is in fact nothing that

[22] *Ibid.*, p. 150.
[23] *Ibid.*, p. 153.

the United States Government can say in defence of its aggressive position."[24]

He noted that Stevenson "had the temerity to refer" to Article 2, paragraph 4, of the Charter — "All members shall refrain in their international relations from the threat or use of force . . ." — and, of course, construed it as prohibiting the blockade and not, as Stevenson had done earlier, as prohibiting the emplacement of Soviet missiles in Cuba.[25]

Zorin explicitly repudiated the claim that any OAS action might add a color of legality to the blockade. Involving the OAS "is openly usurping the prerogatives of the Security Council, which is the only body empowered to take coercive measures."[26]

After declaring that "no self-respecting State will permit its ships to be interfered with," Zorin added these closing flourishes:

> The United States has no right whatever, either from the point of view of the accepted rules of international law relating to freedom of shipping, or from that of the provisions of the United Nations Charter, to put forward the demands contained in the statements of President Kennedy. No state, no matter how powerful it may be, has any right to rule on the quantities or types of arms which another State considers necessary for its defence. . . .

> The Soviet Government calls on all the peoples of the world to raise their voices in defence of the United Nations, to refuse to permit the break-up of the Organization, and to oppose the policy of piracy and thermonuclear warmongering followed by the United States.[27]

In their performances at the United Nations, the representatives of Castro's Cuba have generally displayed a fascinating combination of Latin rhetorical indiscipline, sartorial "deviationism," revolutionary fervor, and Communist fanaticism. All these characteristics were conspicuous, of course, during the missile crisis, but the Cubans also showed themselves capable of engaging in legal offensives as well. And in the atmosphere of the "new" United Nations, with so many of its members newly independent, the apparent legal status of claims made by small states against the real and alleged depredations of big states is likely to be high. Cuba's acceptance of Soviet missiles may

---

[24] U.N., Security Council, 1022nd Meeting, October 23, 1962, S/PV. 1022, pp. 25–26.
[25] *Ibid.*, p. 31.
[26] *Ibid.*, pp. 33–34. The counterarguments to this were outlined above.
[27] *Ibid.*, pp. 35–36.

have shocked most states, but Cuba was, nonetheless, a small state against whom the now-blockading superpower had, only eighteen months earlier, sponsored an abortive invasion attempt.

Thus it was that the Cuban representative, Ambassador García-Inchaustegui, spoke in some detail about all the attacks and indignities for which the Cuban government held the United States government responsible, all of which alleged actions took place "without any declaration of war." Indeed, "the latter-day monarchs, in their imperialist rivalries, proved to be more respectful of international law than is the Government of the United States in this age of the United Nations and of international co-operation."[28]

The Cubans then quoted excerpts from the Convention of 1928 Concerning the Duties and Rights of States in the Event of Civil Strife, to which both Cuba and the United States are signators. The recitation of these "obligations" by the representative of a government that had been actively violating them in Latin America for some time and believed that it had an historic responsibility to do so was one of the more conspicuous and brazen manifestations of how legal norms are applied selectively and with little or no sense of either irony or contradiction.

First: to use all means at their disposal to prevent the inhabitants of their territory, national or aliens, from participating in, gathering elements, crossing the boundary or sailing from their territory for the purpose of starting or promoting civil strife.

Second: to disarm and intern every rebel force crossing their boundaries. . . .

Third: to forbid the traffic in arms and war material. . . .

Fourth: to prevent that within their jurisdiction there be equipped, armed or adapted for warlike purposes any vessel intended to operate in favor of the rebellion.[29]

He also said, and with less hypocrisy and greater prerogative, that he did not understand why it was

. . . that the United States, in its capacity as a military Power and a highly developed country, can promote, encourage and carry out all types of aggression, boycott, sabotage and acts contrary to international law, whereas Cuba, a small but valiant country, may not arm in its own defence.

102. After so flagrant a violation of law has once been sanctioned, what small country will feel secure in its sovereignty and independence? It will

[28] *Ibid.*, pp. 18–19.
[29] *Ibid.*, pp. 19–20.

be sufficient for a great Power, neighboring or otherwise, to decide that the regime of any small state is subversive or that its defences represent a threat to security, for this to constitute a pretext for intervention and for acts of war such as our country is experiencing today. At that rate, no sovereignty will be left intact and only the law of the strongest will prevail in relations between States.[30]

In these excerpts and elsewhere, the Cuban Ambassador talked much more about international legal norms than most of the other speakers; and for obvious reasons. In traditional terms, a strong case could be made for the proposition that Cuba's behavior *was* legal and that of the United States illegal. Moreover, as a small state being pressured by a superpower, Cuba shrewdly invoked the norms that emphasize the "rights" of all states as over against the privileges and presumptions of large and powerful ones. Stevenson, conversely, was forced to take the debate away from a simple invocation of allegedly clear norms and put it in the larger and only vaguely legal context of "the world of the Charter" and who — on the basis of extralegal judgments — really constituted the threat to peace.

It remained for Rumania to score what was probably the most distinct and embarrassing — to the United States — legal point of all. Cuba had remembered a 1928 Convention, but its relevance to the crisis was — as suggested above — questionable at best; and everyone else, of course, invoked the Charter to demonstrate a bewildering and contradictory variety of alleged legal norms. But Rumania had the presence of mind to remember that something called "The United Nations Conference on the Law of the Sea" had been held in 1958 and that some conventions had been adopted. For several reasons, this was from the standpoint of international law perhaps the forensic highlight of the whole debate.

During a lengthy dissertation on international law — in which, *inter alia,* he tellingly chided Great Britain for its sudden lack of concern for the freedom of the high seas — Rumanian Ambassador Mircea Malitza contended that "the Members of the United Nations which ratified the Geneva Conventions on the High Seas and thus recognized their legal force cannot witness such a clear violation of those Conventions without condemning the guilty state."[31]

---

[30] *Ibid.,* p. 20.
[31] United Nations, Security Council, *Official Records,* Seventeenth Year, 1023rd Meeting, October 24, 1962, New York, S/PV. 1023, p. 14. [Cited hereafter as U.N., Security Council, 1023rd Meeting, October 24, 1962, S/PV. 1023.]

The conference referred to had been held from February 24, 1958, through April 27, 1958. Among the items adopted was a Convention on the High Seas and it was, of course, a statement of high-minded "rules of conduct" to which all right-minded nations should certainly subscribe. Excerpts follow.

Article 27

The high seas being open to all nations, no State may validly purport to subject any part of them to its sovereignty. Freedom of the high seas is exercised under the conditions laid down by these articles and by the other rules of international law. It comprises, *inter alia:*

(1) Freedom of navigation; . . .

Article 46

1. Except where acts of interference derive from powers conferred by treaty, a warship which encounters a foreign merchant vessel on the high seas is not justified in boarding her unless there is reasonable ground for suspecting [that the ship is engaged in piracy or slave trade].[32]

If Ambassador Stevenson had responded directly to this, he presumably would have argued that the United States *was* acting under powers deriving from a treaty — the Rio Pact — and that therefore the "interference" was legal. This argument would not have been likely to receive widespread endorsement, and if it had — as stressed earlier — this would open the door to all manner of mischief in the name of the Warsaw Pact, for example, and many future alliances.

However that may be, on September 15, 1958 the United States had quickly signed the convention and it had received enough endorsements to "enter into force" on September 30, 1962, less than three weeks before President Kennedy was to decide to impose a partial blockade on Cuba. Perhaps the most ironic touch of all was that the President officially proclaimed the convention on November 9, 1962, at which time the blockade was still in effect.[33] (The blockade was terminated on November 20, 1962, by which time President Kennedy was satisfied that the Soviet ground-to-ground missiles and nuclear-weapons-carrying bombers either had been or were being removed from Cuba.)[34]

Ambassador Malitza went on to enumerate a whole host of other

[32] United Nations Conference on the Law of the Sea, *Official Records,* Vol. IV, Second Committee (High Seas: General Régime), Summary records of meetings and Annexes, Geneva, February 24–April 27, 1958, pp. 150, 152.

[33] *The Department of State Bulletin,* XXXIX, No. 1006 (October 6, 1958), 554; *ibid.,* XLVII, No. 1223 (December 3, 1962), 862.

[34] *Ibid.,* No. 1224 (December 10, 1962), p. 874.

international instruments that purportedly held, in more traditional and limited terms than the 1958 Convention on the High Seas, that "a military blockade beyond the shores of a State may not be instituted unless war has begun between the Parties to the dispute." Then, in what may have been the unkindest cut of all by this representative of a small Communist government that apparently included some superb international lawyers, he declared that

. . . military blockade is one of the forms of aggression. It has been defined as such in many international instruments; I would cite, first and foremost, the Conventions for the Definition of Aggression concluded in London in 3 July and 4 July 1933, which were recognized or made use of by many States, including the United States of America. In the statement made by the military prosecutor in the course of the Nürnberg trials, a number of allusions were made to these conventions, in which it is provided that in an international conflict "the State which is the first to commit any of the following actions shall be . . . considered as the aggressor," and one of those acts is "naval blockade of the coasts or ports of another State." [Here he cites League of Nations, *Treaty Series*, Vol. CXLVII, 1934, No. 3391, art. II.][35]

If Rumania supplied the most troublesome and scholarly legal indictment of the blockade, Bulgaria's response was perhaps the most humorous. Its representative announced in a letter to the Secretary-General that in response to the illegal threat to the peace posed by the United States and its allies, the Bulgarian government had given "instructions for raising the defence capability of the country and for putting its armed forces in a state of battle readiness."[36]

The Chinese Communist government was less inclined than most to focus much of its response on legal considerations. Could this have been because its pronouncements did not take place in the U.N. chambers, where debates often create an illusory sense that this is where the issue will be resolved and where the inducements for moral and legal posturing are so tempting? However that may be, the Chinese concentrated instead on pledges of solidarity with Cuba and threats against the imperialists. They did, however, with their usual loose regard for linguistic precision, refer to the blockade as

[35] U.N., Security Council, 1023rd Meeting, October 24, 1962, S/PV. 1023, pp. 14–15.

[36] United Nations, Security Council, *Official Records*, Seventeenth Year, Supplement for October, November and December 1962, S/5189, Letter dated October 24, 1962 from the Deputy Minister of Foreign Affairs of the People's Republic of Bulgaria, addressed to the Secretary-General, p. 156.

an "outrageous piratical action," and they asserted with admirable but presumably fleeting fidelity to traditional international law that "what weapons Cuba may have is a matter entirely within Cuba's sovereignty, with which the United States has no right whatsoever to meddle."[37]

The other participants in the debate in the Security Council offered few surprises and demonstrated little legal creativity. Secretary-General U Thant reflected an attitude that was common among neutralist representatives when he remarked that he could not "help expressing the view that some of the measures proposed or already taken, which the Council is called upon to approve, are very unusual and, I might say, even extraordinary except in wartime." He then went on to read a letter that he had sent to President Kennedy and Premier Nikita Khrushchev calling for a voluntary suspension of the quarantine and of the shipping of arms to Cuba.[38] It is therefore not absolutely clear whether his statement was aimed at the blockade alone or at both the blockade and the emplacement of missiles; but it would seem to be concerned primarily if not exclusively, with the blockade. And in vaguely legal terms.

As was the case with the governments most directly involved, the critics of the blockade stressed — besides their fears of a nuclear holocaust, of course — traditional international law doctrines regarding the freedom of navigation and selective interpretations of the U.N. Charter, while supporters stressed "the inherent right of self-defense," the OAS "legitimizing" resolution, and the alleged "threat to the peace" posed by the missiles. The representative of the United Arab Republic, for example, made a lengthy speech in which he outlined the "principles" upon which the U.A.R.'s position assertedly rested. These turned out, not unexpectedly, to be based on the Charter, resolutions from the international conferences of neutralist states held at Bandung in 1955 and Belgrade in 1961, and others such as nonintervention in internal affairs, freedom to choose one's own political system and way of life and "the right and the freedom to bring its [i.e., each each state's] defences up to the standard which will secure its political independence and territorial integrity." The U.A.R. "cannot condone" the quarantine. "This action, we believe, not only is contrary to inter-

---

[37] *Peking Review*, IV, No. 44 (November 2, 1962), 5. The quotations are from an official statement of the Chinese government.

[38] United Nations, Security Council, *Official Records*, Seventeenth Year, 1024th Meeting, October 24, 1962, New York, S/PV. 1024, p. 21. Cited hereafter as U.N., Security Council, 1024th Meeting, October 24, 1962, S/PV. 1024.

national law and the accepted norms of freedom of navigation on the high seas, but also leads to a situation which . . . is pregnant with all the symptoms of increasing world tension. . . ."[39]

It presumably did not escape the attention of many of his listeners that if the United Arab Republic's conduct vis-à-vis Israel, for example, were to be measured against these allegedly deeply held principles, it would be found to be unacceptable on nearly every count. But this kind of thing could be said of most legal posturing in the United Nations and elsewhere, with no apparent effect on the propensity of spokesmen to invoke alleged legal norms.

The representative of Chile supported the quarantine and he went to some lengths to contrast this situation from many others wherein his government had opposed the activation of the OAS security machinery. Needless to say, he found that in sanctioning the use of force this time while usually opposing it, "once again, Chile acted in perfect accord with its juridical traditions, and felt that the moment had arrived when it should contribute its cooperation to the cause of continental solidarity."[40] The reader can be forgiven if he believes that there is a good deal more truth in the second half of the just-quoted sentence than there is in the first.

The British and French governments supported the measures taken by the United States, and their statements at the United Nations reflected the essentially nonlegal sources of this support. The British representative, speaking for a nation that has long given rhetorical allegiance to the "freedom of the seas" doctrine, said that "the real point" was that the Soviet Union had affected the security of the Western Hemisphere in an intolerable way. By contrast, "the real point" was not "as has been pretended here, the right of a Government to take such measures as it may think necessary for its own defence."[41] And nowhere in the rest of his lengthy statement did he refer to anything remotely resembling legal considerations. The French representative took a similar line and took the position that the United States was clearly "striving for a peaceful solution in accordance with the principles of the Charter."[42]

The most dispassionate and straightforward statement in the whole

[39] *Ibid.*, pp. 10–14.
[40] *Ibid.*, p. 8.
[41] U.N., Security Council, 1023rd Meeting, October 24, 1962, S/PV. 1023, p. 4.
[42] U.N., Security Council, 1024th Meeting, October 24, 1962, S/PV. 1024, p. 3.

series of speeches was made by the Irish representative. He appealed for and saw some basis for negotiations; and there is not one reference to alleged legal norms in his entire address.[43]

But the Irish were the only participants to avoid such invocations. The question naturally arises, therefore, as to why almost all governments made at least some use of what they regard as "the principles of international law" during this awesome crisis. While it should be recalled that the foregoing recitation focused on legal references and that most of the rhetoric had to do with more practical matters, nonetheless the near-universality of legal argumentation is presumably indicative of something or other.

Some have contended that the legal claims and counterclaims actually affected or would affect the behavior of the governments, even those with a major stake in the confrontation. As earlier remarked, Llewellyn Thompson, for example, argued in the Ex Com that the Soviets were seriously concerned about legal questions and would be impressed by such things as an OAS sanction for a blockade of Cuba. According to one account, he even characterized the Soviet leadership as "legalistic-minded."[44] Thompson is a respected diplomat with long experience in and regarding the Soviet Union, but this view as attributed to him is of doubtful validity. It surely is true that the Soviets are as adroit as most in invoking international legal norms to support their policies and to discredit those of their adversaries, but to believe that their behavior in the crisis was affected by how they viewed the legal merits of each participant's policies stretches one's credulity too far. Moreover, if the Soviets did or do in fact have such an operational regard for international law, this would not be altogether reassuring. They almost certainly rejected the argument that the OAS sanction legitimized the blockade. Therefore, if legalities were the guide by which they fixed policy — or even if it were a substantial factor — then there would have been a higher degree of probability that they would have rejected and resisted the blockade, with unforeseeable consequences.

Another and more plausible argument to the effect that legal considerations affected national policies is that if the United States had not gone through the motions of seeking OAS support, many Latin American governments would have withheld their support for the blockade. Leaving aside the question of whether that would have

[43] U.N., Security Council, 1023rd Meeting, October 24, 1962, S/PV. 1023, pp. 15–19.

[44] Sorensen, op. cit., p. 706. See also Abel, op. cit., p. 87.

made any practical difference, this has a more plausible ring to it than the above-mentioned claim about Soviet reactions. Whatever its legal status might be, there is little room for doubt that the United States decisions to convene the Council of the OAS, acting as the Organ of Consultation under the Rio Pact, and to delay proclaiming the blockade officially until after the Latin ambassadors had sanctioned it, were politically prudent.

Finally, it should be recognized that a nation's failure to articulate a legal defense of its behavior leaves that manipulable field entirely to the adversary. In addition to being just plain scared about possible developments in the crisis and being concerned to help find a way out of it, presumably most governments — especially the genuinely uncommitted ones — were in search of some balance of equities around which they could build their own position. Legal norms express or imply values that are common to most men and most governments most of the time, at least in the abstract. "Non-interference in the internal affairs of other nations," "the right of self-defense," "discriminate use of force," "freedom of the seas": these and similar phrases have a considerable propaganda appeal because they are widely believed to be associated with fairness and decency in international relations. This condition surely goes a long way toward explaining the nearly-universal invocation of legal norms by government spokesmen in and out of the United Nations. This phenomenon might be called compensatory legalizing.

This still leaves open the question of how seriously any government took "legal constraints" on its own behavior (as distinguished from how useful to them they regarded skillful legal argumentation). Without knowing a great deal more than is now known or knowable about the motives of the involved governments, it is impossible to answer this question definitively. But it is possible to say some rather persuasive things about how seriously one government — that of the United States — took legal constraints during the crisis; and that analysis is undertaken on the assumption that few if any governments under stress and believing that their vital interests (and perhaps even survival) are at stake would treat legal norms in a much different fashion.

II

Some rather ambitious claims have been made by scholars and public officials concerning the extent to which legal norms defined United

States policy. Abram Chayes, the State Department's Legal Adviser, was in Paris when the missiles were discovered but was ordered home on Thursday evening, October 18, and was involved thereafter. About six months later, he was involved in a panel discussion at the 57th annual meeting of the American Society of International Law on the topic "Cuban Quarantine: Implications for the Future." As reported in a third-person summary of the discussion, Chayes dismissed the idea that law had nothing to do with the quarantine:

> In practice, lawyers were clearly involved in their professional capacity from the very early stages of decision-making. Legal analysis was significant, not determinative, but significant among the considerations bearing on the basic action decision. For instance, broad legal notions, such as the principle of least possible use of force, were obviously among important considerations which argued for the quarantine rather than more drastic measures. On another level, after the basic course of action was decided upon, there was a continuous and complex interplay between law and action in, for example, the content and timing of the appeal to the United Nations and the Organization of American States, the formulation and timing of the quarantine proclamation itself, the content of orders to the fleet and in notices of proposed action.[45]

If examined closely, much of this is a modest claim for the role of international law in this crisis. Each of the specifics mentioned in the last sentence quoted is tactical or, to put it another way, has to do with the way in which the basic decision — already made — was to be implemented. It may be that each one of them was in fact influenced by considerations of what international legal norms required. Whether this was really true or whether these matters were primarily or even exclusively determined in the light of prudential political desiderata is open to question. But however that may be, it is a modest claim.

The earlier part of the quotation is more troublesome, however. It is claimed that "legal analysis was significant, not determinative, but significant among the considerations bearing on the basic action decision." Then the alleged "principle" of "least possible use of force" is cited as "among important considerations which argued for the quarantine rather than more drastic measures."

The problem with this claim has to do with the status in international law of the "principle of least possible use of force." This may

---

[45] *Proceedings of the American Society of International Law* at its 57th Annual Meeting held at Washington, D.C., April 25–27, 1963, p. 11. Cited hereafter as *Proceedings*.

or may not be a principle of international law — and there presumably are lawyers who could argue persuasively for either a positive or a negative answer — but it unquestionably is sensible advice for all statesmen, especially the leaders of the two superpowers at a time when there is an increased danger of war between them. Should such prudential prescriptions as this be regarded as "legal principles"? Unless the answer is negative, then legal norms in international affairs and reduced — elevated? — to mere common-sense propositions about what constitutes prudent and civilized behavior in international politics.

Legal scholars have also made some dubious claims about the role of international law in the crisis. Covey Oliver, for example, who is an eminent professor of international law, declared in November, 1962, that the Cuban crisis " 'has been a real triumph for the lawyer and his role in decision-making.' " The manner in which he supported this claim is, because of its candor and sophistication, worth analyzing in some detail.[46]

"It is perfectly obvious to anyone who knows anything about the legal issues involved that they were carefully considered and that plans were made in this crisis with the legal situation in mind," Oliver continued. It is unclear from this sentence whether it is being asserted that the basic decision to employ a blockade or merely the subsidiary decisions about how to gain legal support for the political decision was, or were, affected by legal considerations. If it is the latter only, then the assertion is both true and of minor significance, and hardly constitutes "a real triumph for the lawyer and his role in decision-making." If it is the former, then some evidence is needed.

But none is forthcoming. Oliver notes the reports that Llewellyn Thompson alluded in the Executive Committee to the alleged Soviet concern for legal issues. But, as noted earlier, this is a dubious claim and, in any event, did not inform the basic decision to impose a blockade. And that is all the evidence that is offered. His closing remarks were as follows:

I do not understand why the latter-day Machiavellis of the power politics school of American foreign relations have never understood this obvious fact: that law is, *as used instrumentally*, an important variable in the power process, and *if used intelligently by a master*, can achieve sound

[46] As reported in Tondel (ed.), *op. cit.*, p. 55. All the immediately succeeding quotations from Oliver are *ibid*.

and desirable foreign policy results, I would say in nine cases out of ten. [Emphasis added.]

This sentence proves too much for a proponent of the view that the crisis was "a real triumph for the lawyer." The emphasized passages show clearly that all that is really being claimed is that *after* political decisions have been made, it is prudent to defer if possible to what Oliver referred to earlier in his remarks as "legal niceties." That may very well be true. It probably was wise to refer the matter to the OAS and the United Nations and to induce the regional organization to sanction the blockade, and these moves were probably influenced by the legal minds present in the Executive Committee. But whether such tactical and essentially "public relations" maneuvers constitute a "real triumph" for international law and a refutation of the judgment of the "latter-day Machiavellis" is open to doubt.

In sum, if this kind of claim is not read with considerable care, it appears to be claiming — and to be supporting the claim — that international law affected the basic policy decisions of the United States, i.e., that the decision to blockade Cuba and the decision to withhold conditionally the use of additional force were to an important degree shaped by legal considerations. In fact, however, this is not explicitly claimed and it is surely not supported by evidence.[47]

Leaving aside what has been or has not been claimed about the role of international law, it is time to confront the following question independently: Were President Kennedy or any of his important policy advisers consciously applying legal criteria or "principles" as they worked their way toward the decision to blockade Cuba?

There are three rather authoritative versions of what happened at the highest levels of government during those tense days: the books by Abel, Schlesinger, and Sorenson. The last two were "insiders" who saw and heard much of what they relate; Abel is a responsible journalist who researched his account carefully and interviewed most of

---

[47] In another and less guarded moment, Covey Oliver has written that in the famous November 3, 1962, *New York Times* account of the crisis, "the legal environment had been mentioned as a take-off point in the planning of the response." "International Law and the Quarantine of Cuba: A Hopeful Prescription for Legal Writing," *The American Journal of International Law,* LVII, No. 2 (April, 1963), 374.

There are two things wrong with this statement. In the first place, the *New York Times* account does not say anything remotely resembling what is attributed to it by him, and in the second, as will be argued below, neither does any other authoritative evidence.

the President's closest advisers. On the basis of their evidence, the answer to the above question is an emphatic "no."

Schlesinger describes how, in the early phases of the discussions, there seemed to be only two alternatives: to acquiesce in the presence of the missiles or to launch an air strike against the missile sites. He then sets forth the arguments used against the air strike that encouraged a search for alternatives, and not one of them was even remotely legal in character.[48]

Sorensen's account first relates in a preliminary way the questions that were being asked during that first week and none of them were legal in character.[49] Then ten pages of the book are given over to an extended recounting of how the alternatives were considered and evaluated by the Executive Committee. Only twice, and briefly, are legal considerations alluded to at all. The first time is a fleeting reference to the fact that consideration was given to the desirability of declaring war against Cuba "as a means of building both Allied support and a legal basis for the blockade, but deemed not essential to either."[50] The second reference was equally summary. And the next paragraph makes it unmistakably clear how tangential and inconclusive such considerations were by opening as follows: "But the greatest single drawback to the blockade, in comparison with the air strike, was time."[51]

Sorensen implicitly gives the game away in a later section. He starts with his best legal foot forward by asserting that the quarantine — he candidly puts the word in quotation marks — was "a new form of reprisal under international law, an act of national and collective self-defense against an act of aggression under the UN and OAS charters and under the Rio Treaty of 1947. Its legality, much strengthened by the OAS endorsement, had been carefully worked out."[52] Its legality was, in other words, "carefully worked out" *after* the basic decisions were made; it was merely tactical, prudential. There is no hint here that the blockade was *questioned* on legal grounds; it was merely *buttressed* by the best legal arguments available.

[48] Schlesinger, *op. cit.*, p. 804. It is relevant to note that the arguments put forward against the blockade by air-strike advocates were also devoid of legal elements. *Ibid.*, p. 805.
[49] Sorensen, *op. cit.*, p. 680.
[50] *Ibid.*, p. 682.
[51] *Ibid.*, p. 687.
[52] *Ibid.*, pp. 707–708.

[handwritten margin note: specific blockade — new norm of international law — no declaration of war — OAS determine threat to peace — regional. —]

Abel's account further supports this view of the role of legal considerations in the minds of the members of the Executive Committee. On Thursday, October 18, the problem of legality was explicitly discussed. Abel reports on the positions of three participants. Former Secretary of State Dean Acheson reportedly took the position that "legal niceties were so much pompous foolishness in a situation where the essential security of the United States, its prestige, its pledged word to defend the Americas, was threatened." Undersecretary of State George Ball "argued that a naval blockade, though traditionally regarded as an act of war, would have more 'color of legality.'" And Abram Chayes' deputy, Leonard C. Meeker, "presented a legal analysis suggesting, for the first time, that the blockade might better be called a defensive quarantine."[53]

This scene certainly has its humorous side, and one can select which of these three positions best reflects his own tastes. But the accounts hardly give the impression that anyone was very concerned about legal matters. The purely expediential role of law is perhaps best illustrated by the fact that, as recounted above, on Thursday evening, Attorney General Robert F. Kennedy called his deputy "and asked him to get started on a brief establishing the legal basis for a blockade of Cuba."[54]

It is sometimes hinted that the Attorney General invoked legal norms in his now-famous and apparently influential argument against an air strike.[55] Covey Oliver, for example, has written that "it may be that the Attorney General . . . was as 'legal' as he was 'moral' in reported opposition to an air strike."[56] For better or for worse, the available records do not support this hypothesis. A *Saturday Evening Post* article cited by Oliver has only the following reference to this episode: "[Robert Kennedy] argued passionately that an air strike against Cuba would be a Pearl Harbor in reverse and contrary to all American traditions."[57] Only if one is willing to define "American tra-

[53] Abel, *op. cit.*, pp. 72–73.
[54] *Ibid.*, p. 82.
[55] In Abel's account (p. 64), which is perhaps too popularized, the Attorney General is reported to have "said passionately: 'My brother is not going to be the Tojo of the 1960's.'"
[56] Oliver, *The American Journal of International Law*, LVII, No. 2 (April, 1963), 374.
[57] Stewart Alsop and Charles Bartlett, "In Time of Crisis," *The Saturday Evening Post*, CCXXXVI, No. 44 (December 8, 1962), 20.

ditions" as an element of international law is it possible to construe this as an invocation of such law.

Nor do the other authoritative accounts support the contention that the President's brother and intimate confidant was swayed by legal considerations. Schlesinger, for example, represents the Attorney General as being concerned about "the responsibility we would have to bear in the world afterward" and "a betrayal of our heritage and our ideals," but nothing is said about international legal norms.[58]

In the final analysis, the most important evidence regarding how much or how little legal reasoning went into the basic decisions must, of course, relate to the President himself. And any such inquiry should take place against the background of an understanding of the fact that President Kennedy was not only not a lawyer, but that he was, like most Presidents, a politician and a man preoccupied with very earthy, practical matters such as national security and international peace.

There is, however, one small piece of evidence to support the proposition that President Kennedy did attach some weight to legal norms in his basic decisions. Schlesinger records that on Thursday evening, October 18, the President was "evidently attracted by the idea of the blockade." He goes on to give many reasons for this, including this one: "It could be carried out within the framework of the Organization of American States and the Rio Treaty."[59] *legality of Kennedy*

It could be, of course, that this reconstruction of the President's thinking is not altogether accurate. Or it could be that President Kennedy's reference to the OAS and the Rio Pact was casual comment, reflecting his retention of some other person's rationale. But even if the account is accurate and the President did take the matter seriously, we are still left with the question of whether he mentioned these things merely because of their utility as legal props for a policy determined entirely on other, nonlegal grounds; or whether he meant that the OAS and the Rio Pact legitimized *and therefore made possible* the blockade.

All the evidence points to the former interpretation. Nowhere else in the accounts is he represented as having legal concerns. In his

---

[58] Schlesinger, *op. cit.*, pp. 806–807. See also Sorensen, *op. cit.*, p. 684; and Abel, *op. cit.*, pp. 64, 88.
[59] Schlesinger, *op. cit.*, pp. 805–806.

summary analysis of the President's motives and performance, Schlesinger makes no mention of international law.[60] Nor does Sorensen represent the President as being concerned about legal matters during the crisis.[61] And on the day of his television address, October 22, President Kennedy gave his press secretary a detailed "backgrounder" on why the blockade was being imposed, and he did not allude to legal considerations.[62]

But the most important piece of evidence on this question is the fact that the President was determined to impose the blockade regardless of whether the OAS sanctioned such a move. This is clear both explicitly and implicitly from the evidence available. Sorenson, who should know, states flatly that the blockade would have been instituted without OAS approval "because our national security was directly involved."[63] And this merely makes explicit what was implicit in the fact that the President's October 22 speech announced unequivocally that the blockade was being initiated and this, of course, was before the OAS ministers had met.

In conclusion, it is instructive to note that President Kennedy's attitude toward international legal norms was stated with candor at his first news conference after the crisis on November 20, 1962. He was asked if he would "clear up . . . our relationship with the United Nations. . . ." Could we invade Cuba or take "unilateral action in any way" against Cuba without the approval of the United Nations? The President's awkward, honest, and sensible reply deserves to be quoted in full:

Well, I don't think a question — you would have to give me a much more detailed hypothetical question before I could consider answering it, and even under those conditions it might not be wise. Obviously, the United States, let us take a hypothetical case, which is always better. The United States has the means as a sovereign power to defend itself, and of course exercises that power. It has in the past and it would in the future. We would hope to exercise it in a way consistent with our treaty obligations, including the United Nations Charter. But we of course keep to ourselves and hold to ourselves under the United States Constitution and under the laws of international law, the right to defend our security, on our own, if necessary, though we hope to always move in concert with our al-

[60] *Ibid.*, pp. 840–41.
[61] Sorensen, *op. cit.*, p. 694.
[62] Salinger, *op. cit.*, pp. 262–63.
[63] Sorensen, *op. cit.*, p. 699. See also Salinger, *op. cit.*, p. 259.

lies, but on our own if that situation was necessary to protect our survival, or integrity, or other vital interests.

III

A few words remain to be said about what role international law could conceivably play in crisis situations such as this one. It has already been acknowledged that after the basic decision was made to apply a partial blockade against Cuba, the United States did seek to adhere strictly to its treaty obligations in other and more procedural matters. It did convene the OAS and it called for a meeting of the Security Council and it developed elaborate legal defenses for what it was determined to do. But can and/or should international legal norms play a less subsidiary, more guiding role in such confrontations? How that question should be answered depends on many factors, but among the more important is the degree to which clarity and political relevance can be said to characterize such norms.

One way of approaching this issue is to analyze the arguments put forward by the primary legal spokesman for the United States government at the time of the crisis. Since these arguments have had the overwhelming endorsement of American international law specialists, they carry both an official and a more independent authority. They tell us a good deal about the issue of clarity and relevance.

Abram Chayes was not an international lawyer by training. The fact that a law professor whose specialty was *not* international law was serving as the Department's Legal Adviser is in itself interesting and may suggest something about the seriousness with which legal matters tend to be taken by United States governments. However that may be, Chayes often described himself as "a common lawyer" and he frequently spoke in terms of how international law should be understood in as vital and malleable a manner as common law. His most extensive defense of the legality of the blockade is contained in a speech he made on November 3, 1962, before the Harvard Law School Class of 1962.[64]

The structure of his argument was designed, as might be expected, to support a permissive interpretation of international legal norms. As he remarked some months after the crisis, the question "Was the quarantine legal?" is the kind of question "bound to elicit over-gen-

[64] The speech is reproduced in the *Department of State Bulletin*, XLVII, No. 1221 (November 19, 1962), 763–65.

eralized and useless answers. The object of a first-year law school education is to teach students not to ask such questions."[65] This is very much like saying — and nothing that Chayes has written on the subject contradicts this conclusion — that the question of legality regarding behavior in international affairs is at best cloudy and controversial, and at worst a nonsense question.

In the aforementioned November, 1962, speech, he argued that international realities have changed since the 19th century and that the Soviet challenge in Cuba and the United States's response should be judged in terms of the realities of the 1960's, not those of an earlier period. New conditions, he implied, require new law.

He then went on to argue that the Rio Treaty was adhered to and that such actions by regional organizations "to keep the peace" are consistent with the United Nations Charter. He noted that Article 52 prescribes the use of "regional arrangements or agencies for dealing with such matters relating to the maintenance of international peace and security as are appropriate for regional action. . . ."

He then launched into one of those artful arguments that, like so much of the writing about international law, applies satisfactorily enough when applied to one's own side but becomes uncomfortable if its utility is considered in the hands of an adversary. He began by acknowledging that the activities of regional organizations must be, in the words of Article 52, "consistent with the Purposes and Principles of the United Nations." And he further noted that Article 2 of the Charter commits all members to "refrain in their international relations from the threat or use of force against the territorial or political independence of any state, or in any other manner inconsistent with the Purposes of the United Nations."

But, he argued, "the promise not to use force is not absolute." He then cited, of course, "the inherent right of individual or collective self-defense if an armed attack occurs" of Article 51. However, he went on, there are *other* grounds for legitimizing the use of force beyond self-defense and he reminded his audience of the fact, noted earlier, that Article 51 was not in fact invoked by the United States. So, we approach the clinching subtlety, which follows in his own words:

Obviously, the United Nations itself could sanction the use of force to deal with a threat to the peace. So it did in Korea and in the Congo. We ac-

---

[65] *Proceedings,* p. 11.

cept use of force in these instances as legitimate for two reasons. First, all the members have constituted the United Nations for these purposes. In signing the charter they have assented to its powers and procedures. Second, the political processes by which the U.N. makes a decision to use force give some assurance that the decision will not be rashly taken.

I submit that the same two factors legitimize use of force in accordance with the OAS resolution dealing with a threat to the peace in the hemisphere. The significance of assent is attested by the fact that, though Cuba is now and has been for some time the object of sanctions and hostility from the OAS and has been suspended from participation in its agencies, she has remained a party to the treaties and a member of the inter-American system. . . . The significance of the political processes in the Organization is attested by the fact that, despite the disproportion of power between the United States and its neighbors to the south, it was not until the danger was clear and present that the necessary majority could be mustered to sanction use of armed force. But when that time came, the vote was unanimous.[66]

Both elements of this ingenious argument are open to serious criticism. In the first place, it is a gross oversimplification — to the point of being false — to state that by signing the U.N. Charter, member states "have assented to its powers and procedures." Even the most cursory examination of the history of the United Nations makes it very clear that these "powers and procedures" are constantly in dispute and that assent and dissent vie for prominence in specific instances. But even if this were not the case, the further argument that Cuba in effect assented to the blockade because she was technically still a member of a regional organization that sanctioned it is so bizarre as to require no refutation. Only a painfully literalist, traditional international lawyer[67] or a government apologist with at least a temporarily legalistic and narrow cast of mind could make such an argument.

But these problems are really minor alongside those implicit in the second "factor" mentioned, namely, the "significance of the political processes" employed by the OAS. The implication of this position is that *any* regional organization can, providing its political processes "give some assurance that the decision will not be rashly taken," sanction the use of force "to deal with a threat to the peace." At the risk of becoming monotonous, it suffices to point out once again that the Warsaw Pact powers, for example, might find this bit of mental gym-

[66] *Department of State Bulletin,* XLVII, No. 1221, 764–65.
[67] See, as an example, Quincy Wright's treatment of this argument, as set forth in footnote 20 above.

nastics on behalf of legal sanctions to be handy with their "Berlin problem."

The OAS approval of the blockade may have been "legal" in some sense or other — and it was assuredly wise and sensible — but the official State Department apologia leaves a good deal to be desired.

The quality of the argument does not improve as the speech lengthens.

I suppose that in the original conception of the United Nations, it was thought that the Security Council would be the agency for dealing with situations of this kind. However, the drafters of the charter demonstrated their wisdom by making Security Council responsibility for dealing with threats to the peace "primary" and not "exclusive." For events since 1945 have demonstrated that the Security Council, like our own electoral college, was not a viable institution. The veto has made it substantially useless in keeping the peace.[68]

It will come as a surprise to students of American government to learn that the electoral college is "not a viable institution." It is clumsy and perhaps undesirable, but it lives, albeit admittedly not playing precisely the role the founding fathers envisaged for it. But a much worse flaw in the reasoning quoted above is the alleged impotence of the Security Council. Chayes earlier made reference to two instances wherein the United Nations had sanctioned the use of force to deal with a threat to the peace, i.e., Korea and the Congo. In both of these instances, it was the Security Council that did the sanctioning.

Admittedly, the Security Council could not conceivably have authorized action against the Soviets in Cuba. But this does not justify the use of easily controverted generalizations in order to strengthen an argument for taking an expansive view of the meaning of the Charter.

He then resorted to one of the most beguiling of all analogies, that between the United States Constitution and the United Nations Charter.

You will not have failed to see that the legal defense of the quarantine I have outlined reflects what I would call an American constitutional lawyer's approach to international law.

There is normative content in the system: "Congress shall make no law . . . abridging the freedom of speech, or of the press . . ."; "Member States

---

[68] *Department of State Bulletin*, XLVII, No. 1221, 765.

shall refrain in their international relations from the threat or use of force."
But it recognizes that norms, to be durable, must be subject to growth and
development as circumstances change.[69]

Here are the key words: "growth and development." Others, more
cynical, might say that freely translated they mean "Anything goes."
The analogy with American constitutional development is as untenable and misleading as it is beguiling. This is not the place to go into
the matter in detail, but a couple of central propositions can be
stated: The development of constitutional law, unlike international
law, takes place within an institutional environment and through reg-
ularized procedures that are characteristics of a settled, orderly, sovereign nation. Laws derive from widely understood and legitimate
institutions; they have the support of a relatively cohesive, self-con-
scious entity called a national society; and they are enforced. None
of these things can be said about either traditional international law
or the latest versions of the "growth and development" school.

Presumably, Chayes was aware of the shaky foundations of his defense and was merely playing the role of a loyal administration spokesman. However that may be, his elaborate and often self-defeating
defense of the legality of the blockade points to the central facts about
international law in international politics, namely, its amorphousness
and its irrelevance to important political matters. It follows from the
expediential character of most of the governmental pronouncements
and even scholarly discourses on the blockade, from the susceptibility
of documents and alleged "norms" and "principles" to almost any interpretation, and from the absence of authoritative and legitimate institutions to create, interpret, and enforce the "law" that it can be and
is used in whatever manner governments choose to use it. It does not
have a valid life of its own; it is a mere instrument, available to political leaders for their own ends, be they good or evil, peaceful or aggressive.

International law is, in sum, a tool and not a guide to action.
Chayes once admonished a group of international lawyers to "avoid
the temptation to deal with very different political and moral issues
as though they could be resolved by rather simple and very general

[69] *Ibid.* Chayes is especially fond of this largely specious analogy. He came
back to it in an otherwise more creditable article entitled "A Common Lawyer
Looks at International Law," *Harvard Law Review,* LXXVIII, No. 7 (May,
1965), 1410.

legal imperatives."[70] He went on to declare that the "content and meaning" of the United Nations Charter "are built up by accumulating experience, by developing public attitudes, and by the action of political bodies and other organs charged with the vindication of the norms."[71] The reader can be excused if he fails to see any difference between this candid formulation of "the sociological school" of international legal thought and the proposition that international legal norms are whatever a government says they are.

Chayes concluded the November speech by acknowledging the dangers in this "growth and development" view and called for "professional vigilance so that law is not corrupted by *raison d'état*."[72] But, given the amorphous character of international law, can or should governments or lawyers or anyone else really summon up more concern for it than for "reasons of state"? Skilled legal advocates and apologists never face this problem, because for every "reason of state" they can find or create a corresponding international legal norm. But surely this merely reconfirms the irrelevance of international law in major political disputes. Since it can mean nearly anything, it means almost nothing.

The Cuban missile crisis induced some brilliant statesmanship which was motivated — and should have been motivated — by political and strategic considerations, not by amorphous and largely irrelevant international legal norms.

---

[70] *Proceedings,* p. 12.
[71] *Ibid.,* p. 13.
[72] *Department of State Bulletin,* XLVII, No. 1221, 765.

DAVID WILKINSON

The Article 17 Crisis:
The Dispute over
Financing the United Nations

This is a study of the manner in which three states — the United States, the Soviet Union, and France — used the shapeless body of principles and alleged principles of international law in order to advance their opposed interests in a certain dispute. The dispute was over the issue of whether the Soviet Union and France were to pay for operations of the United Nations which frustrated them and pleased the United States.

The object of this essay is to describe the controversy, to narrate the legal arguments which these states used to justify their policies and decisions, to explain the tactical effects of the legal arguments they chose, and to evaluate the utility of these choices in advancing the self-defined interests of these states.

The study falls into a natural order. The precipitating events — the Congo crisis and U.N. intervention therein — are briefly examined, and provide a background explaining the conflicting interests of the three states in the controversy over financing that intervention. The alleged international legal norms round which the debate raged are set forth, and the debate examined at length. There were changes in the arguments and pressures each side employed, which are noted and interpreted. This noting and interpreting accounts for the main body of the work, and is taken from the start of the argument in 1960 down to the collapse of the American position in 1965. The study concludes with a brief reflection on the significance of the U.N. financing case for understanding the general role of international law in world politics.

The Belgian Congo became independent on June 30, 1960. Riots swiftly broke out; the army mutinied. In the spreading disorder, Belgian nationals were attacked, and Belgium flew in troops. President Joseph Kasavubu and Premier Patrice Lumumba of the Congo asked the United Nations to send troops to expel the Belgians and to restore order. The premier of Katanga province, Moise Tshombe, then announced his secession from the Congo and asked Belgian aid. The U.N. Security Council authorized Secretary-General Dag Hammarskjöld to provide the Congolese government with military assistance for the preservation of order. U.N. troops entered the Congo in mid-July, and the Belgians began to withdraw by agreement.

The Congolese affair, however, had hardly begun, and U.N. troops were not to depart until June, 1964. The internal conflicts in the Congo were seized on by external forces. The Soviet Union and Kwame Nkrumah's Ghana became sponsors of Premier Lumumba; Belgium, more or less involuntarily, was associated with Tshombe, and France defended Belgium's conduct. The United States, making no commitments to personalities, and interested primarily in a speedy end to the situation, gravitated toward lukewarm support of any elements in the Central government of the Congo which seemed (at a given moment) less hostile to the West than Lumumba, and more capable of restoring some order and consensus in the Congo. On September 5, President Kasavubu undertook to dismiss Premier Lumumba from office; the Premier likewise deposed the President; neither was able to enforce his will by force. In the confusion, Colonel (later General) Joseph Mobutu, Chief of Staff, announced the army's temporary seizure of power. The U.N. force on the scene declined to aid any of these parties actively, but took several measures to restrict violence which had the effect of hurting the cause of Lumumba, who was repeatedly arrested and finally murdered. Antoine Gizenga inherited Lumumba's cause and external allies, and set up a rival government in Oriental province. After some two years of alternate negotiation and fighting, the U.N. troops forcibly terminated the secession of Katanga; meanwhile, in one of the intervals of the Katangan drama, the U.N. and Central government troops arrested Gizenga. Despite continuing internal disorders and confusion, the U.N. role in the Congo was ultimately much more satisfactory to the United States than to the Soviet Union or to De Gaulle's France.

Indeed, this was so almost from the beginning of the operation. France at this time was concerned to defend the record of colonialism, which the U.N. majority of the period was inclined to denounce. The U.N. operation was itself an implicit criticism of the Belgian landing of troops, and many members who supported the operation took pains to flay Belgium at every turn. France rejected these attacks. Though De Gaulle permitted the U.N. force to exist and act (by refraining from casting the French veto against the original Security Council resolution), and though the French delegate supported the sending of U.N. troops to replace the Belgians, France resented all slurs on Belgium. Therefore, because the initial Security Council resolution proposed by Tunisia supposedly constituted a condemnation of Belgium (by calling on her to withdraw her troops), France declined to support it, and instead abstained. As ONUC[1] developed, France maintained a cool and skeptical distance from it, at times supporting without enthusiasm (Security Council resolution of July 22), at times hostile or obstructive; at no time did the French assume or feel responsibility for the U.N. efforts, which at best represented in Gallic eyes "undue alarm."

The Soviet Union took a more active interest in the imbroglio. It voted for the original Security Council resolution of July 13, 1960, not because it supported the creation of a U.N. force, but because it sensed and approved an implicit condemnation of Belgium. The Russian delegate, Sobolev, made clear the Soviet position: the Belgian landings were "armed aggression"; the Belgian plot had been supported by the United States; the Belgians ought to be condemned and ordered to withdraw immediately. The U.S.S.R. was able to vote for the resolution of July 22 which called on Belgians to withdraw "immediately." But when Secretary-General Hammarskjöld sought (August, 1960) to make arrangements with Tshombe to prevent a violent clash between U.N. and Katangan troops, and declined (on the strength of provisions in the Council resolutions forbidding ONUC to intervene in internal Congolese politics) to use U.N. forces to compel the Katangese government to accept the authority of the Central government, Lumumba denounced the Secretary-General and sought

---

[1] The French acronym for "U.N. Operation in the Congo."

other (including Soviet) assistance. Soviet influence rapidly began to penetrate the Congo; thus when ONUC's activities during the Kasavubu-Lumumba quarrel worked to the disadvantage of Lumumba,[2] the U.S.S.R. vetoed a Security Council resolution supporting the Secretary-General and calling on "all countries" to supply no military aid to the Congo outside the U.N. framework. The matter then being taken up by the Assembly, Russia declined to support a resolution (September 20) supporting Hammarskjöld, and went further into opposition after the death of Lumumba by demanding the dismissal of Hammarskjöld, the withdrawal of ONUC, and sanctions against Belgium. From this point, the Soviet Union was alienated from, and remained irrelevant to, the U.N. operation in the Congo.

The United States found itself mostly able to agree with and sometimes to lead the majorities in Council and Assembly, the Secretary-General, the U.N. Command, and the post-Lumumba Central government. To no other major power was ONUC so acceptable and (since the restoration of order not coincidentally restricted Soviet influence in the Congo) so useful. America supported ONUC verbally and materially.

Since it had not served their interests, the Soviet Union and France declined to contribute to the financial support of ONUC, as did certain other states. Many states which were less than content with the U.N. operation in the Congo nevertheless virtually consented to help finance it, out of support for the U.N. as such, or for U.S. policy in general. (Thus Britain, as discontented as France, joined the United States and Canada as a leading financier.) ONUC was at first routinely budgeted with other expenses and each U.N. member assessed, not a share of ONUC expenses, but a share of total U.N. expenses. Thus no state was explicitly presented with a bill for its share of the U.N. operation in the Congo. Both ex-imperial states (which disapproved of certain anti-Belgian tendencies of U.N. resolutions and of the public statements of persons in various degrees associated with ONUC) and extremely anti-colonial ex-colonies (which generally had fraternal feelings for Lumumba) could thereby contribute to ONUC without giving scandal to themselves or their publics, if they chose to see the principle at issue as one of paying or not paying their U.N.

---

[2] ONUC closed the air fields of the Congo, after the U.S.S.R. had supplied Lumumba with air transport to be used to send troops to Katanga.

bills in the manner to which they had become habituated. Paying was thereby made easier for such states, since it was necessary for them to take the initiative of discriminating their share of the ONUC expenses from their share of other expenses if they cared to make an issue of the legal status of ONUC expenses. Among those which took such pains were France and the Soviet Union.

Refusal of a U.N. member to pay for a U.N. activity that did not suit it was not unprecedented. In particular, in the case of the United Nations Emergency Force (UNEF) in the Gaza strip, which was arranged in 1956 to separate the military forces of Egypt and Israel in the aftermath of the Suez-Sinai crisis, the Soviet Union declared that it would not consider itself bound to pay any UNEF obligations. Its grounds were that UNEF was created to halt aggression by the United Kingdom, France, and Israel against Egypt, and that to relieve these states of the material responsibility for maintaining these forces would be tantamount to encouraging aggression.[3] This position was taken by the Arab states as well. Nevertheless, the Secretariat continued to assess these states in accordance with the decision of the majority of the General Assembly. They continued to decline to pay. Considerable arrears had already been reckoned against them, therefore, by the time of the events in the Congo.

But the practical consequences of the payment refusals for the financial position of the United Nations had no precedents. The Congo operation was strikingly expensive; thus, while UNEF expenditures for 1961 were estimated at $1.5 million per month and the normal budgetary disbursements of the U.N. (excluding UNEF and ONUC) at $5 million per month, those for ONUC were estimated at $10 million per month. The Secretary-General delivered the first of a series of increasingly disturbing reports on the general financial condition of the Organization in November, 1960, when he estimated that, with arrears of contributions totalling approximately $31 million, the Organization would begin fiscal 1961 with "a virtually empty treasury."[4] Since the arrears were never paid, the financial crisis was chronic; since ONUC continued to eat up funds into 1964, the crisis became more and more painful year by year. By 1964, for instance, the total arrears of the Soviet Union amounted to more than half of

[3] Plenary, 596 (i.e., United Nations, General Assembly, *Official Records, 596th meeting*).
[4] V:796 (i.e., United Nations, General Assembly, *Official Records, Fifth Committee, 796th meeting*).

the annual operating budget of the United Nations as a whole. On more than one occasion, the equivalent of bankruptcy seemed to face the international body, leading to more or less desperate appeals by the Secretary-General and to expedient palliatives (primarily financed by the United States and its friends) which relieved the short-run but not the long-run problem. This period cannot be fully understood unless the constant if subdued frenzy of those international civil servants responsible for keeping the Organization afloat, and those foreign officers (Americans above all) most certain that the activities of the United Nations were especially beneficial to their states' interests, is kept in mind. Such persons, whatever their positions regarding the Soviet, French and other arrears — and they generally deplored, at least, the withholding of funds by these states — were unable to avoid the fear that if matters were not delicately handled, the Organization — to which they were not seldom attached by ties stronger than those of career or *raison d'état* alone — might not survive at all. They were therefore as much — and, finally, more — concerned with getting funds from any likely source as they were with squeezing them out of the wallets of the delinquent nations.

The decisions of all states throughout this crisis were shaped by the broadest considerations of the utility of the United Nations to their foreign policies, as well as by the more immediate question of their attitudes toward the activities of the United Nations in the Congo. Three states are of major interest in this connection as having both the leading roles in the financing crisis and, perhaps, the best articulated general lines of policy toward the United Nations: the chief delinquents, Russia and France; and their chief pursuer, the United States.

The lines of all these powers were influenced by the fact that, culminating in 1960, the United Nations had undergone a "membership explosion." A great number of small, weak, European-ruled colonial territories in the Southern Hemisphere had gained independence and joined the world organization. These states had no particular initial interest in the struggle between "East" and "West," or Soviet-led and American-led blocs, which had dominated world politics, and U.N. politics as well, for a decade, and which had seen the "West," by virtue of superior numbers, dominating the Assembly when it chose to.

For the United States, the threatened political effect of the "membership explosion" was a loss in its dominant or at worst its leading role. For the Soviet Union, the new states represented an opportunity

— if it could only compromise with and influence them sufficiently — to break the grip of its great foe on an international institution in which America had invested much time, hope, love, and cash. The Congo issue was the first major test of skill between the two states in the changed U.N. arena. The United States was successful, the Soviets were deeply frustrated; this outcome was reflected throughout 1961 by bitter Soviet denunciations of the Secretary-General and the structure of the institution, and by more than two years of laudatory speeches from President John F. Kennedy and Ambassador Adlai Stevenson, in which such phrases as "last best hope of peace" were consistently applied to the United Nations to indicate satisfaction and a high good humor. After the Congo decisions, however, the will or the skill of the Americans began to diminish; the new majority showed itself less open to manipulation, more prone on cold-war issues to slip and slide into an "independent," i.e., compromising or noncommittal or vacillating position between the two great states, unwilling to do anything seriously displeasing to one for the benefit of the other. This alignment marked the financing crisis as much as the earlier alignment had marked its prelude. Correspondingly, American enthusiasms tapered off or became more formal and reserved, while Soviet anger was at first silenced. It was then replaced by an optimism even more reserved than the American — for if the Westerners could no longer rely on the Organization to serve their interests, the Russians had never been able to do so and still could not.

French policy toward the United Nations, as all Gallic policy in these years, can hardly be explained without reference to the special animus of Charles de Gaulle. In this man, ego was merged with his political theory: both demanded independence, and even more the appearance of independence, of any leadership from a foreign state stronger than De Gaulle's own, while sardonically contemning all similar manifestations, except such as served his needs of the moment, on the part of lesser nations. He chafed under an American bit, an alliance he had inherited from the regime he replaced; and slowly and conspicuously he worked loose of it, creating a series of dramatized happenings, generally of less material effect than was advertised, which first gave, and then repeated, the impression of a break for freedom. He gradually approached the detached and ineffectual position of the new states. But he could not join them as an equal; his France he deemed a great power, they were scarcely nations at all, mere ex-colonies, often of the great metropolitan power France. Still, in the later years of the financial crisis he did not again treat them to the public contempt with which he had repaid the new anti-colonial majority for its attempts to intervene in France's war against the revolt of the Algerians; and once he had liquidated that war and most of France's colonial empire, he had no grounds to detest or to seek the destruction of the United Nations, though no grounds for loving it either.

Thus in the first years of the financing crisis, the United States was warmly concerned with maintaining the status and role of the United Nations, while as time wore on its fervor waned; and the French and the Soviets moved from angry retaliation to cool tolerance. This changing political climate explains the changing aims of the legal arguments of these states, as well as their changing behavior in the crisis; to these changes, the norms they invoked were supplely tailored.

In accordance with its previous stand on UNEF, the Soviet Union and its East European satellite states early declined to pay any of their assessments for the U.N. Operations in the Congo. Belgium, in the Soviets' eyes, was chiefly responsible for the emergency situation in the Congo; the Belgians should pay the costs, and the Soviet government would pay nothing. On October 21, 1960, Nacvalac, the Czech representative on the General Assembly's Fifth Committee (which deals with administrative and budgetary matters) declared that the activities of the United Nations in the Congo served the interests solely of the "colonialists and the imperialists." A Communist regime could not be expected to finance an "imperialist conspiracy"; therefore Czechoslovakia would not participate financially in those operations.[5] This speech frankly revealed the motivation of the Soviet-bloc states in refusing to pay any of the costs of the operation: it hurt them and helped their enemies, and for them to finance such an affair would be to chew ashes.

But such reasoning, though not without impact in an international arena where each regime feels itself the prime defender of its own interest, is seldom left to stand alone. There is a certain element of community and idealism among states, and a far greater element of hypocrisy, image-making, respect for pretense and admiration of a plausible case. Therefore it is not the habit of statesmen to declare simply, "I do this because it pleases me to do this," or "I take this step because it suits the interests of my state"; they combine such reasons,

---

[5] V:772. (See footnote 4 for the meaning of this abbreviation.)

commonly in their arguments but even in their minds, with the appeal to some right higher than their own reason of state. That higher right may be a set of words represented as symbolizing ideals common to all nations, or it may be a set of sentences represented as symbolizing rules of conduct by which all states are (in some sense) bound to act. The latter set of symbols are the symbols of international law; the manipulating of them is international legal argument, and it is such an argument with which we are here mostly concerned.

The Communist states did not, therefore, leave the Czech's blunt declaration as the sole statement of their position. Nor would France, which in early 1961 informed the United Nations that she would pay no part of the costs of the military operation in the Congo, rest satisfied with the explanation that the United Nations had attempted to intervene in the French war in Algeria, and had too many (anti-colonial) masters to be able to deal satisfactorily with a problem.[6] Even the grander language of De Gaulle — who in April, 1961 declared that the sessions of the United Nations were "tumultuous and scandalous" and that its ambitions to intervene, creating a "worldwide incoherence," made it necessary for France to treat this "dis-Organization" with deep reserve, participating in its military adventures with neither men nor money[7] — even these sentiments, edifying as they might be, were not let alone by the French international lawyers and diplomats. The public to which they were appealing had a taste for legalistic rather than dramatic rhetoric; that public was, first of all, the limited circle of professional foreign-office civil servants and diplomatic corpsmen, foreign correspondents, and prominent public figures of major states, a public which interests itself and has an influence in world affairs and thereby constitutes "world public opinion" — if, indeed, it does not constitute the international community.

The legal issues that were raised by these refusals revolved around a set of articles in the Charter of the United Nations. These include Articles 17(1) and (2), and a portion of 19:

17(1). The General Assembly shall consider and approve the budget of the Organization.

17(2). The expenses of the Organization shall be borne by the Members as apportioned by the General Assembly.

19 [*part*] A member of the United Nations which is in arrears in the

---

[6] *New York Times,* March 29, 1961, Section 1, p. 5.
[7] *Le Monde,* April 12, 1961.

payment of its financial contributions to the Organization shall have no vote in the General Assembly if the amount of its arrears equals or exceeds the amount of the contributions due from it for the preceding two full years.

While the administrative practices of the United Nations made it necessary for the delinquent states to take the first giant step of refusing to pay a specified part of their assessments, once that decision had been made the burden of contriving a countermove fell upon the Organization and its non-delinquent members. It was possible for them to do nothing but make unhappy noises; this is a popular course in international politics generally, and had been followed since the first Soviet bloc refusal to pay (dating back to certain expenses connected with the U.N. role in the Korean War). But the size of the refused assessments for the Congo operation was such that if no one covered the deficit, the United Nations would at length go bankrupt. On the other hand, if states other than the delinquents were tapped for voluntary contributions, the United States would surely find itself the chief volunteer, and would thus be paying the bills of its main antagonist. Only a certain legalism and idealism in the American concept of the United Nations — held in the State Department as well as Congress — together with a sense of justice that was at least mildly spiteful, prevented America from doing precisely that: prevented her, that is, from paying most of the costs of an operation with which she was on the whole well pleased, certainly more pleased than were her rivals. In American eyes, however, the interest taken by the Soviet Union in the Congo was troublesome meddling in an area outside the Russian sphere of influence, and it would be ironic justice if they had to pay toward driving their own protagonist out. Also, the U.S. policymakers considered that the Soviets had, after all, seen fit to ratify the Charter; this committed them to pay their share of what the United Nations spent, *vide* Article 17(2). The funds had certainly been spent, the share of all states had been determined: it was in poor taste and a breach of promise not to pay, and those who would not pay voluntarily should be bludgeoned into paying — thus reasoned the U.S. government. Furthermore, for America and its cohorts to have to pay would damage a delightful and persistent image, held primarily in these days by Americans, of the United Nations as the representative of the conscience of mankind; this image was most flattering so long as that conscience in its impartial judgment on major issues of the day ratified American policy. Financing by the majority that voted a decision through would shake this image, and make it clear that the Organization's banner belonged, not to "mankind," but to whatever shifting coalition could snatch it by mustering both the votes to ram a resolution through and the material power to enforce it. This vision was far out of line with the myths about the nature of politics then and currently subscribed to, in the United States. For one or another of these reasons, the American Congress was known to be more than reluctant to pick up the delinquents' tab, and those in the State Department who valued the utility of the United Nations were compelled to seek means of prodding the arrears out of the defaulters.

Such means were few. Military and economic sanctions were not considered, nor were economic side-payments, nor bargaining concessions on other outstanding issues. The weight of the Charter, of law itself, was the chief instrument; legal argument and diplomatic persuasion were the means used. This selection of tools may account for the outcome. The American line was first to impress the wretched debtors with world public opinion (i.e., with the number of states and jurists that agreed with America's legal arguments), and then threaten them with legal sanctions (i.e., the application of Article 19, depriving them of their Assembly vote). The Russians became the main public target at an early point; the French were never a main target.

The initial line of legal argument for the United States was clear and uncomplicated, based on Article 17. The initial response of the French, who were exempted from the American attack, was to avoid taking a determinate legal position. The Soviets, however, rapidly clapped together a structure of legal argument to serve as a first line of defense. The point of such a defense was, of course, to blunt such diplomatic pressure as the United States could muster from those non-aligned states whose good opinion the Soviet Union sought, and whose opposition on this issue would therefore have been inconvenient. Four days after the delivery of Nacvalac's blunt opinion that the Communist states would finance just what they chose to finance, the Soviet delegate on the Fifth Committee,[8] Roschin, presented a suaver, less candid, and more legalistic case.

The chief element was an attack upon Secretary-General Ham-

---

[8] The General Assembly customarily divides into six numbered committees, and several non-numbered committees, to engage in detailed and specialized debate. The Fifth Committee handles budgetary problems before they are discussed on the floor of the Assembly itself: therefore the Soviet refusal to pay assessments became a matter of debate first in this committee, and then in the plenary session.

marskjöld's conduct in office. The Security Council's resolutions, said Roschin, had directed the Secretary-General to assist the Central government of the Congo; the Secretary-General had violated these directives; the U.S.S.R. would not pay for an operation which was not the one authorized.[9] But during the operation, the Secretary-General had taken care to court the good opinion of the Afro-Asian states at every juncture. Therefore, this Soviet argument proved unconvincing to states which had authorized and supported the activities Russia denounced. The supporters of ONUC were able to secure a vote of 46 to 17 (24 abstentions) for a resolution whereby the General Assembly recognized explicitly the American position on financing: that the expenses of ONUC for 1960 "constitute 'expenses of the Organization' within the meaning of Article 17, Paragraph 2 of the Charter of the United Nations and that the assessment thereof against member states creates binding legal obligations on such states to pay their assessed shares."[10] For what it was worth, this was a victory for the United States; nevertheless the U.S.S.R. did not pay. And the rest of the resolution revealed that there was a voting group of poor states forming — states which were for ONUC in principle, but which in practice sought to avoid ONUC's costs by securing voluntary contributions from major powers.

The issue arose again in the context of the regular Fifth Committee meetings to consider methods of financing the continuing operations. The legal debate was therefore relevant not only to pressures on the Soviet Union (*et al.*) to pay, but also to the more immediate issue of whether or not the Soviets could choke off the operation by preventing its continued financing.

The Soviets at this juncture took a more formal position which rested less on condemnation of the legality of Hammarskjöld's acts and more on a favorite issue of theirs: the power of the Security Council vs. the General Assembly. The Congo Operation had been authorized by the Security Council originally with Soviet consent, but in the Council the Soviets had the veto; in the Assembly they did not. Therefore, when Russia became disenchanted with ONUC, the United States had managed the transfer of its direction from Council to Assembly. The Soviet Union then declared that the only United Nations organ competent to take action on questions relating to the

[9] V:775.
[10] Resolution 1583 (XV), December 20, 1960.

maintenance of international peace and security was the Security Council.

This was an old Soviet position, based on Article 11(2), which states that any such question "on which action is necessary shall be referred" by the Assembly to the Council. Several ambiguities, however, blurred this argument: the same article permitted the making of recommendations to states by the Assembly; Article 24 conferred upon the Council only "primary," not sole, responsibility for these questions; and it was not clear that the Assembly was obliged under 11(2) to *return* to the Council a matter which the Council had referred to the Assembly. Since 1950 a majority led by the United States had been mustered on occasion to override the Soviet position in favor of the American view that the Assembly had a residual responsibility that, in effect, permitted it to take over the Council's function when the latter was paralyzed by the veto. The Soviets had never abandoned their unsuccessful cause, however, and declared, even more tenuously, that the financing of ONUC was just such a question requiring "action" (more often construed to mean military and other sanctions) in the meaning of the Charter. The Assembly could take binding decisions only on the financing of administrative expenditures, not with regard to operations to maintain peace and security. Thus a budgetary decision of the Assembly on ONUC would be invalid and the U.S.S.R. would ignore it.[11]

The delegates were familiar with this argument, and it was routinely pointed out that no article dealt with financing but Article 17, which explicitly recognized the sole competence of the Assembly. Most delegations simply ignored the Soviet contention. But there was another argument, advanced by states seeking to escape the financial burdens of ONUC, that made more headway. These states, led by Mexico, called for a special procedure for financing ONUC, which would rely on voluntary contributions to relieve the poor states of most of their assessments, and they defended this position by proposing that ONUC expenses were expenses of a "special nature" and therefore not "expenses of the Organization" within the meaning of Article 17(2).[12]

Arguments over "natures" are notoriously difficult to settle by means

[11] V:828, 825.
[12] V:841; A/C.5/L. 658 and corr. 1, A/C.5/862 (these are U.N. Document numbers, referring to Assembly Documents of the Fifth Committee).

of an appeal to facts, and this one was no different. The Soviet-bloc states found a certain common ground here which their other arguments did not afford them, since they also denied that ONUC-UNEF expenses were "expenses" within the meaning of Article 17(2). But they could not join the Mexican-led group, since the latter did not deny the Assembly the power to apportion those extraordinary expenses and did not intend to repudiate such assessments as the Assembly might make, but wanted only to shift the burden to richer states. Thus the West was able to fudge the legal issues by means of a pair of resolutions that compromised with the Mexicans (but not with the chief debtors) by giving the poor states a modicum of financial relief and by preparing for the study, with a working group of fifteen, of the reforms which the poor states had demanded in budgetary procedure and in peacekeeping-assessment scales.[13]

Thus, 1961 was a year of expedients. The United Nations was kept afloat by internal borrowing, by American and other voluntary contributions, and finally by a $200 million issue of U.N. bonds. This last had to be approved by the Assembly, and gave occasion for another confrontation of legal arguments, especially since the bond-issuance resolutions included a provision whereby the bonds were to be paid off through additional regular-budget assessments. If the defaulter states acquiesced in this ploy, they would still be in arrears on the Congo payments, but the United Nations would have secured (from them among others) the funds to sustain it through the Congo operation, and perhaps through others of which these states would disapprove.

The U.S.S.R. was, perhaps, caught off guard by the bond-issue resolution. Its ineffectual objections in committee were merely procedural. In the same discussion, however, France began to clarify her position; she chose to take up and to exploit the troublesome potential of the Mexican case. Peacekeeping expenses were clearly, as the Mexicans said, extraordinary expenses. But while Mexico interpreted this to mean that members could not then be assessed in the regular manner by the Assembly and that the Assembly should therefore vote a new scale of assessments, France went on to suggest that if peacekeeping expenses were fundamentally different from the "expenses" contemplated in 17(1) and (2), then the Assembly had no competence to assess for them under any circumstances, and Members had

[13] Resolutions 1619 and 1620 (XV), April 21, 1961.

no obligation to pay them. The French, however, kept a point of distinction from the Russian position: the Assembly might recommend operations, for which it could then recommend payment by voluntary contributions of cash or forces from those who supported such operations (as the Korean War had been financed). The Soviets, of course, considered even such operations inadmissible, since they skirted the veto.

The Assembly was not convinced by these objections. The bond plan was adopted, but not before France had made it clear that it would repudiate all financial liability for any such bonds.[14] The Soviet Union later took the same position. Thus, while the immediate financial shortage was surmounted by the bond issue, it was in fact merely postponed to the time when Franco-Soviet refusals to be assessed for the bonds left the United Nations unable to complete repayment thereon. The immediate purposes of the United States and like-opinioned states had been served, but the delinquents remained unmoved.

Meanwhile the point of the Mexican draft resolution had come up elsewhere and created certain scruples and doubts in the minds of the pro-ONUC majority. In the Working Group created to study U.N. administrative and budgetary procedures mentioned earlier, the United States found that both the Latin American and the African representatives rejected her view. That American view was now legalistically expressed: "the cost of all peace-keeping operations carried out in accordance with mandates given by the appropriate organ must be regarded as expenses of the Organization within the meaning of Article 17, paragraph 2 of the Charter. . . . It is only under Article 17 that the General Assembly has power to assess member states for contributions to peace-keeping expenses." But the African and Latin states joined France and the U.S.S.R. in replying that "the costs of peace-keeping operations by their very nature and basis cannot be regarded as regular expenses of the Organization as envisaged in Article 17 of the Charter." The opposition broke its unity, of course, when alternative sources of funds were to be recommended: France declared that extraordinary expenses should not be included in the regular budget, but in special funds and accounts, all of them financed on a voluntary basis; the African and Latin states tended to reject the voluntary principle and to prefer a special scale of assessments, probably to be imposed by the General Assembly, paid into a

[14] See Plenary 1086; V:908.

special fund or account rather than into the regular budget; Russia declared that procedures for financing peacekeeping operations must in every case be determined by a decision of the Security Council, primarily through fining the state or states whose actions caused the Council to take the measures in question. The U.S. position, of course, was that peacekeeping costs must be shared on the basis of such principles as the Assembly might determine.[15]

Since the objection of the non-delinquent states to the U.S. position was of a principled nature, based less on commitments of pique and interest than on a certain reading of a text, it appeared possible that by a certain tactical maneuver the broken Assembly majority might be largely reassembled and the delinquents subjected to renewed pressure. This maneuver was to have the Assembly apply to the International Court of Justice for an advisory opinion on the specific question of whether the expenditures authorized by the Assembly for ONUC and UNEF were "expenses of the Organization" within the meaning of Article 17(2). The United States thought that they plainly were; but, the Americans declared, the obvious means to settle the doubts of those who might withhold their contributions on legal grounds was to ask the Court for an advisory opinion. The United States was not unfamiliar with the composition of the International Court of Justice, which made it likely that the position supported by America would be approved. The delinquent states were equally aware of this, and therefore objected to this move. The Soviet Union took two lines on the subject: it declared that the problem of legal interpretation had already been settled (settled, that is, by the authoritative arguments of the Soviet Union); it also declared that the problem was not "legal" but "political" and therefore not within the competence of the Court. The first argument did not undermine the Soviet Union's previous position, while the second justified its refusal to be bound by any decision the Court might take. These utilities were more important than the fact that the two lines were, of course, mutually inconsistent. France merely suggested that the Court opinion would alter little except to make the opinions of governments more rigid. The request for an advisory opinion was nevertheless approved by the Assembly.[16]

[15] A/4971.
[16] V:897.

As is usual with the technical language of law, the words used to frame the Assembly resolution requesting the advisory opinion were of political significance. The Western powers were primarily hopeful of setting to rest the doubts engendered by the Mexican position on Article 17(2). They had a strong common-sense or plain-language basis to make for their case; if the Charter was to be taken at face value, an expense is money disbursed, and the Organization had certainly disbursed money, so that it seemed reasonable to say that the Congo expenditures were expenses. The burden of proof lay on those who denied it. Therefore the resolution was phrased tightly; the Assembly asked whether the expenditures it had authorized for UNEF and ONUC constituted "expenses of the Organization" within the meaning of 17(2).[17] In plenary, France submitted an amendment which would also have required the Court to appraise the conformity of the UNEF and ONUC expenditure resolutions with the Charter. This would have required the Court to examine in some detail the rights of the Assembly to initiate and of the Secretary-General to control military operations of the United Nations. On the one hand, this was a matter on which a literal reading of the Charter left the Western powers with a much more difficult case. On the other hand, it was an issue on which the United States was in agreement with most Latins and Afro-Asians and in clear disagreement only with the immovable Russians; for the weaker states had generally been glad to embrace the powers of the Assembly at the expense of the Council, and merely wished to escape the onerous duty of paying for what they were happy to ordain. The United States and its small-power critics were therefore in agreement in seeking a decision on the narrower question, and the French amendment was rejected. As an apparent consequence, France declined to present an argument before the Court, on the grounds that the conditions under which the Court was consulted did not permit the obtaining of the necessary clear-cut legal opinion on the juridical basis for the financial obligations of members.[18]

The International Court of Justice sits in the Hague, and hears cases of two sorts. Contentious cases are submitted by states which accept the Court's jurisdiction as binding upon them, in effect pledging to obey its decision even if it goes against them. The losers on the whole

[17] Resolution 1731 (XVI), December 20, 1961.
[18] Plenary 1086; letter in I.C.J. Pleadings, *Certain Expenses of the United Nations* (*Article 17, paragraph 2 of the Charter*), pp. 130–35.

tend to keep this pledge, though not in every instance and though in practice there is no means to compel them to do so. The Court also renders opinions at the request of the General Assembly and Security Council, when and if the latter, involved in some dispute in which claims based upon so-called legal norms (and particularly upon the provisions of the Charter of the United Nations itself), request it. Neither the Members of the United Nations nor the U.N. bodies themselves are required to follow these opinions, which are merely advisory. Formal acceptance is usually accorded them by the Assembly, but in practice they are sometimes disregarded.

This disregard stems partly from the belief, strong in every foreign office, that the government of a state (and only that government) has the right and privilege of deciding what international law is, so far as that state is concerned. Therefore, every state deems itself sole judge of what its rights and its obligations (if any) are. No external body would make the delicate adjustments and interpretations by which, far more often than not, the sanction of justice and the ages is found to lie upon and only upon the course which it also happens to be most pleasant and most convenient for a state to take at the given moment. The Court, despite the integrity of and general high regard for its members, is not in anyone's foreign office, and is therefore routinely suspect. Even worse, it is made up of men, who are, by statute, drawn from among the most distinguished jurists of various countries. Never does an enemy, seldom does a severe critic of his own government attain this distinction. Despite their independence, it does not often happen that the opinion rendered by a judge differs radically and materially from that which his government expects and desires. Hence many statesmen have doubts about the value of requesting advisory opinions on matters of importance, unless all parties are first committed to accept them. The Court is partly a political body, and while most of its members may be able to achieve impartiality in contentious cases (which generally concern only a few parties, and matters of small material importance), impartiality is less to be expected of the jurists in a dispute which has been fought out in the Assembly and its Committees. In such a situation, most states have had to take a stand of which their Justice (if they have one) will be uncomfortably aware. Split opinions on controversial matters, especially if disregarded, expose the feebleness of international norms and the relentless self-love of governments more than is generally warranted proper. Still, the Court is an instrument made to be used, and it cannot be denied that using it may bring a state some rewards, as may the use of legal argument in a political debate. Therefore the Americans and their allies gambled that the Court would side with them, and that the Soviet Union would be awed by the prestige of the Court as it was not awed by the prestige of the Assembly.

So the expert lawyers made their expert pleas before the international tribunal. The Soviet Union had subtly altered its case; its argument now rested equally on two points, one containing the traditional Soviet position, the other taken from the more generally appealing Mexican position. The Soviets argued that the operations of UNEF and ONUC imposed no financial obligations on U.N. Members, for the reasons (1) that these operations were not carried out in accordance with the requirements of the U.N. Charter, and (2) that the expenses of these operations are not the expenses referred to in Article 17(2) of the Charter. Either of these two points, if sustained, might be sufficient to require the Court to return a negative answer to the Assembly's query, although only the second was strictly relevant to that query.

On the first point, the U.S.S.R. made one case against UNEF and another against ONUC. UNEF, it declared, was set up in violation of the Charter, circumventing the Security Council. The General Assembly resolved that it be set up; but while the General Assembly was competent to "discuss" questions involving international peace and security, and to "make recommendations" to states (Article 11 [2]), it was not within its competence to take *decisions* requiring *action* for maintenance of peace and security. The creation of UNEF, said the Soviets, was a decision, not a recommendation, to take action; but Article 11(2) says that any such question on which action is necessary shall be referred to the Council by the Assembly. Chapter VII of the Charter empowered the Security Council, and the Council only, to set up international armed forces. Since UNEF was set up in violation of the Charter, its financing is no obligation of the members.

ONUC was based on the Security Council's Resolution S/4387 of July 14, 1960. But the resolution was implemented in violation of the provisions of the Charter, the Soviets said; this resolution was a *decision* (under Articles 41 and 42 of the Charter) to use armed forces for the maintenance of international peace and security. However, Articles 43 and 48 stipulate the conditions under which states may participate in implementing the Council's decisions under 41 and 42. Article 48(1) reads, "The action required to carry out decisions of the Security Council for the maintenance of international peace and security shall be taken by all the Members of the United Nations, or by some of them, as the Security Council may determine." Instead the Secretary-General himself had determined the list of states which were invited to participate in ONUC. Further, member states may participate in such action only on the basis of special agreements concluded by them with the Security Council to make available armed forces, and then address the Assembly for appropriations to defray expenses. Therefore, the Soviet Union concluded, the appropriations resolutions were in contradiction to the Charter and imposed no obligations.

It is useful to recall at this point that the Secretary-General refused to invite the major powers to participate in ONUC, and rejected a Soviet suggestion that African states' alone be called on to provide troops, a suggestion which took into account the fact that many African states supported Lumumba.

As for the argument against Article 17(2), it went as follows. Financial obligations for actions such as ONUC must be based on special agreements under Article 43. These expenses are different in their nature from those that fall under Article 17. Article 17 gives general budgetary competence to the Assembly; Article 45 gives an exception, a particular rule which governs expenditures related to peace and security. Furthermore, resolutions of the Assembly, as stipulated in Article 10, are recommendations; thus they are not binding on states; but then all measures (e.g., appropriations) following from such resolutions are also only recommendatory and not obligatory. Finally, the Assembly itself never considered UNEF expenses as falling within 17(2), but instead repeatedly asked for Members' views on how to finance the force and then failed to come to a decision on them; and while ONUC expenses were considered in Resolution 1585 as falling under 17(2), they were seen in Resolution 1732 as "extraordinary expenses . . . essentially different in nature from the expenses of the Organization under the regular budget" requiring "a procedure different from that applied under the regular budget" to meet them. Therefore, the expenses of UNEF and ONUC are not "the expenses of the Organization" as stipulated in Article 17, paragraph 2.[19]

---

[19] I.C.J. Pleadings, *loc. cit.*, pp. 270–74, 397–412.

Of the opposed pleadings, that of the United States was the most extensive, constituting a positive case and a rebuttal. The positive arguments: 1. The General Assembly, in the assessment resolutions before the Court, made it clear that it intended to treat expenditures for ONUC and UNEF as "expenses of the Organization" under Article 17 of the Charter. Special accounts were established for each operation as a matter of accounting convenience, and to permit special scales of apportionment of expenses, not in order to remove the binding character of the expenses, which were always assumed. 2. The language of Article 17 is mandatory: expenses "shall" be borne. Interpretation and practice agree that this empowers the Assembly to create legally binding obligations by levying assessments under Article 17. The fact that the Council has (under Article 24) primary responsibility for maintaining peace and security does not mean that the Assembly lacks power to provide funds to meet expenses in this sphere; only the Assembly is allotted fiscal power in the Charter, and only the Assembly exercises it in practice. As a general principle, the legally incurred expenses of an association must be borne by all its members in common, and the recommendatory character of the basic resolution relates only to the contributions of forces. 3. The validity of the resolutions establishing UNEF and ONUC is not at issue, since the Assembly asked for advice only on the assessing resolutions. But if the Court found this question germane, still the resolutions remain valid. ONUC and UNEF are subsidiary organs established under Articles 22 and 29 of the Charter, and constituted by recommendations to member states that they voluntarily supply troops and equipment. No action of a mandatory character was required, since the participants volunteered forces and the host countries consented to the presence of the force. Therefore UNEF and ONUC were validly constituted.

The United States then went on to rebut Soviet and other arguments: 1. Chapter VII of the Charter provides procedures for adoption in a special case: bringing force to bear to crush the will of an aggressor state. Activities such as UNEF and ONUC do not have the character of enforcement; they involve no "action" to carry out "decisions" in the sense of Chapter VII, whereby the Council can bind states to supply forces or admit them to their territory whether the states consent or not. There is no prohibition of voluntary use of armed force on the recommendation of the Assembly in the Charter, and no provision vesting exclusive responsibility for maintaining peace and security in the Council. 2. The budgetary resolutions of the Assembly are binding, not recommendatory, as the mandatory language of Article 17 demonstrates; and the budgetary provisions of the Charter make no distinction between expenses occasioned by recommendations and other expenses. Peacekeeping operations fulfill an essential purpose of the United Nations; it has the right to undertake them; it has the power to pay for what it has the power to do; and what it lacks the power to pay for it cannot do. 3. UNEF and ONUC assessments are not part of the "regular" budget, but they are special accounts in the budget of the Organization, clearly intended to be mandatory. Hence the contrary contentions are unpersuasive.[20]

The most important fact about this controversy was that both sides were trying to adapt a text to circumstances which the drafters of that text had not contemplated. The drafters of the Charter had chosen to assume that crises in world politics would take one of two forms: quarrels between small powers in which force would not be a decisive factor, and in which the great majority of U.N. members would apply pressures for a single solution; and unprovoked attacks of one state on another, wherein no permanent member of the Security Council would be — or support — the assailant. No provisions were made to govern the dispatch of a U.N. force to separate combatants or to restore order in a country, especially when the permanent Council members were in disagreement as to what that force should do. Since UNEF and ONUC were not clearly based on a specific clause contemplating such forces, their financing had also to be arranged *ad hoc*. Their creation involved a distinct stretching of the Charter, according to a constitutional practice of "loose interpretation" very familiar to Americans: a certain act (i.e., setting up the force) is seen or represented as necessary and vital to the achievement of the broadly and vaguely expressed purposes of the institution (i.e., maintenance of peace and security). Then some specific clause (like the commerce or equal protection clause of the Constitution, or Articles 10 and 11(2) of the Charter) is selected, interpreted freely, and the operation tailored and declared to fit that clause, while other clauses, such as the states' rights or due process clauses of the Constitution, or Chapter VII of the Charter, which seem to stand in the way of the operation are ignored or interpreted very narrowly. Because the drafters of constitutions and Charters do not foresee some controversies and

[20] *Ibid.*, pp. 180–209, 413–27.

cannot agree how to prejudge some others, every such document can be interpreted one way and another after the fact, and few interpretations are so specious as to have no basis at all. Thus, though a literal reading of the Charter was favorable to the Western powers' case, and the record of U.N. practice even more so, a conscientious judge might have decided that there was no intention on the part of the Charter drafters to permit such operations as ONUC and UNEF or to give such a significant role to the Assembly and Secretary-General as both had assumed in these affairs; and a strict-interpretationist might then, without feeling any sympathy for Soviet foreign policy or any antipathy to the American and U.N. roles, have decided to apply the principle that "what is not [explicitly] permitted is forbidden" and to find UNEF and ONUC, and assessments therefor, illegal.

The Court did not do so. Nine members, of fourteen sitting, chose to return an affirmative answer to the Assembly's question: Are these peacekeeping expenditures "expenses of the Organization" within the meaning of Article 17(2)? The opinion of this majority of nine was split into the Court's opinion, sustained by six of nine; the added declaration of one of the six; and three separate concurring opinions. A summary of the Court's opinion follows.

Two objections to the Court's dealing with the case at all were first answered. (The Statute of the Court permits it to refuse at discretion to render advisory opinions.) The first, suggested in Fifth Committee by India and others, contended that an opinion should be refused because the question was of a "political" rather than a "legal" nature. This argument is a classic, and works both ways. Every serious dispute in world politics is *both* "political" in the sense that states are struggling with power for what they want, and "legal" in the sense that some set of international norms could be applied to argue or decide the conflict. To say that this conflict, or any such conflict, is "political" is therefore correct and obvious; to say that it is political rather than legal is a fraud and, superficially, a pointless fraud. All such arguments, however, carry more than one message. The second-level message in this case depends upon the conventional (and false) distinction between the Assembly and Council on the one hand as "political" organs and the Court on the other as a "legal" body. India's contention that the dispute was not "legal" but "political" was actually a request to the Court to send the question back to the General Assembly (a "political" body). And the reason for that request was that India considered that its own goals would be poorly served in the Court.

India was interested primarily in conciliating the U.S.–Soviet quarrel that had been projected into and reflected in the dispute. But India doubted that conciliation would be achieved by a Court opinion — a doubt which is in general and proved to be in this case again well founded. Consequently, India desired to have the Court refuse jurisdiction, and India provided the Court with a plausible-sounding legal argument for refusing jurisdiction, in case the judges were prepared to accede to her conciliatory desires.

The Court replied that it could not attribute a political character to a request which invited it to undertake an essentially judicial task — namely "the interpretation of a treaty provision" — and saw "no compelling reason" not to return the advice requested. The Court majority thereby returned the reply that its interests and attachments in the dispute were not of a conciliatory nature. What the interests of the Court were cannot be analyzed without a review of the character and politics of each of these nine men. However, it is not without relevance that eight of the nine came from countries fairly closely aligned with the United States, and only the ninth (Badawi, United Arab Republic) clearly adopted a position which his government — a delinquent on UNEF — would vigorously repudiate.

The second objection, tacitly answered, was to be found in the dissent of Judge Basdevant. It was a compound argument, as follows: (1) in order to answer the Assembly's query the Court must examine not only the narrow matter of whether the peacekeeping expenses in the Middle East and Congo were "expenses of the Organization," but also the broader issue raised by the rejected French[21] amendment to the Assembly's query, the amendment that would have had the Court consider whether ONUC and UNEF had been authorized "in conformity with the Charter." But (2) the Assembly having rejected the amendment had in effect directed the Court to exclude this essential from consideration; *therefore* (3), the Court, since it must not examine what it was essential to examine, should refuse to examine the matter at all. Certain opinions concurring in the majority judgment — those of Spender (Australia) and Morelli (Italy) as well as Spiropoulos' (Greece) separate declaration — accepted the second part of the French objection and rejected the first and third; that is, they said that the question was narrowed by the Assembly, but that it could be answered even so. The Court's opinion accepted the first

[21] Judge Basdevant, it may be noted, was French.

part of the French objection and rejected the second and third; that is, it said that the Court was not precluded from examining the "charterability" of the resolutions setting up ONUC and UNEF, and proceeded to do so. (It is difficult to attach any political correlation to this separation of the two main lines of the majority's arguments, and it is likely that there is none.) Thus the position taken by the dissent of Basdevant (France), as well as by Moreno Quintana (Argentina) and Bustamante (Peru), was rejected by the Court, and it proceeded to the substance of the matter.

The Court's opinion accepted the U.S. and rejected the Soviet position in every fundamental point and many details. The "action" that is barred to the Assembly by Article 11(2) and regulated for the Council by Chapter VII (including Articles 43 and 48) is coercive or enforcement action; but UNEF and ONUC did not involve the use of force against any state, and therefore escape these strictures (which in Soviet eyes made UNEF illegal in origin and ONUC illegal in its conduct). The text of the Charter and the practice of the Assembly offer no justification for reading into Article 17(1) any qualifying word such as "regular" or "administration" before the term "budget"; therefore there is no special kind of budget which the Assembly lacks the authority to approve. Similarly neither the text of 17(2) nor the context of the Charter (including Article 43) supports a limitation on the budgetary authority of the Assembly with respect to the maintenance of peace and security. The Assembly has repeatedly treated ONUC and UNEF expenses as expenses of the Organization, and since Assembly and Council determine their own jurisdiction the Court does not question the underlying validity of their actions (does not, that is, take up the question of whether these actions really maintained peace and security). So said the Court.

Koretsky and Winiarski, the Soviet and Polish judges, dissented. Winiarski took up the line that a recommendation not binding on a member cannot be "partially binding" on him financially; Koretsky agreed, and went on to reiterate the whole Soviet case.[22]

But it is less important to recite arguments which have already been repeated than to consider the political effect of the opinion of the Court. Seeking the advisory was a calculated risk on the part of the

---

[22] See "Certain Expenses of the United Nations (Article 17, paragraph 2 of the Charter), Advisory Opinion of 20 July 1962," *I.C.J. Reports 1962*, pp. 151–308.

United States and Western states; it might have been highly embarrassing had the Court been in the mood to temporize, but if the opinion were favorable, as it was, the United States hoped to apply added pressure and perhaps cause the defaulters to pay up, and at minimum to repair the U.S.–Latin–ex-colonial front which had been behind ONUC but which the financial burden of ONUC had shattered. The next question, then, was how the Assembly majority and the delinquent states would respond to the opinion of the International Court of Justice.

As might have been expected, the key debtor states were unmoved. The opportunity for them to demonstrate their intentions was speedily provided by a draft resolution whereby the Assembly *"accepts"* the opinion of the Court. The Soviet Union reiterated its position as stated before the Court, and declared that it would not participate in the financing of "those two illegal operations" and did not recognize the validity of the advisory opinion of the Court.[23] France now, at last, specified its legal posture more clearly. Expenses entailed by operations undertaken upon a recommendation of the General Assembly were binding only upon those member states which had approved the operations, and which had formally accepted the financial obligations thereof; any other position would turn the United Nations into a super-state.[24] France had not agreed to the operations in the Congo, and could not therefore be required to contribute to their financing.[25] As for the Court's opinion, it was in any case strictly advisory and therefore had no binding force. The Assembly had no authority to

---

[23] V:961.

[24] It will be noted that this position is supported by the dissent of Winiarski (Poland), while the French technical objection to the Court's delivering any opinion whatever was supported by Basdevant (France).

[25] This has been the French position since their refusal to pay. It is not entirely factual. France voted at the 879th meeting of the Security Council for the resolution of July 22, 1960 on the Congo, and gave as its reason that this resolution was not critical of Belgium. Previously, its delegate had verbally supported the dispatch of U.N. troops to the Congo, but abstained on the initial Security Council resolution of July 15, 1960 because that resolution was critical of Belgium. Later, of course, France became more interested in opposing the United States and its dominance, less intrigued with defending colonialism; correspondingly it rewrote the history of its motives, and even of its acts. The United States (*et al.*) never chose to embarrass the French severely on this score because France was still apparently an ally while the U.S.S.R. was an old enemy and the principal offender; it was hoped that if the chief culprit could be bludgeoned into line, the others, whom the United States had more to lose by offending, would fall into line of themselves.

oblige member states to contribute to the expenses in question, and the Court could not confer on the Assembly a legal power which the Assembly lacked in the first place.[26]

The Arab states took a more politic line. Jordan proposed and others supported an amendment to the draft resolution, whereby the Assembly would not "accept" but would merely "take note of" the Court's opinion; this would avoid the use of the Court's opinion as a means of imposing a majority decision on member states which did not accept those opinions.[27] However, a number of states which might have been expected on the strength of their previous positions to have accepted this lukewarm approach did not do so. States like Ceylon, Nepal, Ghana and India had had reservations about seeking the Court's opinion, whether because of the "legal-political" business or because they felt that Court adjudication would not facilitate a practical settlement; states like Venezuela had had doubts in principle over the whole controversy; and states like Mexico, Brazil, and Argentina had argued that expenses arising out of peacekeeping operations such as ONUC and UNEF were not expenses of the Organization within the meaning of Article 17. All these states had had serious doubts about the American position, which the Court had adopted; all nevertheless decided that in order to uphold the authority of the U.N.'s highest judicial organ, or as a matter of respect for international law, or to demonstrate support for the United Nations, they would accept the Court's opinion.[28] The resolution of acceptance was yoked to a resolution recreating the Working Group — now with twenty-one members — to study and report on ways to wipe out past budgetary shortages, and on means of financing future peacekeeping operations that would weigh less heavily on poorer members. The resolution was passed by a vote of 76–17 with 8 abstentions.[29]

The broken front had reassembled itself, and the delinquents were virtually isolated once again — but still they refused to pay. France rejected a formula under which the Assembly was, through its financial prerogatives, accorded political powers "which it does not possess under the Charter." The Soviets declared the decision to be "contrary to the United Nations Charter" and to have no force whatever.[30]

---

[26] V: 962.
[27] V: 964.
[28] V: 963, 964, 967, 972, 973.
[29] Plenary 1199, Resolution 1854A and 1854B (XVII), December 19, 1962.
[30] Plenary 1199.

There followed a period of more than a year in which diplomatic approaches to the problem of arrears failed, as juridical approaches and prior diplomacy had failed, to budge the immobile French and Soviets, and in which a new legal issue arose and new postures were adopted. In the Working Group, sixteen of the twenty-one members agreed on a proposal which was intended to wipe out the Organization's old peacekeeping debts, save the face of France and Russia, and leave the financing of future operations open to a compromise: "member states who are in arrears and object to making payments to meet the expenses of these peacekeeping operations on political or juridical grounds are invited nevertheless to make a special effort toward solving the financial difficulties of the Organization by making this payment." This issue was separated from the question of special methods for financing future peacekeeping operations involving heavy expenditure. The Soviet bloc was firm: it rejected this compromise and all proposals to solve the future financing problem by means other than referring the matter to the Council under 11(2). France refused to participate in the discussion. Though the proposal was later adopted by the Assembly, it was without effect.[31]

When the Working Group's report came up in Fifth Committee, the Soviet bloc made further gestures of defiance by refusing from then on to contribute to certain portions of the regular budget which they considered unjustifiable or incorrectly administered, including in particular the redemption of U.N. bonds. This last step had already been taken by the French. Meanwhile, arrears had risen to such a point that a new factor intervened. The Charter contains only one sanction prescribed for fiscal delinquents, and it is to be found in Article 19: "A member of the United Nations which is in arrears in the payment of its financial contributions to the Organization shall have no vote in the General Assembly if the amount of its arrears equals or exceeds the amount of the contributions due from it for the preceding two full years. The General Assembly may, nevertheless, permit such a Member to vote if it is satisfied that the failure to pay is due to conditions beyond the control of the Member."

The United States at this time made no statement on Article 19: but a number of other states did so. Several delegations — Colombia, Ecuador, Norway, Thailand, and Iceland — stated simply that if member states did not pay their arrears, Article 19 must and should be

[31] A/5407; Resolution 1877(S-IV), June 25, 1963.

invoked. But others disagreed; Sudan and Guinea and Hungary warned that to apply Article 19 could mean the loss of certain members or the collapse of the United Nations. Other states sought a legal basis for averting the unpleasant consequences of a collision over the sanction of Article 19, Uruguay by declaring that in its opinion Article 19 could not be automatically applied but required an Assembly decision, Mexico and Jordan by contending that arrears under Article 19 should exclude arrears for peacekeeping operations.[32] And the Soviet Union, in reference not to its own arrears but to those of Haiti, which at this time brought that state to the verge of application of Article 19, made a more extended case.

The position of the United States appeared at this time to be that the deprivation under Article 19 was automatic and would consist of the President of the Assembly declaring that a certain member had lost its right to vote. The Soviets rejected this approach and declared that the Assembly itself must decide the question of suspending a member state's right to vote. This interpretation was rested on: (1) a General Assembly Rule 161 providing that the Committee on Contributions "shall advise the General Assembly . . . on the action to be taken with regard to the application of Article 19 of the Charter"; (2) the second sentence of Article 19, which states that the Assembly may make a decision to permit a delinquent to vote; and (3) Article 18(2) which says, "Decisions of the General Assembly on important questions shall be made by a two-thirds majority of the Members present and voting. These questions shall include . . . the suspension of the rights and privileges of membership. . . ."[33]

This argument was an essential protective for the delinquent states if the United States insisted on pressing for sanctions. Although the Soviet Union also maintained that it was not subject to sanctions on its arrears because it had no obligation to pay them, Russia was aware that this argument had worn thin for the majority of U.N. members, and that if it alone were employed the consequences could be summary rejection. At the same time that many states might be willing to accept an "automatic" denial of the delinquents' right to vote, i.e., a denial bluntly made by the President of the Assembly, they might equally be hesitant to give explicit approval to a denial if that were forced to a vote — and if the vote could be conducted

[32] V:985, 986, 988, 989, 992–994, 1003.
[33] U.S.S.R. letter, A/5431.

under a two-thirds rather than a simple majority rule, the sanctions might be defeated. Therefore the Soviet Union concentrated on the case against "automatic" sanctions.

The Haitian episode evolved as follows. The Fourth Special Session of the Assembly opened May 14, 1963. Haiti was more than two years in arrears. The Haitian delegate did not attend the opening session; further, the President of the Assembly, Zafrullah Khan of Pakistan, had obtained an agreement to dispense with any form of voting at the session. Therefore, despite his opinion that Article 19 must be enforced, he did not invoke it. Western delegations, however, pressed for some statement from the President explaining that Article 19 was applicable. Haiti was friendless in the Assembly, and without influence; she could not muster the strength to override such a statement. A statement would have value as a precedent-setting device, which might make a later President more inclined to go along with the Western concept of automatic sanctions if and when the time came to penalize the Soviet Union. On May 21, Zafrullah Khan made public a letter from himself to the Secretary-General stating that "I would have made an announcement drawing the attention of the Assembly to the loss of voting rights in the Assembly of the member state mentioned, under the first sentence of Article 19, had a formal count of votes taken place in the presence of a representative of that state at the opening plenary meeting. As no such vote took place, and as the representative of Haiti was not present, this announcement became unnecessary."[34] Haiti was able to pay in time to avoid actual sanctions, but this letter cleared the way for parallel action against the Soviet Union and prompted the Soviet reply on interpreting Article 19.

The United States now began making psychological and legal preparations for the next painful phase of this struggle with the recalcitrant Soviets. The *New York Times* Washington correspondent Max Frankel reported that the Kennedy Administration "welcomes" the impending constitutional crisis as a way to establish the U.N.'s right "to tax its members," and that the administration intended to press for "a showdown" in 1964 when on January 1 the Soviets would become liable under Article 19. It was anticipated that the U.S.S.R. would more and more violently denounce and threaten to walk out, the better to intimidate those smaller countries, more devoted to the

[34] *The Times* (London), May 22, 1963, p. 11.

United Nations, which the United States was trying to weld into a non-Communist coalition. The American strategy was to isolate the Communist-bloc states by persuading Belgium and France to pay their shares in the Congo and the Arab states to pay for UNEF, while working out some financial formulas to relieve the small and poor states.[35] Conveniently, France would not become eligible for sanctions before 1965. The U.S.S.R. did not fall under Article 19's provisions in the 1963 regular session, which ended before January 1, 1964. But a challenge was clearly thrown down by U.S. representative Adlai Stevenson, who indicated that the United States would insist on suspending the Soviet vote if it did not pay. "Rigid adherence to the law, to the Charter, is essential to the Charter's preservation."[36]

In order to enforce this challenge, certain other delegations must be persuaded to support it. It would be necessary, if Article 19 were to be applied to the U.S.S.R., to convince the new President of the Assembly that he should announce the voteless status of the Soviets. If he were convinced, the Americans would in addition have to muster the votes to defeat a point of order, whereby a simple majority vote could override his ruling. If the President were to remain unconvinced by the American case, they would have at minimum to raise a point of order and to find a majority to override his refusal to rule. At worst, should the Assembly majority accept the Soviet case that Article 19 was neither mandatory nor automatic, the Americans would have to put together a two-thirds majority willing to endorse its application. To prepare for the necessary persuasion, the United States elaborated its legal case. This case had to be all the stronger, in that members' desire to keep the United Nations soundly financed and the Assembly able to set up future peacekeeping operations could easily have been silenced by their fear of a Soviet withdrawal or other fearful consequences of applying sanctions.

The United States therefore met each potential escape-route in some detail: the notion that the no-vote sanction required an Assembly decision rather than being automatic, and the idea that it was permissive rather than mandatory; the correlate that under Article 18 a two-thirds majority is therein required; the suggestion that the Assembly had, before it could apply sanctions, to make a decision that members were in fact in arrears; the hope that a majority might over-

---

[35] *New York Times,* June 8, 1963, p. 1.
[36] *New York Times,* December 19, 1963, p. 1.

ride sanctions on a point of order; and the thought that the second sentence of Article 19 might speedily be employed to remove the strictures if the first sentence were used to impose them. On the contrary, said the United States, the suspension was mandatory and automatic: the Charter clearly differentiated in every one of its languages mandatory from permissive provisions, and Article 19 says members *shall* have no vote. Article 18 is inapplicable because it refers to a decision, and no decision is needed under Article 19. In all previous practice relating to arrears the Assembly had made no decision on the fact of arrears, but had accepted the "arithmetical, not political" decision of · its Committee on Contributions. No point of order could be used to alter the substance of the Charter. And the second sentence of Article 19 was expressly inapplicable to willful delinquencies. Comparable situations in United Nations specialized agencies showed that a member's loss of voting rights was mandatory and automatic and that the fact of its debt was a mathematical calculation rather than a political decision.[37]

But the United States had no real heart for a "showdown," despite all talk to the contrary. America began to seek or accept expedients that might avoid confrontation: a concession plan that would route all future peacekeeping operations first through the Security Council; two postponements of the opening of the Nineteenth General Assembly Session of 1964. Meanwhile the Soviets went to work with threats rather than legal arguments: a move to withhold Russia's vote would be considered an "unfriendly act"; "serious harm" could be done to the United Nations by this move. Soon the Secretary-General became concerned that Moscow would leave the United Nations if denied its vote. This Soviet campaign had rather more impact than the reiteration of the Soviet position that the operations of UNEF and ONUC "lay no financial obligations on the Members of the United Nations, inasmuch as these operations have been conducted otherwise than in accordance with the requirements of the United Nations Charter" and that "expenditure for United Nations armed forces does not come under Article 17 of the Charter . . . even in cases in which their establishment and operation conform to the Charter." Article 19 could not be applied, then, because it regards only obligations of states under Article 17; UNEF and ONUC create no such obliga-

---

[37] Department of State Memorandum of Law, February 1964, *Article 19 of the Charter of the United Nations.*

tions because they are illegal; even armed forces employed in accordance with the Charter create no such obligations, because they are to be financed not under Article 17 but by special agreements under Article 43.[38] Nothing new is to be found here, and so the American reply is repetitious: UNEF and ONUC expenses *are* "expenses of the Organization" under Article 17, and therefore *are* to be included in any calculation of arrears, under Article 19. The only novelty to be found in the American reply is a set of countermenaces. Failure to apply Article 19 would break faith with the Charter-supporting non-delinquent members, would be a repudiation of the International Court, would undermine the constitutional integrity of the United Nations; and it could affect the attitude toward the Organization of its strongest supporters, tempt members to pick and choose with impunity from among their U.N. obligations, and jeopardize not only peacekeeping but economic and social development programs.[39]

These menaces suggest what was the case: the U.S. was now contemplating, marginally if not seriously, the possibility of failure — failure in its attempts to get the Soviets to pay, and then failure in the attempt to deprive it of its vote. The United States was concerned over the vacillating position taken by the (now) fifty-eight Afro-Asian states, and over the decline of Washington's influence with these states since the Congo operation. The UNESCO budget at its 13th General Conference was adopted over the protests of nations paying most of the money. If Article 19 were to go unenforced, but America were to maintain its legal posture nevertheless, the situation could be most uncomfortable; the U.S.S.R. would evade any assessment it disliked, while the U.S. would be trapped by its own legalism into paying for anything and everything the now unruly Assembly majority might choose to charge to its account — including, if special assessment scales were so manipulated, a healthy share of the Soviet debt. This was intolerable to the Americans, and they began to prepare a fallback legal position. In politic language, the United States began to adopt the view that if the Assembly did not impose an equal legal obligation on all its members, including the Soviet Union, America would re-examine its willingness (and obligation) to pay all of its own assessments.[40]

---

[38] A/5729, U.S.S.R. letter.
[39] U.S. memorandum, "The United Nations Financial Crisis," October 8, 1964.
[40] *New York Times,* November 8, 1964, p. 1.

Meanwhile, maneuvers were set underway by states interested in averting a confrontation. The United States was agreeable to any plan under which the Russians would make a voluntary donation, not tied to specific payments, which could nonetheless be figured against Soviet arrears. Plans began to blossom like the flowers of spring, generally withering within three to seven days when the U.S.S.R. rejected them. The twice postponed opening date drew nigh, and an ingenious device was hit on by U Thant: the Assembly would sit without any formal vote being taken, decisions being made by unanimous consent; the President of the Assembly would ask if there were any objection, and if there were none, the President would rule that the Assembly had acted. (This plan replaced an Afro-Asian proposal that would postpone a decision on Article 19 pending negotiations, but permitting voting during the study; the United States contended that if the Soviet Union were allowed to vote on any issue, even the least important, this would violate Article 19.) The Soviets grudgingly accepted the postponement of confrontation beyond January 1, 1965, for beyond this date France would also become subject to sanction, and it was almost certain that the former French African colonies would refuse to take a position against France on this issue.

Next the voluntary-payment U.N. rescue-fund notion was advanced again. The Soviets appeared to agree in principle, but then demanded an Assembly vote on the rescue-fund notion which would break the U.S. position on Article 19; the plan, so altered, was rejected by the United States, whereupon the Soviet Union publicly endorsed it. Meanwhile, the Afro-Asian states were showing a distinct lack of enthusiasm for Article 19 in the General Debate, and pressed for a "suspension" of Article 19 and a return to normal procedures. The volatile majority was further prejudiced against the U.S. position by the American-Belgian operation to rescue white hostages in Stanleyville, Congo, and it became more and more likely that any vote would go against the United States. The confrontation approached on several occasions; a contest for a Security Council seat was decided by the ingenious scheme of an "informal" ballot or "consultation" conducted by the Assembly President (consistently with the waning strength of the United States's position, the Soviet Union took part in the informal ballot); the Assembly President set a date for resumption of voting for Assembly offices, and then postponed it for a week due to the death of Sir Winston Churchill. But at last the Albanians, who cared as little for the Soviet Union as for America, demanded an immediate return to a normal voting procedure, i.e., a showdown. The Assembly had been preparing to adjourn the entire session and reconvene in September, but a vote could not be averted. The United States consented to this vote, as it had to do, but declared that the vote (a challenge to a ruling of the President) was "procedural" and "would not involve or prejudice the question of the applicability of Article 19." This interpretation was highly dubious, since no one had ever previously used the distinction between a procedural and a substantive vote in the Article 19 context. But this retreat again reflected the waning influence of the extreme pro-U.N., pro-Charter group in the State Department, and the growth of a group which considered the Assembly majority intractable and, if armed with the unlimited taxing powers of Article 17, even dangerous. The blessings of Article 19 appeared the more mixed, the more the Afro-Asians broke away from Washington's lead to undermine it; thus the more the Americans failed, the more they came to appreciate the virtues of their failure.

As negotiations dragged on through the summer, the adhesion of the majority of members to the principle of voluntary financing and their abandonment of the notion of collective fiscal responsibility became clearer and clearer, and U.S. resignation increased. At length, the United States decided to give way in principle rather than to face defeat. For all such retreats from exposed positions, a cover is required, and in this instance a legal explanation, adequate if tortured, played that role. On August 16, 1965 U.N. Ambassador Arthur Goldberg declared that the United States would not insist on the application of Article 19, so that the work of the General Assembly might proceed normally in September. But he formally declared that the United States would no longer be bound to pay for U.N. activities to which it objected. The stand which the United States adopted was close to the voluntary-payment stand of Justice Winiarski and of France, rather than to the position of the Soviet Union, which simply could not have been swallowed whole. Goldberg's exact words, however, reveal the U.S. stance in detail: the United States "adheres to the present position that Article 19 is applicable in the present circumstances" — but, because the consensus of the membership was that the Assembly should proceed normally and because the Assembly "is not prepared to apply Article 19 in the present situation," the United States would not force a showdown. At the same time, "there can be no double standard": "if any member can insist on making an exception to the principle of collective financial responsibility with respect to certain activities of the organization, the United States reserves the same option to make exceptions if, in our view, strong and compelling reasons exist for doing so."[41] This statement permitted the United States to maintain the whole of its previous legal position, while abandoning on practical grounds the attempt to enforce it, and while amending it by adding the equal-right-to-violate-Article 17 proviso. As the Soviet delegation promptly noted, there was no statement herein that Article 19 was never to be applied. Likewise there was no admission that the U.S.S.R. was not really in arrears, no concession on the legality of ONUC and UNEF, and no abandonment of the residual right of the General Assembly to launch peacekeeping operations. With this concession, the U.N. constitutional crisis abated. Negotiations on peacekeeping operations continued, with little issue.

The events relating to law in this case are easily summarized. The political objectives of the United States were, sequentially, to use the United Nations to restore and maintain order in the Congo, thereby forestalling Communist influence there; and to maintain the instrumental utility of the United Nations by keeping together a consensus of a majority of U.N. members on the American interpretation of the Charter and specifically on the powers of the Assembly. The Americans put together as part of their persuasive efforts an involved legal case which defined the rights of the Assembly in a broad manner, and were able to convince an Assembly majority of the validity of this case. But their case required them to force their chief opponents to pay for the operations they opposed, or else to further convince the Assembly that these opponents must be penalized. They prepared legal barrages and used further pressure to do first the one and then the other; but their opponents outlasted them on the one score and outmaneuvered them on the other. The Americans then made a tactical retreat which terminated the fruitless engagement, at the cost of a minor revision in their legal case, a significant (but purely momentary) loss of prestige, and the (perhaps temporary) abandonment of their second main goal.

Legal language and the manipulation of norms served all major participants in this crisis who had well-defined interests as means of rallying to their side parties without direct and clear desires. In some cases, these vacillating powers were no doubt actually convinced and

[41] *New York Times*, August 17, 1965, pp. 1, 6.

moved by the force of a legal argument alone; in other cases, the legal argument was a convenient shield and justification for an adhesion otherwise motivated. Making a good case was not, then, a matter of no importance. But it cannot be missed that, under the vague but violent language of menace employed by the Soviet Union, and with no more than a threat of withdrawal, the consensus produced by America's appeals to national interests and by its previously highly successful legalists collapsed and vanished with scarcely a trace. This is most relevant. The case illustrates the general point that law, i.e., taking, arguing, documenting and defending a legal posture, is a customary and serviceable instrument of statescraft; but law is far from being the most important or effective means by which states gain their ends, and it seldom or never works alone.

These limits understood, the U.N. financing case provides examples of how legal cases can be well and not so well tailored to the audiences they have to convince. At this time, both Americans and Soviets were actively seeking the support of a large number of states which had no prior commitment to either side. So long as debate was permeated heavily by legal norms, the Americans had the better of it. Their case flattered the weakness of the majority of member states, where the Soviet case offended it; and the Americans were enabled to do this by a history of carefully tailored political decisions which accorded, as if of right, a role to weaker states which their own power could never have given them. So long as little either of will or of material strength was demanded of them, this art secured the voices and votes of states which would not have deigned or dared to become open allies. The Soviets were willing to give much less for such aid than the United States; but the need to remain consistent with a fairly rigid legal stance hamstrung them in any case. Students of the methods by which great powers cheaply secure the assent of small states to their policies could do worse than to study the orchestration of legal and other pressures employed in this crisis by the United States (before its policy line began to weaken in the fall of 1964). Law is a specialized but useful tool, and this case displays both its uses and its limitations.

❁ ❁ ❁

In writing this essay, I have directed myself mainly to the factual question, "How did the chief parties to this crisis use legal norms to advance and defend their interests?" I judge that this question can be answered without there being too much distortion of the answer by my own academic, political and moral preferences and opinions. But the reader should take into account that I regard the *general* policy of the United States in the Congo as sound, and the outcome of the Congolese affair as a minor but significant American success. The American policy in the consequent U.N. financial-constitutional crisis, on the contrary, I consider superficially bold but actually timid and immobilized by entanglements of our own making. In retrospect it seems a minor failure.

Whether the Americans were in some objective sense "right" or "wrong" in struggling to make the French and Russians pay the bill for the Congo operation I regard as a spurious question. I judge that the U.S. legal argument was, for what this is worth, more in accord with the text of the Charter than were its opponents' cases. Ironically enough, this apparent advantage was a piece of bad luck for the Americans, because they were so impressed by the (real) legalistic credibility of their case that they pressed it beyond the limits within which they were prepared to commit their resources. The United States was not prepared to make dramatic deployments of power to impose its views on those in whose interest it was to reject those views. This is to say that the American government was bluffing. It did not admit the bluff, to itself or to associates. But when its threat was called, it backed off. Its own self-regard thereby received an affront, and so did its "prestige": too bad, but hardly fatal. The only lesson that I see in this experience is this: those who claim as a right what they are not willing and able to get on their own, will be disappointed; if they also believe in the righteousness of their own claims, they will be vexed as well. The Americans were unwilling to use the only sanction in the U.N. Charter that could be applied to fiscal delinquents; the delinquents sensed it, and refused to pay. The Americans were disappointed; being righteous, they were also vexed. They received a minor lesson in political realism. No more should be expected from a minor failure.

The *general* line of U.S. foreign policy in the past twenty years causes me no unease; I have no confidence in the will and ability of other states or of any international institution to enact the values and advance the interests supported by that general line without considerable and conscious exercise of American leadership and influence. Therefore I feel that it is right and judge that it is prudent for the U.S. to forward its policy by using legal argument, as well as by more effective means — and most other means are more effective. But international legal norms are many, mutually and internally inconsistent, vague, and amorphous. Law will be a useless instrument to a diplomacy that fails to lead in the interpretation and development of these nebulous norms. Norms are such shapeless and malleable clay that the first and firmest hand applied will seldom fail to find them apt to its design. For the long run, American diplomacy, and any diplomacy, ought to work to ensure that if a lucid, meaningful, consistent, enforceable international law ever emerges, it will be a law under which it can live at least as comfortably as it now does under today's confused clouds of norms. American policy in the financing crisis was risky and speculative, in the light of this latter principle. The United States fought (ostensibly) to establish the unrestricted taxing power of a General Assembly which the Americans were less and less able to lead or to guide, much less to control. If that taxing power had been confirmed, and later used wildly, the United States would have felt its misuse first and most sharply. What the American government did at last could prudently have been done first: as it paid for the useful Korean operations a decade before, it might have paid for the equally useful Congo venture, and thus have avoided a quarrel which it was as embarrassing to lose as it would have been to win.

STANLEY HOFFMANN

A World Divided
and a World Court Confused:
The World Court's Advisory Opinion
on U.N. Financing

The financial crisis of the United Nations, due largely to the failure of many members to pay for the U.N. operations in the Middle East and in the Congo, has had a judicial phase in the midst of the political developments. On December 20, 1961, the General Assembly of the United Nations requested the International Court of Justice to give an advisory opinion on the following question: "Do the expenditures authorized in General Assembly resolutions . . . relating to the United Nations operations in the Congo . . . and the expenditures authorized in General Assembly resolutions . . . relating to the operations of the United Nations Emergency Force . . . constitute expenses of the Organization within the meaning of Article 17, paragraph 2, of the Charter of the United Nations?" Article 17 (2) of the Charter says: "the expenses of the Organization shall be borne by the members as apportioned by the General Assembly."

The Court asked for written statements from the members of the United Nations, and received twenty-one such statements, as well as three letters whose authors referred to their governments' views previously expressed in General Assembly discussions. In May, 1962, oral proceedings were held before the Court; nine states, whose views had already been communicated to the Court in the written statements, were represented in the oral proceedings. On July 20, 1962, the Court's opinion was announced: by a vote of 9 to 5, the Court stated that the expenditures authorized in the General Assembly resolutions dealing with the financing of UNEF and ONUC "constitute 'expenses of the

Organization' within the meaning of Article 17, paragraph 2, of the Charter." Of the nine judges in the majority, three – Sir Percy Spender, Sir Gerald Fitzmaurice and Gaetano Morelli – wrote separate opinions, and one – Judge Spiropoulos – made a separate declaration. Each of the five dissenting judges – President Winiarski, Jules Basdevant, V. Koretsky, Lucio M. Moreno Quintana and J. L. Bustamante – wrote his own opinion.

This essay will first describe the main issues with which the World Court has been concerned, and then try to give a critical evaluation of the advisory opinion.

I

1. The work of the Court appears to have been dominated by two rather paradoxical question marks: the relation between the question asked in specific terms in the Assembly's request, and two other legal questions not mentioned therein but nevertheless very closely tied to the narrower issue at hand.

(a) One question mark concerns the relation between two kinds of U.N. resolutions: those of the Assembly, authorizing the expenditures for the financing of UNEF and ONUC, and whose nature was at stake in the request – and those of the Assembly and Security Council, setting up the two forces and defining their missions. This problem has to be subdivided into two separate, if related, questions.

(i) Was it *necessary* for the Court to pronounce on the legality of the basic resolutions on the operations, before it could decide whether the resolutions on financing are "expenses of the Organization?" In other words, is the legality of the former a precondition of the qualification of the latter? Strangely enough, it is difficult to find a clear-cut answer in the Court's majority opinion; the reasoning in the first half of this opinion tends to imply that the answer is no: here, the Court merely examines the legal basis of, and the alleged limits on, the financial powers of the General Assembly, and the Court explains furthermore that irregularity of action "would not necessarily mean that the expense incurred was not an expense of the Organization." However, in its discussion of Article 17 (2), the Court does *in fact* examine not only the financial powers of the Assembly but also the powers of the Assembly and of the Security Council with respect to peace and security operations, and in the second part of the opinion, the legality of UNEF and ONUC comes under explicit scrutiny. Among the separate (concurring and dissenting) opinions, three state that an examination of the legality of the resolutions on the operations is indispensable (Quintana, Koretsky, Bustamante), one does so implicitly (Sir Gerald Fitzmaurice), two do not address themselves to the issue (Winiarski, Basdevant), and three explicitly consider that the two problems are sufficiently distinct to allow the Court not to pronounce on the issue of the resolutions on the operations (Spiropoulos, Spender, Morelli).[1]

(ii) Whether one thinks that this issue must be considered or not, there arises a second question: Was the Court empowered by the request to examine it or not? Not only did the Assembly's request omit to mention this issue, but the request was formulated after the rejection of a French proposal which would have amended its terms so that the Court would have been asked to indicate first whether the expenditures were "decided in conformity with the provisions of the Charter" and *if so,* whether they constitute expenses of the Organization. The rejection of the French amendment has been interpreted in diametrically opposed ways by the judges. The majority, pointing out that even this amendment did not explicitly refer to the Court the issue of the legality of the resolutions on the *operations,* considered that the Court remained free to "consider the Charter as a whole";[2] but Judges Spiropoulos, Spender, Morelli, Quintana, Koretsky and Bustamante believe that the rejection of the French amendment precludes the discussion of this issue by the Court. However, of those six, the first three consider that the question of the legality of the basic resolutions does not command the question of the nature of the expenses; the latter three consider that it does: consequently, those three conclude that the Court cannot adequately answer the request.[3] Without giving his own opinion as to the relationship between the two questions, Judge Basdevant uses the fact that the majority went beyond a commentary on Article 17 (2), into a discussion of the Charter as a whole, to make his point that the request was so badly phrased as to justify a refusal by the Court to answer.

(b) The second question mark concerns, not what one might call

---

[1] The latter, however, does not refrain from declaring them valid.

[2] *Purchase of UN Bonds: Hearings before the Committee on Foreign Affairs, House of Representatives, 87th Congress, 2d session, on S.2768,* p. 474. [Hereafter cited as *Hearings.*]

[3] However, all three actually discuss the legality of the basic resolutions: Koretsky brands them invalid; Quintana strongly suggests that they are; Bustamante has his doubts.

the "previous question" of the resolutions on the operations, but a "following question": if the expenditures authorized by the Assembly are "expenses of the Organization," does it necessarily follow that every member must pay the sum apportioned to it by the Assembly? Obviously, the majority of the Assembly must have been convinced that this is indeed the case;[4] perhaps because of this, the request did not explicitly ask the Court to say so: if the majority had not taken it for granted, the phrasing of the request would have made little sense, for it is hard to see how a mere qualification of the UNEF and UNOC expenditures as expenses of the United Nations would otherwise help solve the financial crisis of the Organization. However, the results of this omission were as confusing as those of the Assembly's failure to raise explicitly the issue of the legality of the basic resolutions.

(i) The majority opinion and two of the dissenting ones expressly asked the question, "ought the Court to distinguish between the issue raised in the request, and the subsequent issue of the states' obligation to pay?" But whereas the majority opinion answers by restricting the Court's role to a discussion of the nature of the expenses of the U.N., then states that neither the problem of apportionment nor that of obligation are of concern to the Court here, and changes accordingly the title of the case from "financial obligations of the members of the UN" to "certain expenses of the UN," Judge Fitzmaurice and Judge Winiarski both believe that the Court should have examined the issue of obligation: "except in so far as there is an obligation to contribute to expenditures which duly rank as 'expenses,' there is no point in determining whether these expenditures are expenses or not," according to Sir Gerald Fitzmaurice;[5] and Judge Winiarski writes that the limitation of the Court's reply prevents the Court from offering the legal guidance which the Assembly had requested, concerning the obligations of the member states.

(ii) However, things are even more complicated! Although the majority opinion explicitly restricts itself to the first of the three issues involved in Article 17 (2), *actually,* as both Judge Fitzmaurice and Judge Basdevant point out, the Court's reasoning concerning the financial powers of the General Assembly was aimed at refuting the argument that those are merely powers of recommendation.

[4] After all, Article 19 could not be put into effect unless the obligation exists.
[5] *Hearings,* p. 506.

Thus, the Court *implicitly* assumed that "once it is established that certain expenditures constitute 'expenses of the Organization,' it follows necessarily and automatically that every member State is obliged to pay its apportioned share . . . in all circumstances" (Fitzmaurice).[6] Judge Spender's opinion on this point is pretty close to that of the majority. Indeed, it is precisely this implicit settlement of an issue not explicitly raised in the request that provides Judge Basdevant with his second argument for his demonstration of why the Court ought not to have answered the request. Judges Spiropoulos and Morelli explicitly assert that the resolutions on financing the two operations have created obligations since they concern expenses of the United Nations. Sir Gerald Fitzmaurice comes to the same conclusion, but only after examining the issue *separately*, i.e., after refusing to assume that all expenses validly incurred by the United Nations are *ipso facto* obligatory; he chides the majority for having done so. On the other hand, Judge Winiarski writes that even if the expenditures for UNEF and ONUC are expenses of the Organization, he does not believe that they are obligatory for those members who have not accepted the basic resolutions; and Judge Bustamante thinks that there is need for the Organization itself to pronounce on the matter.

2. An idea of the opinions' disarray may have been suggested already. However, a more detailed examination of the issues requires a classification of the replies to the request. I propose the following one.

(*a*) According to the majority opinion and to the concurring one of Judge Fitzmaurice, the expenditures for UNEF and ONUC are expenses of the Organization under Article 17 (2), because both the basic resolutions and those authorizing the expenditures are legal; consequently, the members are obliged to pay their apportioned shares.[7]

(*b*) According to the concurring statements or opinions of Judges

---

[6] *Ibid.*, p. 514. The implicit assumption on which the majority opinion rests is particularly obvious on pp. 483–84: "The obligation is one thing: the way in which the obligation is met — that is from what source the funds are secured — is another," and is merely a "matter of bookkeeping or accounting" without "legal significance."

[7] In the case of Judge Fitzmaurice, "consequently" means "necessarily" only when the purposes of the expenditures are essential purposes of the United Nations — which is the case here.

Spiropoulos, Morelli and Spender, these are expenses of the United Nations because the resolutions authorizing the expenditures are valid; there is no need to examine the legality of the basic resolutions and the states are obliged by the resolutions on financing.

(c) According to Judge Koretsky, these are not expenditures of the United Nations because the basic resolutions are "incurably" illegal, and consequently there is no obligation at all.

(d) According to Judges Winiarski and Bustamante, the request cannot be legally answered one way or the other by the Court; even if these could be considered expenses of the United Nations, obligation would not necessarily follow.

(e) According to Judge Quintana, just as for Judge Bustamante, the exclusion of the issue of the legality of the basic resolutions from the request is the decisive reason why the Court ought not to answer, but Judge Quintana indicates more strongly than either Judges Winiarski or Bustamante that he thinks that the resolutions on the operations are illegal — although he does not explicitly say so. Consequently, he suggests that there is no obligation.

(f) According to Judge Basdevant, the inadequacy of the way in which the request frames the question is sufficient reason for the Court to decline to answer.

3. The fundamental issue at stake can be defined as follows: Does the General Assembly have the power to include among the "expenses of the Organization" the expenditures incurred for operations designed to maintain or restore peace and security undertaken either by the General Assembly under the Charter or in accordance with the Uniting-for-Peace resolution, or by the Security Council outside of the mechanism of collective action of Article 43? It is almost impossible to systematize the replies. However, the following main lines emerge.

(a) The majority and the concurring opinions argue in effect that the General Assembly has the powers to include among the expenses of the Organization all expenditures incurred on behalf of the United Nations in furtherance of its purposes. The financial powers of the General Assembly extend to all financial requirements of the Organization: the word "budget" in Article 17 (1) does not refer merely to the administrative or regular budget, it applies to operational expenses as well.

(i) Thus, what is decisive is the purpose of the expenditure, not the legality of the basic resolutions. Even if the regularity of those resolutions is open to challenge, the Assembly's financial decision as to the character of the expenses "cannot legally be challenged by any member state" (Spender).[8] The majority opinion states that even if an action was taken by the wrong organ, the expenses incurred might still be expenses of the United Nations. In the case of UNEF and ONUC, the purpose was the maintenance of peace and security, which is the U.N.'s "primary" purpose. This form of reasoning gives decisive priority to the Organization's need to avoid financial chaos: a need so great that, in Judge Morelli's words, the violation of the rules of competence of an organ of the United Nations cannot entail the nullity of that act.

(ii) But this argument is open to the challenge, made by Judges Winiarski, Quintana and Koretsky, that the purposes of the Organization cannot be met by *any* means, for the founders of the United Nations intended those purposes to be reached by a certain balance of powers and responsibilities between the Organs; the rules of competence of the organs are thus just as fundamentally important as the goals. Indeed, Judge Winiarski's point — a perfectly pungent one, if we remember the San Francisco discussions on collective security — is that the founders preferred to have certain purposes *abandoned* rather than having this balance sacrificed.[9] Or, to put it in another way, the maintenance of such a balance, which corresponds to a certain (hierarchical) conception of world politics, was both a prerequisite to the pursuit of the purposes, and a purpose in itself.

(*b*) The majority (and Sir Gerald Fitzmaurice) do not stick simply to the *dictum* mentioned above. In order to determine whether the expenditures were validly incurred, they examine not merely the statements relative to purposes found in the resolutions on financing, but the language and the legal validity of the basic resolutions as well.

(i) Thus, they go beyond a discussion of the financial power of the Assembly into an examination of the peace-making activity of

---

[8] *Hearings,* p. 494. "In my view it is not possible to suppose that the Charter leaves it open to any State Member to claim at any time that an Assembly resolution authorizing a particular expense has never had any legal effect whatever, on the ground that the resolution is based on a wrong interpretation of the Charter or an incorrect ascertainment of situations of fact or of law." *Ibid.,* p. 528 (Judge Morelli).

[9] See I. L. Claude, *Power and International Relations* (New York, 1962).

the Assembly and the Security Council in general, and in the Middle East and the Congo in particular.

The Assembly may legally play a role in peace and security operations. First, the Charter itself entrusts the Assembly with certain peace-keeping activities. Secondly, the majority defines restrictively the kind of "action" that the Assembly is barred from taking under Article 11, paragraph 2: it "must mean such action as is solely within the province of the Security Council," i.e., "enforcement action" in the cases to which Chapter VII refers (note below, a further restriction by the majority). Recommendations by the Assembly which are merely "in connection with the maintenance of international peace and security" and which establish subsidiary organs for that purpose are not action in the sense of Article 11 (2).[10] Specifically, the resolution setting up UNEF is not "patently on [its] face" "enforcement action under Ch. VII," and, furthermore, the resolutions establishing UNEF could find a legal basis in Article 14.

The Security Council's role in facing threats to peace or breaches of peace is not limited to Article 43; consequently the argument according to which the costs of Security Council operations must be handled by "Article 43 agreements" is not acceptable. Specifically, the Security Council resolutions setting up ONUC are not to be considered as an enforcement action under Chapter VII: the majority, debatably, restricts such action to measures taken against a state. It cannot be argued consequently that the Assembly, by providing for the financing of ONUC, violated the barrier of Article 11 (2).

(ii) These arguments are challenged in the dissenting opinions of Judges Koretsky, Bustamante and Quintana. The most drastic position is that of Judge Koretsky. According to him, the General Assembly is not entitled to destroy the balance established by the Charter between the Security Council and the Assembly — a balance which gave the primary role to the former in peace-keeping operations. He interprets the Middle Eastern and Congo operations as enforcement actions whose nature corresponds closely to the words of Article 39 and following, since there were breaches of peace and acts of aggression involved; he rejects the majority's narrow interpretation of enforcement actions as actions against a state only,[11] and he sees in the Assembly and Security Council's basic resolutions, not evidence

---

[10] *Hearings,* p. 480.
[11] See also his refutation of the majority's opinion that UNEF might be based on Article 14. *Ibid.*, p. 557.

of the fact that the organs of the United Nations were involved in operations of a "non-enforcement" nature, but evidence of their illegal determination to avoid the procedure prescribed by Chapter VII – that of Articles 43 and 47. The key point concerning financing is that it is the Security Council's responsibility to determine the way in which expenses of peace-keeping operations ought to be met, according to Article 43.

Judge Quintana's analysis, though less explicit, runs pretty close to this line: Article 17 (2) covers only ordinary expenses; the actions undertaken in the Middle East and the Congo are enforcement actions, for any operation involving the use (for military purposes or not) of armed forces is an enforcement action;[12] and expenses for them are "by their nature" the exclusive responsibility of the members of the Security Council.

Judge Bustamante's own position can best be described as a mixture of law and practical considerations. His attempt at defining the nature of the action, which under Article 11 (2) the Assembly cannot take, leads him to the conclusion that the majority rightly assumes the Assembly could not legally take comminatory enforcement action against a state, but also that the legality of Assembly police or security actions of a non-comminatory nature is not at all evident. Thus, he is not sure whether the Middle East operations were legal or not.

(c) The existence of the Assembly's financial powers having thus been discussed, there remained the issue of the legal nature of this power.

(i) According to Sir Gerald Fitzmaurice, even though the basic resolutions may be mere recommendations, the states are obliged to finance those operations (insofar as the costs "duly rank as expenses of the Organization") because of the intention of the founders who, at San Francisco, inserted Article 17 (2) to establish this obligation. The only exception to the principle of financial obligation concerns the case of activities which are "merely permissive"; thus the criterion lies not in the legal nature of the basic resolutions (i.e., recommendations or decisions) but in the nature of the activities (essential, such as the preservation of peace, or nonessential, such as the various activities carried out through voluntary programs: Special Fund, EPTA, UNICEF, etc.).

---

[12] See his allusion to Katanga. *Ibid.*, p. 546.

(ii) It is on this point that Judge Winiarski concentrates his dissent. He refrains from challenging the validity of the basic resolutions, but he presents an argument which had been forcefully made in the written statement submitted by France. It concerns the relationship between the Assembly's financial powers and the Assembly's "operational" powers: Can the former exceed the latter?[13] The basic resolutions were mere recommendations; if the resolutions on financing are obligatory, then the difference between binding decisions (those which the Security Council only can take) and recommendations, "one of the bases of the whole structure of the Charter," would be subverted. It was Judge Fitzmaurice's point that this was exactly what the founders had wanted; Judge Winiarski's reasoning suggests on the contrary that the financial powers of the Assembly cannot go beyond the basic design of the Charter, which entrusted peace-keeping operations primarily to the Security Council. Otherwise the Assembly could enlarge its powers far beyond what many states would accept, as long as these powers are stated as being used to meet U.N. purposes, and given a financial expression.[14]

The same point is made by Judges Winiarski and Quintana. Judge Bustamante also stresses that the basis of the Charter is the conditional link between the states' duty to accept institutional decisions and the conformity of those decisions to the Charter; one of the reasons why he is dubious about the obligatory nature of financial resolutions "which approve mere recommendations of the Assembly or Security Council" is the cost of operations such as those of the Middle East or the Congo: it is so high that a need for special regulations arises.

4. Another important issue raised by the opinions concerns the legal weight to be given to U.N. organs' practice, both in financial matters and in the setting up of operations for the preservation of peace and security. The majority opinion relied heavily, though not exclusively, on practice: first, in order to interpret the word "budget" in Article 17 (1) and to determine whether the Assembly had considered the expenditures of UNEF and ONUC to be "expenses of the Organization";

---

[13] Cf. the debate in American constitutional law about the treaty-making power and its relation to the balance between federal and state powers.

[14] On the same point, see Judge Quintana, *Hearings*, p. 547. For the French position, see ICJ, *Financial Obligations of Members of the UN, Written Statements*, p. 152.

secondly, in order to assess the nature of the basic resolutions.[15] In their written statements, Denmark, the Netherlands, Canada, Japan, the United Kingdom and the United States had strongly emphasized the relevance and the conclusiveness of U.N. practice. Mr. Chayes, referring to the basic resolutions, wrote that "the interpretation that such a body [as the Assembly or the Security Council] gives of its own powers in practice is entitled to the greatest weight in any subsequent judicial review."[16] This reliance on practice has given rise to two sorts of objections.

(*a*) In the first place, Judges Winiarski, Quintana and Bustamante have had little trouble in pointing out that the practice of the United Nations has been ambiguous in a variety of ways. The legal qualification of the basic resolutions is anything but simple (Bustamante). As for the resolutions on financing, not only have many members refused to pay because they have challenged the legality of the U.N. practices (Winiarski), but also the resolutions themselves are not crystal clear as to the qualification of the expenses: they do preserve a separation "between the normal administrative expenses of the Organization and those called for by exceptional circumstances." Judge Koretsky's long and embattled account and recount of the financial resolutions stresses that those dealing with UNEF never referred to Article 17, and that those dealing with ONUC, with the exception of the one of December 20, 1960, emphasized the essential "difference in nature" between the regular budget and the expenditures for the Congo. After all, if the practices of the United Nations had not been a subject of controversy among the members, the question would not have been referred to the Court.

(*b*) Secondly, to the extent to which the legality of the U.N. resolutions is at stake, the use of statements appearing in those resolutions as evidence is, as Judge Fitzmaurice puts it, "question-begging": if it is the validity of the practices that has to be judged, the argument drawn from practice is perfectly circular.[17] After all, what the Court

---

[15] The most sweeping dictum is (*Hearings,* p. 482): "when the organization takes action which warrants the assertion that it was appropriate for the fulfillment of one of the stated purposes of the United Nations, the presumption is that such action is not *ultra vires* the Organization." This is not a miracle of clarity: Whose assertion? What action?

[16] *ICJ, Financial Obligations of Members of the UN, Written Statements,* p. 152.

[17] For instance, if, under the majority opinions, the only "action" the Assembly cannot take is enforcement action under Chapter VII — since Chapter VII refers to the Security Council only, it is hard to see how *any* Assembly move could ever be taken under this chapter!

was supposed to decide was whether the expenditures in question were legally expenses of the United Nations, not whether the majority of the Assembly considered them to be so: otherwise, they would not have been voted!

II

It is necessary at this point to move from analysis to evaluation.

1. My argument is simple: the Court was faced with a task which is practically beyond the capacity of international judges. This is not so much because of the political *nature* of the question: every important political issue in world affairs has legal aspects which it is legitimate to ask a court to clarify, and every major legal issue in international law has political implications. It is because of two closely connected factors. One, the Court was asked to deal with a set of political developments of a revolutionary character from the viewpoint of law-making and law-amending procedures. Thus the Court found itself caught in the dilemma of having either to declare those developments illegal on the basis of a strict interpretation of the texts, therefore condemning a long evolution of overwhelming political importance, or to sanction those developments, thus recognizing in effect the capacity of states and international bodies to revise the law by *de facto* practices. The usual canons of legal interpretation are put to an unbearable test in such circumstances. Secondly, the political developments submitted to the Court are not only revolutionary from the viewpoint of formal legality: they are also the cause of a violent controversy among states, involving two diametrically opposed conceptions of international politics; thus, the Court found itself caught in the dilemma of either having in effect to give its blessing to one of those conceptions, or else refusing to answer altogether.[18]

The embarrassment of the Court is obvious. I have never before come across a legal opinion in which judges communicated so pathetically their awareness of the inadequacy of legal reasoning to the problem in question. Out of fourteen judges, there are ten different statements. The majority opinion accumulates the sins of obscurity,[19]

---

[18] See Judge Spiropoulos' statement on this point, *Hearings*, p. 492.
[19] Obscurity: see fn. 15. Also, the Court, by assuming implicitly that expenses of the Organization are obligatory, fails to deal with the crucial issues analyzed above, part I, 3c.

confusion,[20] debatable legal reasoning,[21] apparent inconsistency,[22] and circularity.[23] The phrasing of the request drew from the judges a bewildering variety of reactions. Practically every one of the opinions betrays to some extent the judge's sense of applying inappropriate tools to an intractable object. Indeed, the judge's dilemma is quite explicitly laid out by Judge Quintana at the end of his opinion. The Court, he concludes, has three options. It might choose to give a "trifling" answer, i.e., the kind given by Judges Spender and Morelli — a purely formal answer to the question, saying in effect that since the expenses were allegedly incurred for the fulfillment of a U.N. purpose and authorized by the requisite majority, they are *ipso facto* expenses of the United Nations. Or else the Court could give a "substantive" answer which would deal with the basic legal issue (the legality of the

[20] Confusion: (i) see above, part I, 1a (i), my reference to the way in which the Court discusses the *political* powers of the Assembly under the guise of discussing its financial powers. (ii) The worst example concerns the definition of "action" under Article 11 (2) — on p. 480, the majority defines it as enforcement action solely within the province of the Security Council, under Chapter VII; on p. 489, enforcement action is defined as action against a state under Chapter VII. Now, *primo,* Chapter VII does nowhere limit the Security Council to action against a state; *secundo,* if *any* action against a state with respect to threats of peace, breaches of the peace and acts of aggression (cf. p. 480) is action in the sense of Article 11 (2), then the Uniting-for-Peace Resolution and the Assembly resolutions on Korea are invalid; *tertio,* if what the Court means is that the only actions that would be invalid are actions against a state, referring to such cases and amounting not to recommendations but to decisions (which are reserved to the Council), then all the Assembly's past actions are indeed valid. But this amounts to a highly roundabout and involved way of saying that the Assembly can do politically anything it likes as long as it is not legally a decision (decisions by the Assembly being limited to the financial domain), i.e., a detour for giving the Court's blessing to Assembly practice, and making practice prevail over the San Francisco system. This third explanation would reconcile the Court's reasoning on "action" with its sweeping *dictum* quoted in fn. 15.

[21] Debatable legal reasoning: the reduction of Chapter VII to actions against a state.

[22] Apparent inconsistency: the *dictum* of fn. 15, and the sentence (p. 484) according to which the reasoning on Article 17 (2) and on the purposes of the United Nations "might suffice as a basis for the opinion of the Court," are followed by a scrutiny of the specific resolutions on the operations and on financing; it is hard to say whether this scrutiny modifies in any way the previous *dicta,* or merely applies them.

[23] Circularity: the reliance on practice to determine legality (cf. Judges Fitzmaurice's and Spender's criticisms). To the extent to which the majority accepts as expenses of the Organization all expenses incurred in furtherance of U.N. purposes, and considers them to be obligatory, reliance on practice means in effect that the presumption mentioned in fn. 15 will be almost impossible to disprove.

operations). But it would force the Court to pass judgment on the whole evolution of the United Nations, i.e., to assume the exercise of an activity *de lege ferenda* if it gives its blessing, or to condemn a long "politico-legal phenomenon." Consequently, the Court ought to refuse to deliver any opinion. And the judge's inadequacy is highlighted by Judge Bustamante's opinion, in which he gravely lists all the controversial issues — which he would like the United Nations, not the Court to settle — so that his pages read like a Court's request for an advisory opinion from the General Assembly.[24]

2. The first difficulty lies in the nature of the U.N. evolution. There has been a clash between the Charter and political realities; in order to have the United Nations survive and play whatever role those realities allow it to perform, the majority of the members have engaged in a *de facto* revision, or adaptation, of the Charter. In particular, there has taken place (1) a massive transfer of authority from the Security Council to the Assembly, under the Uniting-for-Peace Resolution, and (2) a tacit burial of the sharp distinction made at San Francisco between mere disputes and "Chapter VII cases." Consequently, both the Assembly and the Security Council have resorted to procedures that do not fit the categories listed in Chapters VI and VII. If the Versailles Treaty, in Jacques Bainville's words, was too soft for what was tough in it, and too tough for what was soft in it, the techniques of "international neutralization" developed by the United Nations in crises such as those of Suez and the Congo are too "tough" to be mere investigations or procedural suggestions *à la* Chapter VI, and too unlike collective action to fit Chapter VII or even the Uniting-for-Peace Resolution, patterned after Chapter VII.[25] The combination of the two develop-

---

[24] Judge Bustamante's request for a clarification by the United Nations itself either means nothing, or it means that since each organ is *actually* the master of its jurisdiction, it might as well avoid exporting its troubles to the Court. For it is hard to see the Assembly "clarifying" the legal issues in any way other than that indicated by its practice in the past!

[25] In the Charter's conception, enforcement action was *most likely* to be (although not legally limited to) action against a (minor) state, preceded by explicit recognition of the breach of peace, threat to peace or act of aggression; and Article 43 was consequently the heart of the system. The Uniting-for-Peace Resolution tries to substitute Assembly rule for the rule of Article 43, and to extend collective action legally to breaches by large powers. Political expediency has led to a tacit abandonment of any "enforcement against" states in a world of interlocking powder kegs, and to the use of the Uniting-for-Peace Resolution to very different hypotheses. However, if Chapter VII fits nothing any more, the cases in which

ments mentioned above explains why the U.N. resolutions, whether adopted by the Assembly or by the Council, studiously avoid referring to articles of the Charter.

Now, a judge asked to review such transformations must find himself in a quandary.

(*a*) If he declares them illegal — as Judge Koretsky alone does explicitly — he is obliged to say, in effect, that everybody is out of step except a handful of states, which, furthermore, have been anything but consistent in their legal protest. (See Judge Koretsky's painstaking and painful interpretation of Soviet abstentions or Soviet participation in unanimous Security Council resolutions, so as to be able to argue that the Soviets do not have to pay even though they failed to disapprove!) He is also obliged to say, in effect, that the intentions of the founding fathers are a straitjacket that must be imposed on their sons — and on strangers who have joined the family late because they were not born in 1945 — even if the result is death by strangulation.

(*b*) On the other hand, in order to declare them legal, he may choose between two forms of reasoning. He can either interpret the original document in so broad and permissive a way that all the subsequent changes magically appear compatible with the provisions of the text (such a technique requires that the intentions of the founders be laid to rest); or else he may explicitly recognize that Constitutions (national or international) evolve and that practice actually makes and revises law. One of the weaknesses of the majority opinion is that it uses both procedures in order to reach its positive conclusion. The trouble with the first procedure (as demonstrated by the majority opinion) is that it saves the law by twisting — some might say debasing — it.[26] The trouble with the second is that its realism does not save it from political controversy: whereas it is *relatively* safe to be realistic about the law-making effects of practice in domestic constitutional evolution, the very essence of such majority-imposed practices in international organizations is that they will be resisted by a minority which cannot be compelled to submit. The practice which is being

---

the Assembly has acted do not correspond to the mild language of Article 14 either: all Article 14 fits, is the occasion of this Opinion. On this evolution of the United Nations see the author's "Evaluation of the UN," *Ohio State Law Journal*, 22, No. 3 (Summer, 1961), 472–94.

[26] For an attempt even more heroic and far more questionable than the Court's, see John W. Halderman, "Legal basis for UN armed forces," *American Journal of International Law*, 56, No. 4 (October, 1962).

approved is the very center of controversy, hence the "question-begging" aspect of its invocation as evidence.

(c) The insoluble contradictions in which judges bog down amidst such dilemmas are particularly evident in the three concurring opinions. Judge Spender proclaims that a continuing violation of the Charter by an organ would remain a violation "no matter how frequently and consistently" repeated; however, his own answer to the request gives such overarching importance to the purposes of the United Nations that he considers the legality of the operations irrelevant to the issue of the legality of expenses. Now, it is this very argument of the need for the United Nations to reach its goals that has served to justify all the departures from the Charter — including one which an *obiter dictum* of Judge Spender roundly condemns: the dismissing by U.N. organs of domestic jurisdiction. Moreover, Judge Spender himself writes that "the Charter must . . . be interpreted, whilst in no way deforming or dislocating its language, so that the authority conferred upon the Organization and its various organs may attach itself to new and unanticipated situations and events."[27] How does this differ from the evidential use of practice which Judge Spender rejects? Judge Fitzmaurice writes that he cannot accept the view that invalidly authorized expenditures "would nevertheless stand automatically validated by the act of the Assembly" in apportioning them, for this would indeed mean, as the French written statement had warned, that the Assembly could do anything. But Judge Fitzmaurice, in order to determine whether an expenditure has been incurred for a valid purpose, is satisfied with formal validity: he gives a *prima facie* presumption of validity to any resolution adopted by a two-thirds majority, authorizing or apportioning expenditures "in the apparent furtherance of the purposes of the organization," unless its invalidity is "apparent on the face of the matter or too manifest to be open to reasonable doubt"[28] — a singularly unmanageable standard. Moreover, in order to establish the legality of the basic resolutions, Judge Fitzmaurice (endorsing the majority opinion) has to assert that the Assembly did not violate Article 11 (2), and the Council did not violate Article 43 — i.e., their actions were voluntary, nonenforcement measures; but whereas the basic resolutions must appear strictly nonobligatory in order to be valid, the financial ones must be presented as obligatory in order to reach their goal — hence the discrepancy which

[27] *Hearings*, p. 497.
[28] *Ibid.*, p. 511.

the majority simply avoids discussing, and which Judge Fitzmaurice labors so hard to eliminate. In the process, he interprets the intentions of the San Francisco drafters with reference to obligatory character of the Assembly's financial resolutions, in a way which is not only debatable (as shown by Judge Quintana) but which also, when combined with his interpretation of validity, amounts to that very financial quasi-omnipotence of the Assembly denounced in the French statement. Finally, faced with the consequences of declaring all "expenses of the Organization" obligatory, he introduces a distinction between essential and nonessential activities that has no basis at all in the Charter which lists economic and social tasks among its purposes as forcefully as it mentions peace. Similarly, Judge Morelli, after having said that it was not up to the Assembly to decide whether an expenditure is or is not an expense of the organization, reaches exactly that conclusion — in the most drastic terms: "each organ of the UN is the judge of its own competence . . . the Charter confers finality on the Assembly's resolution irrespective of the reasons, whether they are correct or not, on which the resolution is based . . . even in a field in which the Assembly does not have true discretionary power";[29] the only exceptions would be cases in which the resolution was not adopted by the requisite majority, or would be "vitiated by a manifest *excès de pouvoir*" not of an organ but of the Organization. The reason for this stringent conclusion is, according to Judge Morelli, that in the conflict between the two needs of legality and certainty, the latter must prevail; since in international affairs, at the difference of domestic legal systems, the only sanction of invalidity would be absolute nullity, perpetual uncertainty must be avoided by restricting absolute nullity to very exceptional cases.

3. This point brings us to the second problem faced by the Court: that of the political implications of its opinion.

(*a*) The problem can be seen in a narrow way by looking at the relations in the United Nations between the majority and a minority that contests the legality of the majority's action. The Court had to face the fact that precisely because "proposals made during the drafting of the Charter to place the ultimate authority to interpret the Charter in the ICJ were not accepted,"[30] each organ is *in fact* free to determine its own jurisdiction, and the protesting minority, as Judge Spender put it,

[29] *Ibid.*, p. 528.
[30] *Ibid.*, p. 483.

can do little except to protest and to reserve its rights. However, the point at issue here is whether the protesting minority can do *more* than protest, and refuse to pay for operations which it dislikes and whose legality it challenges, or whether the organization's need for financial security overrides the minority's interest. This is not just a vital issue for the financing of the United Nations: it is a fundamental issue in world politics.

(*b*) The issue can really be described, in its broadest form, as one of majority rule vs. state sovereignty. To reply that the minority has the right to refuse payment would be to uphold what one might call a traditional view of the international system: restrictions on sovereignty, such as those of the Charter, must be interpreted restrictively (cf. the old *Lotus* decision of the Permanent Court of International Justice). To the extent to which the above-mentioned changes in practice were imposed by majorities (both in the Assembly and in the Council), the minority is entitled to reject them (Koretsky, explicitly; Quintana, implicitly). To the extent to which resolutions on financing pretend to impose obligations on the members, dissenting states can apply the traditional sanction of illegality in international law. "It is the state which regards itself as the injured party which itself rejects a legal instrument vitiated, in its opinion, by such defects as to render it a nullity" (Winiarski); otherwise "the financial power of the Organization would be substituted for the national power of each of its members"; but the United Nations is "not a super-state," it is "an association of states with the view to the achievement of certain common purposes, and of which the constitutive instrument recognizes the sovereign equality" (Quintana).[31] On the other hand, to reply that the minority has no such "financial veto" is to recognize that the U.N. Charter is not just any sort of multilateral treaty, that "it was intended . . . to endure . . . for all time" (Spender), that its purposes are of crucial importance, that its provisions have to be interpreted in such a way as to give effect to, not to frustrate, those purposes (Spender). Indeed, it amounts to interpreting the Charter so as to give to the purposes priority over the distribution of the organ's powers,[32] so as to read into the Charter a special obligation to contribute to the expenses

---

[31] *Ibid.*, p. 548.

[32] See the majority opinion, *ibid.*, p. 482: It cannot be said that the Charter has left the Security Council impotent in the face of an emergency situation when agreements under Article 43 have not been concluded.

incurred for those purposes, and so as to make this special obligation prevail over the "general element of non-obligation" under Assembly resolutions (Fitzmaurice). The metaphor which the latter uses is, most significantly, that of "membership in a club."

(c) Now, to ask judges to settle such a debate is not only to ask them to take what are in fact violently controversial political sides: it also amounts to asking them to declare what the state of the world is.[33] Since their answer was limited by the request to yes or no, the judges' choice seemed reduced to two alternatives they could take. One position makes of traditional world politics the permanent norm, thus freezing international affairs in their classical mold and discounting or devaluating the changes — timid, debated, volatile but undeniable — performed by U.N. practice. Or else they could take a position that assimilates the states of the world to a domestic society in which there is so much centralized power that the minority's right to challenge the majority is limited to attempts at becoming the majority at some future date, while obeying the majority's rule in the meantime. The trouble is that the world — independently of what one wishes it to be — is at present neither quite the traditional state system in which the only *political* rule is that of superior power and in which the legal norm is sovereignty, nor is it yet the club to which Judge Fitzmaurice alludes and for which all members must either pay dues or resign their membership. The very nature of the present state of world affairs is flux: we are not moored any longer to the old shore, but we have not reached the promised land either. And while we are being tossed on the high seas, any attempt to say where the ship belongs can be no more than an attempt to indicate where one wishes it to go. It is therefore not surprising that the judges from Poland and the Soviet Union opt for one interpretation, and those of the United States, England, Australia and Italy for another.[34] Nor is it too surprising that a Peruvian and an Argentinian judge should be concerned with the financial burdens which a majority might impose on lesser members. Just as the world is politically somewhere between the old and the new, financial

[33] For a not very helpful comment, see the majority opinion, *ibid.*, p. 482: "save as they have entrusted the Organization with the attainment of . . . common ends, the member States retain their freedom of action." The question consists precisely of knowing where that freedom stops, and how far the Organization can limit it — the majority's answer, in the next sentence, is the one quoted in fn. 15.

[34] Not every judge voted in what might be called a national way: the Egyptian judge voted for the majority opinion.

common sense suggests some intermediate position between the financial chaos that the majority of the Court wants to avoid, and the potentially unrealistic dictates of majority rule — unrealistic because many members are likely to continue either to contest the legal and political validity of the "club" analogy, or to be unable to bear the financial burdens of membership.

4. For all those reasons, this writer confesses that he sympathizes most with the judges who, realizing, as Judge Koretsky put it, that the case was "saturated with political considerations" of a particularly unjusticiable nature, would have liked the Court to avoid doing what Judge Koretsky and the majority opinion both did, i.e., wallowing in politics and giving it the name of law. The attempts of Judges Spender and Morelli at answering the request positively without engaging in politics prove that this simply cannot be done; so does Judge Bustamante's Hamlet-like listing of arguments and objections. It is with Judge Basdevant's position and with Judge Winiarski's and Judge Quintana's conclusions (if not with all of the arguments of the latter two) that I find myself in agreement.

(a) It seems to me that the opinion merely indicates that the majority wishes the world to move toward the distant shore, and uses the principle of "institutional effectiveness" to that effect.[35] The problem remains, however, whether institutional effectiveness is served by an opinion that manages at the same time to be so sweeping legally and so controversial politically. For if the immediate goal is to help the United Nations survive the financial crisis resulting from its peacekeeping operations, it may be argued that the task has been complicated. By deciding that the expenditures for UNEF and ONUC are "expenses of the Organization," and by assuming that they are obligatory, the Court has made it more difficult for the Assembly to adopt for the future financing of those operations any voluntary scheme similar or comparable to the solution used during the Korean War or to the various economic programs: any such compromise, however wise po-

---

[35] The Court had already applied this principle in its 1949 opinion on *reparations for injuries* in which the Court asserted the international personality of the United Nations. But the circumstances and implications were radically different: in the 1949 case, what was at stake was the Organization's capacity to present claims so as to protect its agents; the issues of majority vs. minority, of internal balance of the organs and of Charter-extending practices were not involved.

litically and financially, would appear as a disavowal of the Court. On the other hand, to the extent to which the Court's opinion continues to be an anathema to many states, the Assembly has, since 1962, faced the following alternatives.

The Assembly could have insisted on the obligation and revised the assessments; the trouble here is that some states have continued to reject any hint of obligation; others could have aimed at the same result by the different method of preventing agreement on a new scale of assessments. When the Working Group of Fifteen was revived by the General Assembly in its December, 1962 resolution, the terms of the resolution, which asked the Group to take into account the special responsibilities of the permanent members for peace and security operations, indicated a continuing unwillingness of many small and new nations to carry a burden they deemed excessive, and foreshadowed the bitter and fruitless debate which ensued, since two of the permanent members considered the whole procedure illegal!

Second, the Assembly — having revised or not revised its scale of assessments by majority rule — could have decided to apply sanctions of Article 19 to financial delinquents. But this remained a *political* decision whose effectiveness, both politically and financially, was open to skepticism: one does not increase one's finances by cutting down one's membership, in a world in which nonmembers (or nonvoters) may be at least as dangerous as the voting members. Of course, the opinion of the Court provided the majority in the United Nations with a judicial basis for applying Article 19 if this were the majority's desire. The only merit of the judicial basis lies in its existence. It is better not to talk too much of its solidity. And the unwillingness of a large number of states to use this basis for political sanctions against two great powers was demonstrated in spectacular fashion during the 19th General Assembly.

Finally, the Assembly could have insisted on the obligatory character of expenses, stuck to the established assessment system and resigned itself *in practice* to the unenforceable character of the obligation; the political merit of this solution would be to facilitate relations with those members (in huge quantities) who do not challenge the legality of U.N. actions but who plead a financial *non possumus;* but otherwise, this would be a pretty disastrous financial and legal expedient, especially if no devices or no *Deus ex* (or in) *machina* are found to deal with peace-keeping operations that may become necessary. The paralysis of the Committee of 33 established by the 19th Assembly has put the United Nations into the unhappy position of this third alternative. An expedient had to be found, in 1964, for the U.N. force in Cyprus.

Ultimately, there are only three real solutions to the crisis. Either the United Nations finds independent revenues — i.e., revenues which would be available, independently of the members' whims and promises; the least one can say is that such income is not forthcoming. Or else the United Nations adjusts its operations to its resources: the political consequences would probably be calamitous, and the Court's own emphasis on the importance of U.N. purposes does not make honorable retreat much easier. Or, finally, the United Nations receives voluntary contributions from states eager to see it play its role well, i.e. (since altruism is not of the state's essence), from governments that have an interest in keeping the United Nations afloat *and also* value it highly enough to make financial sacrifices — the two judgments are, alas, quite separate. This would probably mean subsidies from the United States — if it is true that the U.S. government is as convinced as its representative to the United Nations of the efficiency with which the body has served American interests. But here again, the political implications are far from happy, and domestic opposition within the U.S. would be able to use the Court's arguments about the nature of the expenses as a shield. If they are expenses of the United Nations, why should the United States bail out the other members, and if the United States has to pay anyhow, why not resort to diplomatic or military channels it can control better?

(*b*) Moreover, in one respect the opinion may not only have made a solution of the present crisis more difficult, but even have made a worsening of the financial and constitutional problem possible. The opinion provides a judicial basis to eventual majorities eager to push vast economic or social programs, impatient with the purely voluntary solutions adopted until now, and determined to try to break the resistance of a small number of rich states by deciding that such expenditures are "expenses of the Organization," "appropriate for the fulfillment of one of the stated purposes of the UN," to quote from the majority opinion. The briefs submitted by the United States and the United Kingdom contain arguments that could haunt those hardy perennial opponents of SUNFED. The sweeping dicta of the majority opinion and of at least two of the concurring ones, the weakness of Judge Fitzmaurice's attempt at defining "nonessential" activities, the massive reliance by the Court on statements of intent drafted by the political majorities in the United Nations are goads to irresponsibility. Too broad an interpretation of the requirements of "institutional effectiveness" amounts to a blanket endorsement of majority rule in a milieu of world politics, where it is not majorities that rule, and where numbers and power (financial as well as political) remain very far apart. Precisely because of this, and especially after the fiasco of trying to apply Article 19, the idea of the Security Council's *primary* responsibility in peace-keeping has been strengthened — a paradoxical by-product of the Court's opinion.

(c) The majority of the Court had in effect given its approval to Dag Hammarskjöld's conception of the United Nations as a "dynamic instrument" capable of "executive action" toward "increasingly effective forms of active international cooperation," as against the notion of the United Nations as a mere "static conference machinery."[36] Yet the objection one may raise to this approval is not only that it entails a kind of abdication by the Court of its judicial role — just as too much emphasis on self-restraint and majority rule would entail it for the U.S. Supreme Court — but also that in the international milieu, as Hammarskjöld himself had stated, the nations' support of the United Nations, the Charter and the Secretariat remains purely utilitarian, and the divergent distribution of votes and money keeps plaguing the Organization. Having made the Court's wish the father of its judgment, the Court provides a prize example of both the dilemma of international judges faced with world-constitutional problems of vital importance to states in controversy during a revolutionary period, and the danger of compromising the prestige and the effectiveness of the one, fragile and restricted international judicial body by dragging it into storms in which such a body can only either drown, or share the jumpy fate of corks, but it cannot steer the nations' course.

[36] Introduction to the Annual Report, 1960–61, in *International Organization*, XV, No. 4 (Autumn, 1961), 549.